Body, Mind, Behavior

Body, Mind, Behavior

Maggie Scarf

The New Republic Book Company, Inc.
Washington, D.C.

Published in the United States of America
in 1976

by The New Republic Book Company, Inc.
1220 Nineteenth St., N.W.
Washington, D.C.

Library of Congress Cataloging in Publication Data

Scarf, Maggi.
  Body, mind, behavior.

  Includes index.
  1. Psychiatry—Addresses, essays, lectures.
  2. Psychology—Addresses, essays, lectures. I. Title.
  RC458.S26   616.8'9   76-9079
  ISBN 0-915220-14-8

Printed in the United States of America

For Herb, My Husband and Friend

Contents

Introduction

Every once in awhile I'm asked to come and talk with groups of people who are thinking about possible careers in writing, and I've always found it intriguing to notice that there are two basic questions the audience wants to have answered. The first is: Where do your ideas for articles come from? Are they your own or are they given to you on assignments? And the second one is: How did you ever get started? How does one go about *becoming* a free-lance writer in the area of the behavioral sciences?

The answer to the latter question is, in my own case, in the nature of a long shaggy-dog story. Some seven years ago, as the mother of three small children who were at last in school most of the day, I decided to look around for that "interesting part-time job" so dear to the hearts of many women in my position. I had already published several books for children and was committed to continuing with my writing on a daily basis—but I wanted experience in doing things that were more "practical," more outside, more in the real world as well.

Since my husband is a faculty member at Yale University, the nearby campus seemed to be an obvious place for exploring possibilities; and I actually could think of a couple of good places to try. The *Yale Alumni Magazine* had recently been metamorphosing from a dull throwaway into a cleverly edited and lively journal; they might want to take me on as a part-time articles writer. My other notion had to do with the Yale radio station (WELI): They could, perhaps, use me as an editor, or perhaps arranger, of some of the discussion programs that were their steady fare.

Almost as soon as I began mentioning these ideas to friends, however, I was cautioned against the crudity of going to the Yale employment office directly. So much more discreet and sensible, I was advised, to go through what were termed "channels"—to reconnoiter the situation from above, so to speak—in advance of any potential refusals. This sounded like a sensible, tough-minded, *realpolitik* line of approach; and accordingly, at the next faculty cocktail party, I sought out the name of the administrative official whose power and domains encompassed both the alumni magazine and the radio station. To my delight, he was someone with whom I had a slight acquaintance. I phoned his office the very next day.

He could not have been more receptive, more cordial. Our conversation was "high-Jamesian" inasmuch as little had to be stated directly. He understood perfectly my reasons for calling him, and the kind of work I was looking for: He would check out the situation both at the magazine and the station. Then he would get back to me. Our short chat ended with an exchange of friendly compliments and on a note of warm civility.

But unaccountably, a period of silence followed. The day or so that I had expected the matter would require merged into a period of weeks; "channels" seemed to be clogged. Growing impatient at last, I went directly to the editor of the *Yale Alumni Magazine,* carrying a brown Manila envelope which contained some samples of my writing. He read them that evening; and the next day, over coffee, he gave me an article assignment. After leaving his office, I went straight over to the building which houses the offices and studios of the Yale radio station. WELI was, as it happened, quite short-staffed at the time; I was hired, on the spot, to help organize, record and edit a series of programs (this job, by the way, sounded a lot more glamorous and interesting than it turned out to be).

I started working for my two part-time employers almost immediately, and it wasn't until the following spring that "channels" finally got around to coughing up a response. He apologized, in a brief note, for taking so long to get back to me: He had now checked with both the radio station and the magazine and there was absolutely nothing available in either place; he was sorry. (His letter made me smile and wonder if, when he'd finally gotten around to looking into the matter, both jobs had already been filled by me!)

Shortly after publishing my first article in the *Yale Alumni Magazine* I had what seemed to me to be a really nice idea for a radio program. A friend of ours, Dr. Thomas Detre, was the director of an inpatient mental ward at the Yale-New Haven (then called Grace-New Haven) Hospital: Why not organize a discussion of the type of treatment that was being offered to patients there? My immediate superior at WELI liked the idea and suggested that I contact the speakers, or discussants. I went ahead, therefore, and made arrangements with Detre, with psychologist Kenneth Keniston (who was then carrying out research on that particular ward), and with another Yale psychologist, Daniel J. Levinson. The program format also included an introductory skit in which ward staff members, playing both "patients" and "therapists," enacted an engrossing little dramatization of a typical treatment-situation.

The skit, and the highly explanatory discussion between the psychiatrist and two psychologists that followed upon it, added up (I thought) to a truly remarkable program. To my surprise, however, the station's director didn't much care for it—he kept scheduling other things ahead of it, and ultimately it was never used. I had, in the meanwhile, read and edited the skit and the entire conversation; my own interest in the ward—Tompkins 1—had grown during the process. I was, in fact, toying with the idea of trying to write an article about it.

Shortly afterward, I spoke to Tom Detre (who was not only the director, but the founder and organizer of the ward) about this notion; I found him not only agreeable, but enthusiastic. He was, however, just stepping out of his present role to become director of all psychiatric services, both inpatient and outpatient, for the hospital. He offered to introduce me to the new director of Tompkins 1, Dr. Gary Tucker.

Tucker was, when I met him, equally receptive to the idea of an article that would describe the particular kind of treatment offered on the ward. But I found him a very straight-faced joker, and hard to read. During our first conversation, I was taken aback when he suggested that I check myself in as one of the patients and do my research as an undercover agent, working from inside.

I couldn't tell whether or not he was serious (and am still not sure). "How much does it cost," I asked quickly, to hide my confusion, "to *be* a patient here? I mean, what's the daily rate?"

Tucker puffed impassively on his pipe. "It's just gone up; it's about eighty-five or ninety dollars a day, I think."

"Oh, well," I said, shaking my head. "As far as I'm concerned, if I were willing to put out that kind of money to be here, I guess I'd actually *need* to be . . . ." He rewarded this remark with a smile.

I had thought that as a nonmedical person I would feel like a real outsider on the ward: I was neither patient, nor therapist, nor nurse, nor social worker; I was simply there. This proved to be no problem at all, however, for Tompkins 1 (which everyone called T-1) was a teaching, training and research facility; and there were numerous random comers-and-goers a good deal of the time. One more body present simply didn't have much of an impact. Furthermore, I found the patients astonishingly forthcoming; they seemed eager to co-operate, even moved by the idea that I was planning to write about the ward. It was as if they believed that whatever I wrote was going to make sense of, explain, or perhaps even validate the things they were experiencing and that were happening to them within the framework of that totally engulfing environment. At any rate, what I had feared most in advance—possible hostility or suspicion on the part of the patients—never did materialize at all.

But I was having other problems. My early days on T-1 were filled with the greatest sense of bewilderment and with the kind of tension that prolonged confusion arouses. The daily life of the ward was, as I soon perceived, highly structured in such a way that every interpersonal exchange in which a patient became involved might have a potentially "healing" effect. The patient's existence was, in other words, "programed" (as far as was humanly possible); and Tompkins 1 itself was like a complex and carefully-geared mechanism designed to reward and support "healthy" kinds of behavior and to punish (by means of social disapproval) and suppress "sickness."

The goal of the treatment was not to effect profound personality change, but simply to get the person up and functioning as soon as possible. The idea was to return the individual to the larger community before he or she became adapted to the role of "mental patient"—which has its own set of seductive qualities, such as lack of responsibility, being taken care of by others, and the like. Active efforts were directed, therefore, toward getting the person involved with others, helping him or her to assume responsibility for others; and finally, taking responsibility for his or her own self. As far as the long-term psychological repair work was concerned, this was better done afterward, on the outside.

I found it hard to communicate to outsiders the passion, purpose and intensity of the life that was being lived on Tompkins 1: When I myself returned home in the afternoons, I felt spent and drained. Events on the ward seemed to be happening so fast, I despaired of ever fully understanding the import and meaning of what was going on.

The kind of therapy being used on T-1 was, I'd learned, called *milieu therapy*: In the late nineteen-sixties, when I was researching the article, it was still considered a revolutionary approach to the treatment of mental illness. (Tompkins 1 was, in fact, one of the two hospital wards in America using "therapeutic community" techniques; the concept of the structured or "healing" environment is far more widely accepted now.) There wasn't a great deal written about milieu therapy either, just a couple of short books by the psychiatrists who had originated and pioneered use of the method in English psychiatric facilities just after World War II. I had stumbled, it seemed, into a relatively little-known area . . . and wasn't quite sure what it was all about, what I was doing there, or that I'd ever be able to make any sense of it at all. I began, after several weeks on the ward, to think that I'd made a serious mistake and had let myself in for much more than I could possibly handle.

After taking a few days more in which to settle the matter in my mind, I came to the conclusion that I ought to abandon the idea of trying to write about T-1; and that I should, therefore, let my friend Tom Detre know of my decision forthwith. I went to his new office, on which his name and new title were just being lettered (Director: Psychiatric Services), and asked his secretary if I could see him for just a moment. She hesitated, saying that he was having a difficult, pressured day. "It'll really take no more than a moment," I promised, "and it's important."

She allowed me a few minutes in which to say whatever it was I'd come to say, and I went into Detre's office. I sat down quickly, thanked him for his past assistance, and told him that I had decided to leave. He stared at me, not answering. The whole thing was, I went on, far more complicated than I'd originally imagined; it would require someone with a real background, with serious training in psychiatry, to write an adequate article about Tompkins 1. I was sorry.

Tom Detre, seated across the desk from me, simply peered out from behind his glasses. His expression had become one of amazed harassment. "Why are you telling me this kind of crap?" he demanded, in an elaborately reasonable and objective-sounding tone of voice. "There's absolutely nothing going on out there"—he gestured with his hand—"that you couldn't, that *any intelligent person* couldn't understand." He stood up abruptly, came around the desk, and raised me from my chair by the back of my shirt collar. "And now," he said, literally giving me a shove in the direction of the door, "I'm busier than you can imagine, so please leave me alone and get on with your work.

. . . And *don't* come around with this kind of nonsense again." The next thing I knew I was standing outside in the hospital corridor. I went back to the ward floor, and he and I never discussed the matter again.

After that incident (which had an oddly restorative effect) I began to develop a more coherent system for doing a number of things that I'd been doing somewhat haphazardly before. For one thing, instead of attempting to interact with *all* of the patients, I began limiting myself to following the daily routines of one small group in particular. This group was, in turn, under the supervision of a designated "team" of staff members—senior psychiatrists, residents-in-training, social workers, etc.—and I arranged to have long and relatively uninterrupted periods of conversation with these people. I had long talks with a number of the ward nurses, as well, and spent many hours with the woman who supervised the patients' recreational and "community government" activities (hers was actually a key role in the system). I interviewed the ward's director, Dr. Gary Tucker, at periodic intervals; and I spoke to a number of psychiatrists who had no connection whatsoever with Tompkins 1 . . . several of them were, by the way, strongly critical of the whole therapeutic-community approach.

I was sorting out a variety of assessments of and points of view concerning the kind of therapy being used on T-1; at the same time I was continually gathering suggestions for books and articles that I might read. I had soon moved away from concentrating solely on milieu therapy and was now reading about other types of inpatient care; I was also learning something about the history of treatment of mental disorders, and about the mental asylum in general. A better understanding of the particular ward I was studying and researching— and of that ward in the context of the many other kinds of mental hospitalization—was beginning to take on some preliminary form and shape.

At first, I had meant to write about Tompkins 1 for the *Yale Alumni Magazine*; but, as I became more involved in and fascinated by the material, I began to think about submitting whatever I wrote to the *New York Times Magazine*. If it came out well, I decided, I might give it a try. . . . But in the meanwhile, the main thing was to get it all out and down on paper; after that, I could see. . . . This very rational decision was, however, overridden about two days after I'd sat down to do the actual work. I became so excited by the things I was writing that I simply dashed to the telephone and called the *Times* directly.

I was put through, at once, to a frozen-sounding editor, whom I tried (unavailingly) to thaw out in the warmth of my own enthusiasm. But all that I could get from her was an agreement to look at the piece once it was finished; I was not to imagine, she warned me sternly, that there had been any soupçon of a commitment from the *Times*. She hung up after suggesting that I direct the finished article to her desk.

This conversation convinced me that there wasn't the breath of a chance at the *Times* . . . nevertheless, having made an arrangement, one might as well give it a try. When I'd finished a couple of drafts of the piece, therefore, I wrote to that same editor, inquiring about the usual length of an article. A brief message came to me by return mail: The usual length was in the range of five to six thousand words; but I was to recall that the *Times* had promised absolutely nothing.

I sent in the finished manuscript shortly afterward; and a couple of weeks later (long before I'd expected to hear anything one way or the other), I received a telephone call from the same woman. "Well, we're buying your article," she told me. Then she paused and added: "Uh— now—*who* was it, exactly, that you said you were?" She sounded surprised.

After that time, like an actor who seems suited for a certain kind of role, I was type-cast somehow; I had sprung into existence as an essayist in the field of behavioral science, and an essayist in the field of behavioral science is what I became.

My pattern of researching and writing a piece has remained essentially similar to the one I fashioned while working on that first T-1 article. (See "In the Therapeutic Community the Patients Are Doctors," page 181.) I tend to come blithely into a new area or discipline, get bowled over by the difficulties I experience in trying to understand the basic concepts the scientists are working with—and the unfamiliar lingo they're using—and finally, I cope with the situation by going through a massive process of self-instruction. This invariably begins with a preliminary conversation with an expert working in the field on which I'll be concentrating—frequently that expert is someone working at Yale. To take an example: When I agreed to write an article on sex hormones and behavior I was somewhat troubled by the fact that (come to think of it) I wasn't really sure about which hormones did which things, and for that matter, what hormones actually *were*. . . . My first move, therefore, was to get in touch with Dr. Leon Speroff, an assistant professor at the medical school whose research interests centered on hormone-functioning and who also happened to be the friend-of-a-friend. Speroff generously offered to deliver himself of an extemporaneous lecture on the topic; and so one evening shortly afterward we met in a small seminar-room near his laboratory, which had one long wall that was all blackboard.

The blackboard was necessary. For the next two hours, Dr. Speroff drew lines, arrows, diagrams; he explained not only the functioning of the major sex hormones but of the other bodily hormones as well (which, as soon became evident, it would be imperative for any writer on this topic to know). I was deluged with names of various hormones, some of them familiar, such as the male hormone, testosterone, and the female hormone, estrogen—some fairly familiar, such as epinephrine and norepinephrine—and some of them unknown to me (e.g., a female hormone called 17-*beta*-estradiol, adrenocorticotrophic hormone, the gonadatropins, etc.). When I left Leon Speroff he seemed in a state of mild dejection about how much of the information he'd actually managed to *communicate* to me; and my own head was so crammed full of information I felt that if I leaned to one side, some might spill out of my ears!

I was armed, however, not only with a list of readings and reprints on the subject, given to me by my mentor, but with a number of suggestions about the major researchers in the field whom I might want to consider interviewing. My next step was to go at once to my local library and get out a children's book on the hormones—a trick of the quick-learning trade that I used to think I alone had discovered; I've now found that many of my colleagues use it as well! I also purchased a popular, fairly simplified book on physiology, Isaac Asimov's *The Human Brain*. I began to read these in tandem with the more esoteric works and the reprints on recent sex-hormone research borrowed from Dr. Speroff.

It was those scientific reprints, however, that enabled me to make a choice about which of the researchers to interview first. Dr. Robert Rose of the Boston University School of Medicine was at that time working on the intriguing hypothesis that the dominant males in monkey colonies might be those with the highest levels of testosterone in their bloodstreams (*i.e.,* more male hormone=more aggression=more dominance). Rose had already gathered some evidence supporting this notion, and I found the idea so curious, so picturesque in a way, that I simply wanted to know more. By the time I met with Rose, I was familiar enough with the workings of the endocrine system to carry on a moderately reasonable conversation. And from him I obtained more readings, more reprints, and more suggestions about other authorities in the field whom I might interview. Those next conversations led, in turn, further outward, in ever-expanding circles of reading and understanding. . . .

If I can be said to have a research method, this is pretty much it; I start the actual writing when I feel ready to write, but the learning and talking goes on the entire while. This method, though strenuous, does entail a couple of fine advantages. For one thing, I enter an area with no particular biases (because much or all of it is quite new to me.) Secondly I can—because I, myself, have had to learn the material from the ground up—more easily "translate" it and make it accessible to the general reader. (Scientists in a given area tend to communicate with one another in their own special language, a kind of shorthand, which can be quite incomprehensible to those working outside that particular field.) A term, for instance, such as *milieu therapy*, while conveying a fairly precise meaning to the psychiatrist or other therapist, needs to be explained to the intelligent layman who may be unfamiliar with the concept. And sometimes the same word—*normality* is an example—is used by differing experts in radically differing ways. (See the essays on R. D. Laing and Thomas Szasz, and the article called "Models of Sanity and Madness" as well.) After much experience in plowing through many unfamiliar terms and concepts in a variety of areas of the behavioral sciences, I have found Tom Detre's words to be true: There's nothing going on out there that any intelligent person can't easily understand. Translated from the "scientese," much of the fascinating and important work now going on in the behavioral sciences becomes readily and easily accessible.

There is yet another advantage to working "across" areas in the behavioral sciences. One comes to see, as I hope will be recognized, some interesting interconnections as one moves from an article originating in one field of study to another which may come out of a quite different-

seeming kind of discipline: This is because there are really cor-
respondences between, say, attempts to understand and control
behavior by means of electrical stimulation of the brain and attempts to
do the same thing by means of behavior-modification techniques. And
there is, similarly, a genuine overlap between the work of ethologist Jane
Goodall and the work of a psychiatrist like John Bowlby (compare
"Goodall and Chimpanzees at Yale" and "Human Attachment").

As far as the question of how I find or choose my topics is concerned:
They often, as was true in the T-1 instance, simply happen. The article
on electrical stimulation of the brain resulted from my noticing a short
column in our local newspaper about Dr. Delgado's bullfighting
exploits. The sleep-clinic piece arose from a fascinating conversation I
had (it actually took place·at a cocktail party) with the director of that
clinic, Dr. Peter Hauri. The article on the mid-life crisis in males came
about when I happened to hear that Dr. Daniel J. Levinson was doing
an in-depth study of men between the ages of thirty-five and forty-five
(Dan had been one of the discussants on that ill-fated radio program
about Tompkins 1).

Others among the essays in this collection were generated by ideas
brought to me by my friends and editors at the *Times*, such as Lewis
Bergman and Harvey Shapiro (who is now editor of the *New York
Times Book Review*); these have included the pieces on Thomas Szasz,
on transcendental meditation, on Alfred Adler, on hangovers, and
others.

These pieces were all written over the course of the past six years, and
some details given about the researchers involved may have changed.
Tom Detre, for example, has left Yale and gone to the University of
Pittsburgh to become Director of its Western Psychiatric Institute and
Clinic. Gary Tucker is now a Professor of Psychiatry at Dartmouth
Medical School; and Dr. Delgado has left the United States and is back
in his native Spain. But in general what is said about the research itself
remains unaffected—and the work described still occupies frontier
territory in the different disciplines.

The essays range, I believe, over a broad sampling of the exciting and
important work now going on in psychology, psychiatry, anthropology,
sociology and allied areas, but one ought not to see each of them as being
firmly fixed within its own particular disciplinary niche. They are far
more profitably viewed as appearing under that one broad and very

general heading—Behavioral Science. They are the stuff of new and ingenious attempts at that most difficult of understandings, the understanding of ourselves as a species. This is research directed toward comprehending that most mysterious of creatures—the behaving human being.

New Haven, Connecticut   Maggie Scarf
September 1975

Part 1

The Fetus as Guinea Pig

I can remember a situation in which a woman entered the hospital with a miscarriage. It was a case of spontaneous abortion, and she came in because she'd been told it was about to happen. The baby, however, was born alive. It weighed less than 500 grams, or just under a pound— which was below the legal definition of a live birth (this was in Baltimore). No birth certificate was made out, therefore, and it wasn't legally born. Since it *was* alive, however, it was taken over to the premature unit where it survived for two days. Eventually, being at that very borderline weight, it did die. . . . As it happened, the woman had given birth on December 31; and so the two days of infant care had been during the first two days of the New Year. The parents, when they received the hospital bill, were unable to claim any tax deduction. The father was incensed and he took the position that since there never had been any legally born "person"—no birth certificate and no death certificate—they couldn't hold him responsible for the costs of treatment. Why should he be made to pay for the care of a child who had never even existed? The hospital, on its own part, was put in the odd position of having spent forty-eight hours treating an individual who wasn't even, technically speaking, born. They finally did cancel the charges, I believe, and they agreed to forget the whole thing. . . .

> DR. RICHARD E. BEHRMAN, Medical Director,
Babies Hospital (Columbia University), in an interview.

hen does a fetus become "a person"? At what point in the slow continuum of fetal growth—from fertilization, to implantation in the uterine wall, to the time of the first heartbeat, to "quickening" (when the mother first perceives movement within her womb), to "viability" (the stage of fetal maturation at which the organism becomes capable of surviving outside the mother's support system, outside the uterus), to birth itself—does it become possible to say that, yes, from here onward, the fetus is to be regarded as a fully human individual, endowed with status as a person and a set of protectable human rights?

Legally, the position of the fetus was stated clearly in *Roe v. Wade,*

3

one of the Supreme Court decisions on the abortion issue, which was handed down in 1973. The Court said that the fetus is not to be regarded as a "person in the whole sense" prior to the age of viability. Viability, as defined in the *Roe-Wade* decision, is the point in fetal development at which the growing organism is "potentially able to live outside the mother's womb, albeit with artificial aid"; the Court placed the stage of fetal viability at "seven months twenty-eight weeks," but noted that it could occur earlier, as early as twenty-four weeks. The Court took the view, in short, that a fetus that is born alive is not to be construed as a "person"; the fetus that can maintain a biologically independent existence—that can live, grow and develop outside the womb—is to be so regarded.

As one may readily see, the *Roe-Wade* decision has a curious impact upon our perception of the fetus prior to the age of viability. It places that fetus not only in an odd legal limbo, but in a metaphysical and moral one as well. For, by defining the fetus in the first two trimesters of pregnancy as "not a person in the whole sense," the Court leaves open the entire question of what it actually is—and, more importantly, what may be done with it.

Since the time of the Supreme Court abortion decisions, live and dead fetuses, fetal tissues, fetal organs and similar materials have become widely available for use in a dizzying array of scientific investigations. At the same time, antiabortion forces, who believe that fetal work "legitimizes" abortion practices, as well as people who are simply opposed to this experimentation on moral and ethical grounds, have been pressing for legislation that will impede or halt fetal research entirely. Opponents of this work have decried it as a form of "mad science" and an assault on human values and human dignity. Scientists, for their part, have been protesting what they view as persecutory tactics, spearheaded by "anti-science" fanatics.

In 1974, in response to a surge of public concern over fetal and other kinds of research that utilized "human subjects," Congress enacted legislation to establish a National Commission for the Protection of Human Subjects of Biomedical and Behavioral Research. The commission, whose members were selected by the Secretary of Health, Education and Welfare, was entrusted with the task of studying the various types of human research and suggesting possible regulations for experimentation that might go on in the future. While the National

Commission was to have no legal power to enforce its decisions, the Congressional legislation did require the Secretary of H.E.W. to respond to whatever report it made (either negatively or positively) when he drew up his guidelines for the protection of human subjects.

The same act of Congress that established the National Commission also provided for a ban on all experimentation involving live, whole fetuses, before or after an induced abortion—and it instructed the commission to investigate fetal research in advance of all other kinds of human research, as its very first order of business. As if these moves were not sobering enough for scientists working in this area, the Department of Health, Education and Welfare then suggested that a voluntary "moratorium" on any even mildly questionable fetal studies be entered into by investigators whose research they were supporting.

It was thus in an atmosphere of some apprehension and a good deal of bitter misunderstanding that the National Commission for the Protection of Human Subjects was appointed; it consisted of three lawyers, three physician-investigators, two medical ethicists, two psychologists and one "public representative." Perhaps the thorniest issue they had to consider was that of the fetus's humanity: Does fetal work involve research on "human beings," or are fetuses, prior to viability, "nonpeople," and therefore perfectly legitimate subjects for use in potentially valuable scientific studies?

The question of what the fetus is, as one philosopher working as a consultant to the National Commission remarked to me, is not so much a moral and ethical as it is a pre-ethical issue. "You have to define what it is you're talking about," he explained, "before you can define whatever you're doing as right or wrong. . . ." The word "person" is variously defined, but generally signifies a being characterized by the ability to experience consciousness of self, to communicate, to experience sensations of pain and pleasure, to reason, to behave autonomously both in the moral and physical sense, and so forth. If the fetus cannot do that, then to what else may it best be equated? Is the fetus, for instance, more nearly similar to an animal than it is to a fully human "person"? The ancient philosophers, in point of fact, did so characterize it—they took the view that the developing organism moved from the merely vegetative stage to the animal and finally to the rational level. If it is true, as recent researchers at Albert Einstein Medical School have suggested, that "brain life"—the capacity for human intelligence, including consciousness, self-awareness and other generally recognized cerebral functions—does not come into being until after the twenty-eighth week of fetal life, then can experimentation on the fetus up until the end of the seventh month of pregnancy be seen as nothing too different from experimentation on a monkey or a rabbit? We, as a society, certainly do permit and find morally justifiable a wide range of biomedical investigations that make use of living animal subjects. And such experimentation has yielded impressive medical and scientific benefits—the human community has clearly profited from them.

Perhaps the fetus might, in the early months of pregnancy, more profitably be viewed as something that is simply a part of the mother's body—something similar to her gall bladder or her appendix. If she should choose, due to some pressing set of reasons, to have her gall bladder, appendix or her fetus removed, then she might give consent to have the excised part of her body studied. Isn't her permission—since the fetus was once a part of her—all the moral justification the investigator needs in order to proceed with an experiment?

Many scientists think so. But in a paper on fetal experimentation prepared for the National Commission, Dr. Leon Kass of the Kennedy Institute of Bioethics at Georgetown University said flatly: "The assertion that the fetus is a part of the mother is simply false. The fetus, in its varying stages, is a self-developing, self-changing whole, which assimilates and transforms food supplied by the mother, and grows and differentiates itself according to the plan encoded in its own DNA. . . ." Other experts consulting with the commission have attacked the validity of maternal consent on different grounds. If the mother has determined to abort her fetus, they argue, isn't the meaning of her consent highly equivocal? Generally speaking, in cases involving experimentation on a living, human child, the parent's proxy consent is required—i.e., the parent of a four-year-old child suffering from leukemia would have to give consent if the physician wished to treat the child with a new and unproven drug. The parent is assumed, in such an instance, to "speak for the child," to be the one who has the child's best interests at heart. In a situation in which the mother has already decided upon abortion, however, her own interests (wanting to terminate her pregnancy) would appear to be in some conflict with the interests of the fetus. Is she, then, the person who may most properly "speak on behalf of the fetus," the person who can be assumed to hold the best interests of that fetus closest to heart?

Paul Ramsey, the Princeton theologian and ethical philosopher, has suggested that a good deal of biomedical research involving the human fetus can be seen as similar to experimentation upon unconscious or dying patients. For the fetus, like the unconscious or dying person, is a nonconsenting, vulnerable and helpless human subject. In his recent book *The Ethics of Fetal Research* (Yale University Press, 1975), he carried this analogy further: "In cases of induced abortion," he wrote, "the fetal human being resembles not only the dying; it also closely resembles the condemned (even if necessarily and justly, but tragically, still the condemned)."

Dr. Ramsey, sixty-three, has been serving as one of the battery of consultants to the National Commission for the Protection of Human Subjects over the course of the past year. "One might argue," he pointed out, during the course of a talk we had in his Princeton office, "that capital punishment presented us with a similar 'golden opportunity' to do high-risk medical experimentation. After all, the condemned prisoner, like the living previable fetus, was going to die anyhow. . . . So why is it that we didn't research someone in that position to death? Such experimentation could, you know, have been seen as 'ennobling' the death of the human subject by using him to make great contributions to mankind. . . ."

Ramsey smiled briefly: "I think we all know that would be a morally degrading use of the condemned for us, as a society, to make."

I suggested to Ramsey that the classes of persons to whom he was comparing the fetus—that is, the unconscious, the dying, the condemned—were all among the more "helpless" kinds of human beings. This seemed to beg the whole question of the "personhood" of the fetus; and hence its eligibility for the customary human rights and protections. "I myself," he responded at once, "am of the opinion that the unborn fetus is a protectable human being."

Professor Ramsey leaned forward: "What we're *really* discussing here is not an object called the live but nonviable fetus. We're *really* discussing a tragical case of a dying baby—and the concern I am expressing is about the dying; that is, about imposing research upon this dying creature, who cannot consent. All of a sudden here are these 'things' that can be used for scientific experimentation—and the human fetus may soon become the most unprotected primate in medical research."

Fetal research is not something new under the sun—embryonic

human tissues taken from live but nonviable, spontaneously expelled fetuses were, for example, vitally necessary for culturing the viruses that led to the creation of polio vaccine back in the nineteen-forties. What *is* new is the extraordinary growth and vitality of this area of study: Fetal experimentation is a "hot" field in medicine, not only because of some striking recent advances, but because the ready availability of fetuses and fetal organs—as a result of the 1973 abortion decisions— has itself stimulated a good deal of work.

Some medical ethicists have, as a matter of fact, contended that if we as a society do condone abortion, then there can be no earthly reason for refusal to condone experimentation on the fetus. If, as in the *Roe-Wade* decision, we are making the claim that a mother has the right to abort her previable fetus because the fetus is not yet a "person in the whole sense," with its own set of rights and protections, then why defend and protect the fetus from experimental procedures? Drs. Willard Gaylin and Marc Lappé, of the Institute of Society, Ethics and the Life Sciences, have asserted that such a position—*i.e.*, permitting abortion but drawing the line at much or all fetal experimentation—has "an element of the irrational about it." Writing in the *Atlantic Monthly* in May of 1975, the two authors observed that the fact that some people do hold these mutually contradictory positions "perplex[es] many of us. Such absolute and complete defense of the dignity and autonomous rights of the fetus seems bizarre, when . . . in abortion, we condone procedures which subject the fetus to dismemberment, salt-induced osmotic shock, or surgical extirpation. No experimentation so far imagined would do the same. If society can condone abortion procedures which subject the live fetus to these unimaginable acts of violence, how can it balk at giving a mother an aspirin prior to those procedures in order to determine if the drug crosses the placenta—with the hope that the knowledge thereby gained will prevent damage to future, wanted babies? . . ."

Why not indeed? Critics of the Gaylin-Lappé position have pointed out that their moral justification for experimentation on the live fetus seems to be predicated on the fact that we're going to be committing "unimaginable acts of violence" upon it anyhow. In other words, because the worst will be visited upon the fetus ultimately, lesser acts along the way ought (rationally speaking) to be tolerated. This is a worrisome kind of argument to use in defense of any type of research.

It is true, furthermore, that experimentation can sometimes involve a good deal more than simply having mothers swallow aspirins just prior to abortion procedures. In that instance, the moral costs of the research would appear—in my own view—to be low, and the possible benefits to be high; there are, however, other instances in which the weighing-up of costs and benefits might tilt the argument strongly in the other direction. An experiment called "An Artificial Placenta," for example, involved an attempt to simulate the role of the placenta in supplying oxygen to the immature fetus. For that experiment, eight fetuses were obtained by hysterotomy—an abortion procedure often used after the fifth month of pregnancy—which is much like a Caesarian operation. The living fetuses, ranging in weight from 300 to 980 grams, were then placed in tanks filled with warmed, saline solution (to mimic amniotic fluid). Small cannulas, or tubes, were inserted in the umbilical arteries and veins—for pumping in and removing oxygenated blood. The researchers had constructed an elaborate circulation system, which, they hoped, would prove able to play the mother's role in supplying oxygen to the fetus. In the case of the wanted fetus, this could be the means of assisting the premature infant to survive until its lungs had matured enough to allow for breathing; the experiment described here was simply intended to test out the oxygenation circuitry. The following is taken from the investigators' report, and details the death of the largest (980 grams) fetus used in the study:

For the whole 5 hours of life, the fetus did not respire. Irregular gasping movements, twice a minute, occurred in the middle of the experiment but there was no proper respiration. Once the perfusion [i.e., the pumping-in of oxygenated blood] was stopped, however, the gasping respiratory efforts increased to 8 to 10 per minute. . . . After stopping the circuit, the heart slowed, became irregular and eventually stopped. . . . The fetus was quiet, making occasional stretching limb movements very like the ones reported in other human work . . . The fetus died 21 minutes after leaving the circuit.

"An Artificial Placenta" is a study that has provoked a storm of ethical criticism: Not only does it smack uncomfortably of research on the dying, but it brings to mind old tales of mad science, the "living beings preserved in tanks." This makes it all the more interesting to note that, shortly after this research was completed, it won the Foundation Prize

Award from the American Association of Obstetricians and
Gynecologists.

A more recent fetal investigation, which has not yet attracted much
attention and criticism—but which undoubtedly will —was reported
upon in a 1975 paper innocuously entitled: "Oxidation of Glucose and
D-*beta*-OH Butyrate by the Early Human Fetal Brain." This research
was directed toward ascertaining whether or not the fetal brain is
capable of utilizing the breakdown products of fat bodies when the usual
source of "brain energy" (which is glucose, a sugar) happens to be in
short supply. It was already known that when an adult was starving, D-
beta-OH butyrate, a breakdown product of fat stored in the liver, could
be taken up and used by the cerebral tissues; thus, when the adult brain
was not being nourished by its usual energy source, glucose, it could
survive on derivatives of the body's stored fats. But, given a state of fetal
emergency—say, if a diabetic mother were failing to provide adequate
glucose to the growing organism—was it possible for the fetus's brain to
function in the same way?

In order to answer this question, twelve human fetuses between twelve
and twenty-one weeks of gestation were studied. The fetuses were, at
these ages, nonviable; all died soon after delivery. Once the fetal
heartbeat had ceased, a catheter was inserted into the major artery
leading to the brain (the carotid). The head of the fetus was then, as the
investigators phrased it "isolated surgically from the other organs"; in
other words, the fetuses' heads were cut off. The fetal brains were then
perfused, first with the glucose, and then with D-*beta*-OH butyrate, and
the rate at which the cerebral tissues took up each of these substances
was carefully measured. In this way, it was possible to demonstrate that
the fetal brain can support metabolism of D-*beta*-OH butyrate as an
alternative "brain fuel" in the event that normal glucose supplies are
unavailable. (It should be explained that while the fetuses were officially
dead at the outset of this experiment—heartbeat having ceased—their
brain tissues were living, for death at the cellular level had not yet
occurred.)

Shades of *Donovan's Brain*! It is undeniably somewhat strange to
read, in the researchers' account of this experimentation, that the fetal
heads were placed in something they referred to as an "organ chamber."
And one cannot help but wonder if, on balance, it is worth doing this
kind of experiment in order to obtain this bit of knowledge of fetal

physiology. Some types of scientific research, particularly those that may serve to harden or brutalize the investigator (and the society he or she serves as well) may simply not be worth the moral price they exact.

But this is my own opinion; others would view this work as totally unobjectionable biomedical research. As the author and bioethicist Dr. Joseph Fletcher complained (in *The Ethics of Genetic Control,* Anchor Press, 1974): "Many people's belief propositions are entirely visceral, not rational—witness, for example, the repugnance some people feel at perfusion of a separated fetus head while feeling none at the perfusion of its kidney. Where we start from is essentially important in understanding our own moral judgments and others. . . ." In Fletcher's opinion, as stated repeatedly both in his book and in a paper prepared for the National Commission, the great advances in health and welfare that may accrue to the human race as a direct result of this experimentation are justification enough for such research on the human fetus.

According to Dr. Maurice J. Mahoney, Associate Professor of Human Genetics and Pediatrics at Yale University, experimentation involving the use of the whole, living fetus after an abortion—or, as may also occur, during the abortion procedure itself—represents well under 1 percent of published fetal research. Dr. Mahoney, another of the consultants working with the National Commission, has compiled an overview of all fetal work carried out between the years 1969 and 1975. "Most fetal research has actually addressed itself to diagnosing the fetus that is sick inside the uterus," he told me, "and to finding ways to help and treat that fetus." He himself, Dr. Mahoney said, takes a negative view of the small amount of fetal experimentation that falls into the "artificial placenta" and "severed heads" category. "I think there's something about invading the human body in these ways that makes most of us feel uncomfortable." Nevertheless, he noted, even such morally dubious studies as these have been motivated by sincere attempts to solve real and urgent medical problems.

Is it possible that the living fetus suffers during experimental procedures? Could the eight fetal subjects used in the "artificial placenta" research, for example, have been experiencing pain during their hours in the fluid-filled tank? It seems to be impossible to answer this question with total certainty.

However, in the opinion of every medical expert that I spoke to, it seems extraordinarily improbable that the fetus—at least before the age of twenty-eight weeks—could have the capacity to suffer. The central nervous system is apparently still too underdeveloped. The nerve endings in the skin have not yet extended outward with any of the degree of the affluence to be seen later on; the surface of the brain is relatively smooth, showing little in the way of the convolutions seen in the mature human brain cortex. The nerve endings have not yet developed their fatty myelin sheaths—and without these sheaths, which play some crucial role in the transmission of nervous "messages" from one nerve cell to the next, it is hard to imagine sensations of pain "getting through."

The fetus's "incapacity for experiencing pain" is one of the four major reasons set forth by Sissela Bok in support of continuing—though carefully regulated—research involving living fetal subjects. Dr. Bok, who is a lecturer on Medical Ethics at Harvard Medical School, is another of the consultants working with the National Commission for the Protection of Human Subjects. In a position paper prepared for the commission last March, she cited four major reasons for *not* permitting experimentation on nonconsenting human subjects. These were: (1) because we would not want to cause harm or suffering to the victim, (2) because we would not want to cause grief to those who were bound to the victim by ties of affection, love or economic dependence, (3) because we would not want to permit brutalization of the researcher and (4) because we would not want to permit the brutalization of society—since we all have a stake in the protection of human life.

In the case of the nonviable fetus, Bok pointed out, the organism is not capable of experiencing pain, and is dying as well—the researcher can, therefore, do it no serious harm. If consent for experimentation is given by the mother or both parents, no suffering will be caused on the part of those who might otherwise experience sadness, loss and anguish. The researcher will not be brutalized by the work he is doing, because he is experimenting on a "not-yet-viable" subject—an organism related to the human community in potential, but not yet in fact. Lastly, the society that permits such research will not be brutalized—as we would be, were we to permit experimentation on other kinds of vulnerable, nonconsenting subjects, such as the unconscious or dying person, the infant, the condemned prisoner—because we will not have violated our own strong sense of the worth, protectability and value of the individual human life.

In a conversation with Dr. Bok at her home in Cambridge, I asked when, in her estimation, the developing fetus becomes "a person." Bok, who has the wide blue eyes and blond haircut of a Dutch schoolgirl—so that the force and determination of her personality take one slightly by surprise—shook her head quickly. "I think that's a wrong question to ask," she said. "People have become simply mesmerized by that question, and it's really a question that has no answer. Because we are, after all, talking about something that is biologically 'human' not only after fertilization, but before—the ovum cell and the sperm cells are certainly both living and human even before they meet.

"But if we are talking about 'personhood,' then I believe it's impossible to speak of the fertilized egg, early in gestation, as 'a man,'" she continued, "although I realize that some theologians and others do. . . . It's as if one were to have to contemplate having funerals for two-or three-month fetuses that had miscarried or investigations for murder each time a fetus died *in utero* for reasons that weren't completely clear."

What is essential to do, suggested Dr. Bok, is to draw a line—"an artificial line, admittedly, because as I said, nature hasn't provided us with a biological one"—at some point early in pregnancy, and to say that beyond that stage of development no experimentation will be allowable. The line must, she stated, be drawn at a time in pregnancy when there can be no question whatsoever about the possible viability of the fetus to be used as subject in biomedical research. "I think," she added, "that we'll always have to be very careful anyhow, and that it will be essential for us to continue having experimentation committees that can oversee and regulate all proposals for this kind of research."

Last May, the National Commission for the Protection of Human Subjects, headed by Dr. Kenneth J. Ryan, submitted a full report on their deliberations and conclusions concerning research on the fetus to the Secretary of Health, Education and Welfare (and most of their recommendations were subsequently adopted and incorporated into new guidelines set by the Secretary in August). They suggested that the total ban on experimentation involving the living human fetus be lifted; they also called for the end of the moratorium on H.E.W.-supported fetal research. At the same time, they set the "age of viability" at twenty weeks (four and a half months) and 500 grams; this was much more conservative than the Supreme Court's definition had been. What this means, in essence, is that any fetus above the age of twenty weeks is "possibly viable," and therefore not a candidate for use in biomedical studies.

The commission also proposed a set of guidelines that would serve to restrict and carefully regulate (in some instances, prohibit outright) certain types of fetal experimentation. One kind of research procedure, for example, involves injecting the pregnant mother—who has already decided upon abortion—with drugs whose effects upon the fetus are not fully known. Then, following upon abortion procedures and the fetus's death, an autopsy is performed in order to ascertain the extent to which the drug was able (if it was able) to cross the placental membrane and affect the fetus. This kind of information is often invaluable to the physician treating the pregnant woman who plans to bring her baby to term.

In research such as this, the commission has now ruled against the "testing out" of potentially harmful drugs on fetuses whose mothers have decided upon abortion. The fetus whose mother plans to abort it, the commission has asserted, is no different in itself and in its own essence from a fetus whose mother plans to bring it to term; the only distinction between them is our knowledge of the impending abortion. This ought not, in the commission's opinion, serve to render the fetus-to-be-aborted into a testing animal. Mothers do sometimes change their minds about going ahead with a planned abortion—and for this reason, the commission has proscribed all experimentation involving the fetus *in utero* that entails anything more than "minimal risk."

It is interesting to note at this point that fetal work carried out by the defendants in the "Boston Grave-Robbing Case" would be permissible under the commission's new ruling, even though it is now about to be prosecuted by law. The case involved an attempt to find out what kinds of antibiotics might best be prescribed for pregnant women who had syphilis and who were allergic to penicillin. The syphilis, left alone, would invade the fetus and cause congenital defects; the penicillin, while capable of treating the fetus *in utero*, could not be tolerated by the pregnant mother. The question was what other antibiotic might most effectively be used in its place. In order to find out, researchers performed routine experimentation with fourteen pregnant women, all planning abortions, who agreed to accept injections of two different antibiotics while their fetuses were still *in utero*. Later on, after the nonviable fetuses were aborted and had died, the investigators did autopsies to find out which of the two substitute antibiotics had penetrated the placental barrier most effectively. The doctors who performed this research apparently neglected to get the mothers' signed permission to do the autopsies, which left them vulnerable to prosecution under grave-robbing statutes. Three of the doctors were indicted more than a year and a half ago, but their trial date has not yet been set.

One of the most sensitive issues to be discussed by the National Commission was the whole problem of research involving the intact, living fetus—in practical terms, an aborted fetus that is alive after delivery, but not viable and predictably going to die. Such a fetus must, the report of the commissioners stated, be viewed as a "dying subject." Stating that "issues of violation of integrity are . . . central," the commission recommended that "out of consideration for the dying subject," no experimental procedures be permitted that would alter the duration of the fetus's existence, either shortening its life by methods that might literally research it to death, or prolonging its life. (Enforcement of this regulation would, obviously, serve to prohibit research of the type reported upon in "An Artificial Placenta.")

In a section of their report entitled "Deliberations and Conclusions," the commissioners reviewed some of the complex problems that were debated during their effort to set some reasonable medical-social policy in this truly formidable area. But it is fascinating to note that nowhere in their summing-up document does the commission try to define the nature of the fetus (nonhuman? prehuman? animal-like? "somewhat-human"? "person"?); aside from the fact that the fetus is discussed under the rubric of "human subject," they remain silent on this question. But consultant Paul Ramsey, his sharp blue eyes glittering humorously, observed: ". . . the fact that the National Commission has drawn up *any* protective legislation concerning the human fetus has demonstrated that they do consider it to be a vulnerable, nonconsenting subject of research which is entitled to rights and protections of *some kinds*. It seems to me," he added, with a sly pursing of his lips, "that once you've conceded that much—I mean that you are talking about something which is, in some sense 'human' and protectable—why you've obviously conceded quite a lot."

Why do fetal experimentation at all? Why not, given that this research has ruffled so many moral feathers and aroused such antipathy among certain portions of the population, simply drop the enterprise altogether? The issue need not be linked to the question of abortion—we could, for example, think of continuing to permit abortions to women who want them during the early weeks of pregnancy, but prohibit the use of the abortuses (or the products of spontaneous miscarriages) as material for study in biomedical experimentation. Is there, in fact, some technological imperative urging us implacably onward? Is this research really necessary?

The fact is that fetal experimentation has become important in medicine because it seems to be exploding in a number of different directions, and many real advances have already been made. One of the most important among these, according to Professor Richard E. Behrman, M.D., chairman of the Department of Pediatrics at Columbia and director of its Babies Hospital, has been the development of *amniocentesis.*

The word means, literally, "piercing of the amnion," the sac enclosing the fetus; and the procedure involves sending a fine needle through the mother's belly and into her womb. By withdrawing a sample of the amniotic fluid and subjecting it to careful analysis, physicians are able to diagnose the presence of any of several dozen known genetic (and other) fetal diseases. For instance, Down's syndrome—called *mongolism*— one of the common causes of mental retardation, can readily be detected *in utero* by this means, and the prospective parents can then be forewarned of the danger and make their own choice about whether or not to terminate that pregnancy. "Now the whole development in this area did involve fetal research," observed Dr. Behrman. "I mean, someone did have to take the risk of putting that needle into the mother's uterus. And it had to be done not only in instances where the fetus was thought to be suffering from a disease, but in cases where it was known to be perfectly healthy—so that we could make the necessary comparions between the 'sick' and the 'normal' fetal cell."

The development of amniocentesis, Behrman continued, was crucial to the discovery of effective treatments for Rh-diseased fetuses and infants. Rh-disease, known also as Rh-incompatibility, used to result in the births of scores of severely damaged—retarded and deaf—children, and in the delivery of many dead infants as well. The problem arises when a mother and her fetus are of differing blood types, and cells in the mother's blood have become sensitized to the red blood cells of her developing offspring.

What occurs is essentially an immune reaction on the mother's part. She forms antibodies that literally attack and destroy the red blood cells of the fetus much as they would attack and annihilate an invading virus. By means of amniocentesis doctors are now, however, able to detect the distressed fetus before too much harm has taken place, and take steps to treat it while it remains lodged in the womb.

Fetal research whose effects will be felt in the future is directed mainly toward precise measurement of several dimensions of behavior *in utero*: For instance, the fetus's ability to perceive sound (and the subsequent effects upon heart-rate and brain activity), its swallowing and breathing and gasping patterns, its pattern of urination and its periods of apparent sleep are all currently under study. More exact knowledge of these fetal functions can make a life-and-death difference in circumstances where an early delivery may be indicated and the doctor is uncertain about the maturity of the fetus and therefore its capacity to survive outside the womb. Such information may also be vital to the earlier detection of fetuses that have become ill inside the uterus.

A number of fetal scientists, sensitive to recent criticisms, assert that a failure to pursue such research at this point would be an abandonment of the fetal patient; they add, too, that there has been far too little public awareness of the real gains that have been made in fetal medicine. For instance, researchers have learned to peer directly into the womb and identify structural defects in the developing fetus (such as *hydrocephalus*, or "water on the brain," and *anencephaly*, the failure of the brain to develop). These increasingly sophisticated diagnostic techniques do suggest that more sophisticated methods of treatment will be in the offing.

And many questions about fetal life and development, some of them of a pressing nature, remain unanswered. In numerous instances, for example, it is not known how the drugs a pregnant woman is taking are going to affect her fetus. If the mother is taking antidepressants (which cause changes in her mood by effecting alterations in her brain chemistry), are those drugs entering the brain of the growing fetus as well? And if so, do they affect brain development and functioning—and in what ways? Much more needs to be learned about the effects of maternal psychotropic drug-taking, maternal smoking and environmental pollutants that the mother may be ingesting. A recent study has, for instance, linked the taking of common aspirin with the incidence of stillbirths.

Thus far, it appears to me, the real advances in fetal knowledge have not come from the more brutal, invasive "cutting and chopping" experimentation, or research protocols that call for maintaining live fetuses in amnionlike brine; but rather from the standard kinds of medical research that are more or less directed towards caring for and helping the particular fetuses involved. The major gains (thus far) have really been in areas in which the fetus was the "subject to be treated," not the "object to be studied." Undoubtedly, however, we are now moving into a time in which critical choices are going to have to be faced and made. We do, on the one hand, share a strong presumption that experimentation on dying people is wrong, and that human life is not to be treated casually. On the other hand, many of us also do have doubts regarding the "personhood" of the fetus and realize that we may be balancing its welfare against that of untold numbers of babies who will live to enter the human community, and who can be benefited vastly from this research. On the one side are our concerns about permitting medical researchers to make use of something human; on the other, the promise of great scientific good to be obtained. There is an element of ultimate conflict in this whole, peculiar situation.

                                                                              1975

He and She

Sex Hormones and Behavior

Freud always maintained that human psychology had, as one of its components, some unknown biological "bedrock." He thought that we all, male and female alike, were captives of our physiology: that inborn propensities and tendencies exerted a profound effect upon behavior—and that these inner propensities were different in the two sexes. (Hence his now-infamous remark: "Anatomy is Destiny.") This belief is, however, not popular in the present, more "environmentalist" intellectual climate. The common assumption nowadays appears to be that where male behavior and female behavior are different they are so because of acculturation: that the display of either "masculinity" or "femininity" is by and large the result of social training.

Recent research on the sex hormones suggests that it is Freud's ideas which may be the more valid approximation of the reality. Endocrine studies have now established the critical role played by the sex hormones during prenatal life: These hormones are not only crucial to differentiation of the (male or female) sexual organs; but they "program" the brain, during fetal development, for the later display of either masculine or feminine behavior.

Numerous animal studies have confirmed that there is a curious link between the male hormone, testosterone, and levels of ongoing aggression. In the mouse, for example, fighting among males commences with the onset of puberty, when hormone levels are rising abruptly. Female mice fight only rarely, as is the case for males that have been castrated. When male mouse castrates are given testosterone injections, however, they display normal male adult fighting behavior within a matter of hours.

Does high testosterone level in the male bear a direct, one-to-one relationship to high levels of displayed aggression? In a study published last year, Dr. Robert Rose of the Boston University School of Medicine used new hormone assay techniques to take precise readings of male hormone levels in the bloodstreams of thirty-four male rhesus monkeys. At the same time, Rose, working with colleagues Irwin Bernstein and

19

John Holaday, measured the frequency with which each monkey became involved in aggressive interactions with other members of the colony; and also assessed the dominance rank of each rhesus within the entire group.

Rose and his co-workers found that there was a high correlation between the levels of the animals' testosterone and the position which each held within the dominance hierarchy. The higher a monkey's male hormone concentration was, the higher his position in the "pecking order" tended to be. Those monkeys who were the more dominant were those who were more aggressive. And testosterone levels related, with almost startling simplicity, to levels of displayed aggression: The five animals showing the greatest degree of threat and confrontation behavior were the five with the highest hormonal level. If a clear-cut principle can be said to have emerged from the Rose study it was that, at least among male rhesus monkeys, Testosterone Rules.

Dr. Rose, thirty-five, who trained as both a physician and a psychiatrist, is chief of Boston University's Department of Psychosomatic Medicine. He is currently, he notes, trying to investigate some of the questions raised by last year's male rhesus study. For example, was the superior status of the more dominant monkeys predicated on the fact that their male hormone levels were high in the first place? Or had testosterone levels risen as a *result* of dominance? Or both: Had raised hormonal levels meant more aggressiveness, which in turn lent itself to a higher dominance position, which in turn had the effect of raising testosterone level—a question of the rich getting richer?

Rose and his colleagues, in order to test these possibilities, took several of the male monkeys and placed them, individually, into new colonies consisting only of females (thirteen or more). The lone male, in each instance, assumed the highest dominance position immediately. He had frequent copulations and, says Rose, had "what appeared to be a fairly blissful existence. After several weeks in these paradisiacal circumstances, we tested each male for levels of testosterone circulating in his bloodstream. We found that, across the board, the levels had risen—something like a fourfold increase."

It seemed that male hormone levels were not set and fixed within the body; they could be "turned up" as a consequence of environmental stimuli. The next question was, would the reverse also hold true? The researchers took each of their experimental monkeys and introduced them into new and far different groups—colonies of strange males in which the dominance hierarchy was already well established. In this situation, each lone "new boy" in the colony was set upon by the other males, outnumbered and subjected to total defeat. After a mere half-hour of such treatment, the monkeys were rescued from their respective fields of disgrace, and testosterone measurements were taken once more. In all cases, hormone levels had fallen sharply.

"Defeat was associated with behavioral withdrawal. The monkeys all did, after their experience with the strange males, show every sign of real depression," says Rose. "And that withdrawal involved a concomitant drop in sexual levels." Rose is now interested in finding out what happens to a male rhesus's level of displayed aggressiveness, and to his position within the social hierarchy, when testosterone levels are manipulated upward or downward by adding or removing fixed amounts of male hormone.

Is the human male, like the male rhesus monkey, likely to behave more aggressively if his male hormone levels are high? In a study of a young criminal population at a Southern prison, Dr. Rose, working with Dr. Leo Kreuz, attempted to correlate degrees of expressed aggression (threats, refusals to obey orders, fights, etc.) among a group of young male prisoners with the levels of testosterone measured in their bloodstreams. He could not find, in this group of human males, the same direct relationship that had appeared in the male rhesus study. The only link between high testosterone and aggressive behavior appeared to be the odd fact that those men with the highest male hormone values were the ones who had committed more violent crimes during adolescence: Indeed, the higher a prisoner's testosterone level was in adulthod, the earlier in life he had tended to commit a violent crime.

Rose's fairly negative results are, however, at variance with the findings of a slightly earlier study (1971) of young college men, carried out by Dr. Harold Persky at the Albert Einstein Medical Center in Philadelphia. Persky and his co-workers measured testosterone production rates in a group of eighteen healthy males; at the same time, they administered a battery of psychological tests to their subjects designed to indicate degrees of hostility. In comparing results of endocrine and psychological measurements, the Persky researchers found a positive and direct correlation. In fact they found that those men with the highest testosterone production per unit of time were the very men whose sums of aggressive responses added up to the highest scores.

One of the great problems demonstrated by the conflicting results of the Rose and Persky research projects is—how does one define aggression? Is it observable outward acts, as specified in the Rose study; or is it negative aggressive *feelings* as defined by Persky? One writer, trying to sort out what is meant by "aggressive behavior," has suggested that there are least nine different kinds, including fear-induced, territorial, intermale, etc.

A further complication for the researcher trying to correlate hormone levels and aggression in humans is that the human male, unlike the male rhesus monkey, has learned to have a variety of complex feelings about showing aggressiveness—and has also a far greater awareness of the consequences that can follow. Thus, behaving aggressively may in itself be a stressor—and stress is another variable which, as further work of Rose's has demonstrated, appears to affect testosterone production in both monkeys and men.

In a study published in 1971, Rose and a group of five colleagues (which included the eminent Dr. John Mason) compared testosterone concentrations in urine samples of three disparate groups of men: The first were Vietnam soldiers awaiting an imminent attack; the second were infantrymen undergoing a stressful basic training period; and the third was a "control group" of Army volunteers—men working at routine jobs, and undergoing no stress at all. Rose and his co-workers found that the testosterone levels of the men under great stress were dramatically lower then the testosterone levels of the men in the unstressed group. In fact, male hormone readings for the Vietnam soldiers and basic-training groups were similar to the lowest testosterone values reported in studies of normal male subjects.

In a subsequent research effort, Rose studied a group of men in Officer's Candidate School, as they passed through the first twelve emotional, stressful weeks of training. He found that during this initial period, when anxiety about failure was intense, testosterone levels predictably dropped. Later on, in a more relaxed phase of training, when it was clear to the remaining candidates that they had "made it," male hormone levels rose once more—and so did levels of reported libido. "Stress seems to have an inhibiting effect on hormone secretion," remarks Rose. "It almost looks like a see-saw relationship: as the stress goes up, the testosterone goes down. In fact," he adds with a smile, "it's my hunch that, where those Vietnam soldiers were concerned, you couldn't even *give* away a copy of *Playboy!*"

The word *hormone*, in the Greek, means "to arouse"—and this is what hormones do. They are chemical substances, secreted first in one place (usually, but not always, a gland or organ), then released into the bloodstream to move through the body and exert their ultimate effects elsewhere—on other "target" organs. The hormones and hormone-producing glands are part of an interrelated chemical system, as intricately balanced as the body's "electrical" system (brain, spinal cord, nerves, sense organs). Hormones must be present in order for the initiation—or in some cases, inhibition—of a multitude of complex chemical processes. They are involved, for example, in the vital maintenance of correct blood sugar in the body; of the over-all rate of metabolism; in the regulation of water retention, of growth, of body responses to stress; and in the mediation of reproductive behavior.

The major sex hormones are secreted either in the testes in males (testosterone) or in the ovaries of females (progesterone and the estrogens, the important ones being 17 *beta*-estradiol and estrone). The adrenals, small yellowish organs lying just above each kidney, also secrete some sex hormones, including small amounts of testosterone and larger amounts of the weaker male hormone androstenedione (AD)—as well as a variety of other important hormones, including cortisol, cortisone and the "fight-or-flight" epinephrine (adrenalin).

Both sexes produce hormones of the opposite sex. In fact, men produce as much of the potent 17 *beta*-estradiol as adult women early in their menstrual cycle (when estrogen levels are at a low ebb). Men also have as much, or more, 17 *beta*-estradiol and estrone in their bloodstreams as do most postmenopausal women.

It is not the lack of estrogens which make a male a male, but the far higher levels of testosterone, antagonizing and nullifying the biological effects of the female hormones. An interesting little example of this is the recent finding that women after puberty have a greater sensitivity to odors than do men; and that this sensitivity is lost if male hormones are administered. (It is also lost when women are deprived of estrogen; and regained if the estrogen is replaced.)

In both males *and females*, testosterone appears to be the hormone which most strongly influences levels of libido. Incongruous as this idea might seem in the case of the female, it is now well supported by documentation from many sources. Studies of women who have had their adrenals (where most of the male hormones produced by females are secreted) removed indicate that these women suffer a dramatic loss in sexual desire; women who have had their ovaries removed rarely respond to loss of estrogens with loss of sex drive. In a report on a group of women who had had both operations (adrenalectomy and ovariectomy) it was found that virtually all were affected postoperatively, some merely reducing the frequency of intercourse, some losing interest in sex entirely. A subgroup of the same patients, who had the ovariectomy earlier in a separate and prior operation, reported experiencing no change in sexual interest or desire at that point.

Studies of women receiving testosterone injections also confirm the current hypothesis that male hormone mediates libidinal drive in the female. In one survey of a group of women receiving massive male hormone dosages (in the treatment of breast cancer), it was found that 99 percent of the patients were experiencing a marked surge in sexual desire. In another study, more than one hundred women were treated with male hormone for such symptoms as frigidity, dysmenorrhea, etc. More than three-fourths of these women responded with a reported rise in libido: some even complained that their sex drives had become excessive. (A small group of the same patients, treated for a period of time with estrogens, experienced no apparent change in libido whatsoever.)

In the male, testosterone has sometimes been used as a "maleness-bolstering" medication. Doctors have attempted to treat a variety of problems, including impotence, decreasing libido in aging men, and homosexuality with extracts of this most potent of male hormones. However, the efficacy of such treatments remains unclear. A massive review of efforts to counteract impotence with male hormones, published in 1947, concluded that physically healthy men did not respond to stepped-up dosages of testosterone; the problem was psychological. Where sexual performance did improve after male hormone injections, it was suggested, the improvement came from the easing of psychological anxieties.

A more recent (1970) research report suggests, however, that adding testosterone may after all have more than a placebo effect. In the study described, two groups of male patients with problems of impotence were compared: The men in the first group, receiving a placebo, showed improved sexual performance among less than half of their number. The second group, receiving real medication in the form of oral testosterone doses, responded with more adequate sexual functioning among more than three-quarters of the men taking part.

As to whether or not testosterone is useful in combating the sag in sexual drive sometimes experienced by aging males, the answer, simply, is not known—information on the results of such treatment is largely anecdotal and not, it should be added, particularly optimistic. Attempts to overcome homosexuality with added male hormones have, of course, been doomed: Testosterone influences libido strength in both sexes, but has nothing to do with determining the sex of the individual toward whom heightened sexual interest will be directed.

Puberty is a time when the sex hormones are said to be "awakening." The pituitary or "master gland" (an organ just under the brain, not much larger than a small pea) now begins sending increasing amounts of hormones called *gonadotropins* into the bloodstream. These are chemical messengers which, in the case of the male, stimulate sperm production and the secretion of testosterone by the cells of the testes. In the female the same gonadotropins (chemically identical to those of the male) are released by the pituitary; but in females they appear in sequence, rather than simultaneously. The first of these hormones stimulates the growth of the egg and its nest cells within the ovary, with an accompanying rise in estrogen secretion. The second gonadotropin, appearing slightly later in the cycle, subserves the production of progesterone, the female hormone which prepares the uterine lining to receive the fertilized egg. The sex hormones bring about, in their turn, the onset of secondary sexual characteristics—breast development in girls, growth of facial hair in boys, etc.—as well as the behavioral changes seen in adolescence.

Puberty, however, it now appears, does not constitute an "awakening" so much as it does a *reawakening*. Research during the past several decades has demonstrated that the sex hormones are, in fact, present during prenatal development. The concentrations in which they appear *in utero* are crucial not only to sexual differentiation (to produce a male or a female) but, it now appears, to differentiation of central nervous system tissues which will mediate masculine or feminine behavior during adult life.

The primitive gonad, it should be mentioned here, is sexually bipotential: it contains everything necessary for the fetus to develop either as male or female. There is a "rind," capable of becoming an ovary; a "core" which can develop as a testis; and two sets of internal duct systems, male and female. (One of them will become vestigial during sexual differentiation.) The "genital tubercle" grows into either a clitoris or a penis; the tissue above the urogenital groove either fuses, in the male, to become a scrotum or remains separate as the lips of the vagina.

What makes the embryonic gonad move toward differentiation as male or female? Surely it is genetic sex which sets a "direction"—and, it used to be assumed, determined everything that followed. But a series of brilliant experiments begun in the late forties by the French physiologist Alfred Jost gave definitive proof that it was in fact the prenatal hormones which played the decisive role in sexual differentiation of the developing fetus.

Jost, using surgical methods so delicate that they have been difficult for other investigators to imitate, castrated a male rabbit *in utero*. The infant male, when it was born, had completely *female* external genitalia: It appeared that in the absence of the testes (and therefore, testosterone) a genetic XY male fetus had developed in a female direction.

What would happen, then, to an ovariectomized female fetus? Jost removed the ovaries of a developing female rabbit fetus: At birth, she had normal female internal ducts and external genitalia. It seemed that the ovaries—and therefore, prenatal estrogens—were not vital to the female in order to ensure her normal differentiation. Indeed, given that no interference (such as the presence of testosterone) occurred, the fetus would always develop along female lines. Jost's work suggested that Nature had some fundamental bias in favor of producing females. Femaleness thus could not be—as Freud had suggested—some state of incompleted maleness; it appeared to be the basic form of life. Maleness was itself the correction: to achieve it, something had to be added on— male hormones.

(One psychoendocrinologist tells a story of how he explained to a very religious friend that the Adam and Eve story in Genesis was unlikely— that all biological evidence now available suggested that if one sex arose from the side of the other, it would have had to have been Adam who came from Eve. "Isn't God wonderful?" retorted his friend. "When He created the sexes, He even did it the hard way!")

Later work of Jost's, and a variety of other studies, have now demonstrated that testosterone must not only be present *in utero* in order for normal male differentiation to occur; it must be present during a sensitive "critical period." A male rabbit fetus, castrated by the nineteenth day after conception, will develop a completely female internal duct system and female genitalia. If castrated on day twenty-four, however, when the crucial phase is over, its development will be completely male.

Similarly, a male rat castrated *in utero* (this can now be done using chemical methods) will differentiate in a female direction—with a vaginal pouch, unfused scrotal tissues and a miniaturized penis which is indistinguishable from a clitoris. If castration is delayed until the critical period has passed, however—in this species, several days before birth—the rat will be irreversibly male.

In females, the presence of testosterone during the sensitive phase is as dramatic as its absence in males: A female rat receiving injections of male hormone during the critical period will become virilized, develop male-appearing genitalia, grow at an increased (male-type) rate, lose her reproductive cycle and become sterile. The same hormone doses, given ten days after birth, will achieve none of these effects.

Hormones—the right concentrations at the right times—are decisive to normal sexual differentiation. In the middle fifties, the group of researchers working with the great pioneer in hormones and behavior, Dr. William C. Young (who died in 1965), began to wonder: Was it possible that fetal hormones also had some determining effect upon the type of sexual behavior that would be shown much later on, at puberty? What actually caused males to show masculine sexual responses during mating, and females to display feminine responses? It had always been assumed that the reason, in each case, was genetic. A genetic male simply looked like a male and was expected to behave like one.

But if prenatal hormones could feminize his genitalia, and masculinize those of the female, could they also affect the two complementary sets of behavior and the type of sexual responses each would show?

In a now-classic experiment, Young and his colleagues demonstrated that a female guinea pig which had been virilized during prenatal life (through testosterone shots to the mother) would, when given male hormones at puberty, respond with startling amounts of male behavior. In subsequent work, Dr. Arnold A. Gerall showed that such females would not only mount other females and display pelvic thrusting, but (granted that genital development had been sufficiently anomalous) even intromission and ejaculation. In contrast, even when given high doses of estrogens, the capacity for showing normal female behavior— such as the "lordotic" response, typical in female rats and guinea pigs, in which the back is deeply arched and the genitals raised and presented to the male—was dramatically diminished. It was as if, during the period of prenatal life, some inner behavioral dial had been set at "male."

Experimental studies of the past ten years have now established that, at least in lower animals, there are sensitive neural tissues which (like the primitive gonad) are bisexual in potential. These tissues, located in the hypothalamic region at the base of the brain, differentiate during fetal development to produce an unequivocally "male" or "female" brain; that is, they become imprinted during prenatal life to mediate either masculine or feminine mating behavior at puberty. Again, the key to what happens is testosterone. If it is present, the "female" pattern will be suppressed and the "male" tissues will become organized for the steady release of gonadotropins at puberty, and for male sexual responses during reproductive behavior. If, on the other hand, testosterone is absent in uterine life, the sensitive brain areas will differentiate as "female." They will become programed for the cyclical release of pituitary hormones at puberty, and for female sexual responses during mating.

Might homosexuality in the male be tied to a less-than-adequate supply of testosterone during the critical period when brain tissues are differentiating and becoming "programed" for the display of later sexual behavior? A number of researchers, intrigued by a vast animal literature on the subject, have recently begun looking for a possible correlation between homosexual behavior and the actions of fetal hormones.

In a British report, published last fall, it was found that a group of homosexual males had lower levels of testosterone in their urine than did a comparison group of heterosexual males; and that a group of lesbian women had higher testosterone in urinary samples than did a control group of female heterosexuals.

This past year, in an investigation carried out at the Masters and Johnson research institute in St. Louis, the blood plasma testosterone values and sperm counts of thirty young homosexual college students were carefully analyzed. It was found that among the fifteen men in the group who were totally, or almost totally, homosexual, testosterone readings were much lower than they were among the other half of the men, who had definite heterosexual proclivities also. Sperm scores were also astonishingly lower among exclusively homosexual males. There appeared, interestingly enough, to be no great difference either in hormone levels or sperm counts when the bisexual males were compared with a "control" group of heterosexuals. According to the director of this research project, Dr. Robert C. Kolodny, the important question to be studied now is whether diminished testosterone supply is somehow a *result* of homosexual behavior—or whether it reflects an endocrine makeup that is simply different from that of heterosexuals in the first place.

A fascinating addendum to the recent research on human homosexuality—and, certainly, food for speculation—is the work of Dr. Ingeborg Ward of Villanova University. In an experiment reported in *Science*, Dr. Ward demonstrated that severe stress to a mother rat during pregnancy can block the normal behavioral development of her male offspring—and in effect, demasculinize them.

Dr. Ward, trained as a psychologist, proceeded in this experiment by placing the rat mothers-to-be, periodically, into clear plastic tubes. The tubes, from which it was impossible to escape, were then illuminated from above by implacable, glaring lights. The animals responded with every sign of distress: urination, defecation, hair standing on end. (Rats fear these lights so greatly that, initially, when they were too bright, several of the animals died.) Other pregnant females, kept in a nearby vivarium, were not placed under stress, and served as control animals.

After birth, some of the male "pups" from the stressed mothers, and some from the unstressed mothers, were subjected to further adversities—they were placed in ice-cube trays which were shaken periodically on a vibrating metal rack. When the male offspring all reached the age of puberty (ninety days in the rat), they were paired with females in heat.

Those males which had been stressed prenatally showed low degrees of masculine response, and little sexual interest (as did males which were both prenatally and postnatally stressed). They mated far less frequently than did the group which had been subjected to stress only after birth, or those which had not been stressed at all.

All of the rats were then castrated. Some ten days later they were given injections of estrogen, which were followed up with shots of progesterone. The males were then paired with "stud" male partners. In this situation, those pups which had been stressed *in utero* displayed striking amounts of female sexual behavior, including the lordotic arch. The same high degree of feminine receptivity could not be elicited from males stressed after birth, or those not stressed at all.

It is Dr. Ward's belief that the nonmasculine behavior shown by the prenatally stressed pups resulted from abnormal neural tissue-imprinting during the critical period of fetal development. "In response to high degrees of environmental stress," she explains, "the pituitary began stimulating increased production of the adrenal 'stress' hormones. Included among these is a weak male sex hormone, androstenedione (AD). As a side effect of this situation, the testes also slowed down their production and release of the far more potent testosterone."

The weaker but more plentiful AD then competed with the more powerful testosterone, theorizes Dr. Ward, for control of the same chemical resting sites within the sensitive neural tissues—and the weaker AD won out. "The net result was that testosterone was unable to do its normal job of programing the brain," she says. "The tissues developed under the influence of the weaker hormone, and thus the animals were unable to differentiate as normally functioning males."

Dr. Ward is now trying to determine whether male rats will become feminized simply by being given large doses of AD prenatally. But at present the ingenious experiment described above stands as the sole demonstration that, by manipulating the prenatal environment, one can obtain exactly the same awesome alterations in male and female behavior as have been obtained previously only through direct manipulations of the fetal hormones.

One cannot of course generalize from rats to humans. (And the psychoendocrinological journals are as full of cautions about this temptation as the old temperance tracts once were about the dangers of drink.) Nevertheless, as one researcher remarked privately: "We do, in fact, work with the implicit assumption that what is found to be true in one species will hold true up and down the phylogenetic scale. It's usually an exception when one discovers a physiological mechanism in one species and then finds it absent—or totally reversed—in others. After all, aren't we making the same sorts of assumptions when we test out our drugs on rats?"

The presumption is, then, that the higher animals including monkeys, apes and human beings are, like the rat and the guinea pig, *not* psychosexually neutral at birth: That they are, even before the onset of learning and social experience, "programed" or predisposed by early hormonal influences to acquire specific, either masculine or feminine, patterns of behavior. In a study carried out in the late nineteen-sixties by Dr. Robert W. Goy, it was demonstrated that female rhesus monkeys, exposed to male sex hormones during prenatal development, would later behave in more malelike, than femalelike, fashion. Dr. Goy, working at the Oregon Regional Primate Research Center, injected a group of expectant monkey mothers with periodic doses of testosterone. The result was, not surprisingly, a generation of female offspring whose genitalia were male in appearance. These female "pseudoher-maphrodites" were separated from their mothers at birth, and henceforth socialized only with their agemates.

Goy carefully studied the behavior of the virilized females as they grew into childhood. It had already been well established, through the famous monkey studies of Dr. Harry Harlow and others, that the play behavior of juvenile male monkeys was measurably different from that of the young females (and that these differences were not "taught" by the parent monkeys, because they manifested themselves even when the juveniles had no contact whatsoever with the older generation). The young males, for example, showed much more social threat behavior; they initiated play more often than did the young females; and they engaged in rough-and-tumble and pursuit play to a far greater degree. The males also withdrew less from threats and approaches made by others; and they engaged in more sexual play, including the frequent mounting which was in effect a "game" in which the future sexual role was being rehearsed.

The impressive thing about Goy's experimentally masculinized females was that they too behaved in all of these ways. They displayed the elevated levels of energy and activity commonly seen in young male monkeys: In fact their play behavior was much more similar to that of the male than to anything normally encountered in the behavior of the juvenile female.

In a 1967 study carried out at the Psychohormonal Research Unit of Johns Hopkins Medical School, the same unusually high levels of energy and activity were found in a group of ten young girls who had been accidentally masculinized *in utero*. This research investigation was carried out by Dr. Anke Ehrhardt, working in collaboration with the Psychohormonal Unit's well-known director, Dr. John Money. The ten young females taking part had all been virilized as a result of what was essentially a medical mishap: Their mothers were given progestin, a synthetic hormone, during pregnancy (in order to prevent unwanted abortion). It was not known at the time—during the nineteen-fifties— that certain progestins have a masculinizing effect on the developing female fetus. Nine of the ten girls had been born with malelike genitalia, including an enlarged clitoris and a fused, empty scrotum. They received surgical correction early in life, and development proceeded normally from that point onward; psychosexual development, carefully evaluated by Dr. Ehrhardt in extensive tests and interviews, was certainly within the normal female range also. But it did seem to point toward some interesting questions about what the influence of those masculinizing fetal hormones had been.

Of the ten girls, ranging in age from almost four to almost fifteen, nine were out-and-out tomboys. They preferred trucks, guns and other boys' toys to dolls. They loved being outdoors, climbing trees, playing football and baseball. They preferred being with boys to being with girls; they wore boys' clothing styles and were more or less indifferent—some were actively opposed—to skirts and more feminine modes of dress. All displayed a high frequency of self-assertion and self-reliance, some of them to such an extent that their mothers were concerned about their behavior. "My daughter acts like a boy," complained one woman. "It might be because of the hormones. She is the opposite from me. I was the dainty type." Another family was having problems because their fetally virilized daughter was far better in sports than was her older brother.

Says Dr. Ehrhardt, who is now an assistant research professor of pediatrics and psychiatry at the State University of New York at Buffalo: "The girls were consistently less interested in doll-playing than were a 'control' group of ten girls, who were matched with them in every possible way—age, race, socioeconomic level, I.Q., etc. Also, the 'control' girls did a great deal of bride-fantasying, and involved themselves frequently in those sorts of games which are actually childhood rehearsals of the future maternal and wifely roles. In contrast, the fetally masculinized girls tended to fantasize about future careers."

In studies which she and Dr. Money have done on girls suffering from adrenogenital syndrome, notes Dr. Ehrhardt, the same tomboyish element and high-energy level regularly appear. Adrenogenital syndrome is a genetically transmitted condition which causes masculinization of the female fetus during prenatal development. The condition is due, briefly, to an error in metabolism which causes the adrenals to become overactive and produce too many hormones, including too many male hormones. It is now possible to stabilize this dysfunction with cortisone, so that overproduction of male hormones in the adrenogenital girl can be stopped postnatally, and her genitals can be surgically feminized. Still, psychosexual development of these girls, similar to the progestin-induced masculinized girls, is toward the more "malelike" end of the normal female spectrum—high degrees of activity expressed in more masculine kinds of behavior.

In assessing which behaviors were to be called "masculine" and which were to be called "feminine," Drs. Ehrhardt and Money relied on criteria such as energy expenditure (much higher in boys), toy and sports preferences, career ambitions, maternalism (girls are usually fascinated by infants and infant care; boys are usually not) and several other items, including body image, clothing choice, etc. In statistical analyses of responses of large groups of boys and girls, sex-related "male" and "female" clusters about these items do reliably emerge.

"Nevertheless, isn't it possible," I asked Dr. Ehrhardt, who is a fair-haired, pretty German-born woman in her early thirties, "that these 'sex differences' are merely artifacts of our culture? Most psychiatrists and psychologists (and of course, most Women's Liberationists) believe that they result primarily from social experience. That is, a small female child is taught very early, or learns by imitation, those 'feminine' ways in which she is expected to behave—and responds by doing it."

"I would agree," she answered, "that the most powerful factors in the shaping of gender identity are probably experiential and social. In other words the primary thing is whether a person is called and thought of (and calls himself or herself) male or female. This is of course fundamental to identity. But within the broad spectrums of behavior which we call either masculine or feminine, there are certainly very wide variations. You can have, on the one hand, a woman who is totally domestic and maternal; and on the other, a person who is uninterested in children and wants only a career. My speculation would be that there is a fetal hormonal history, in both these cases, disposing the individual in one direction or the other. In other words, what I'm suggesting is that there may very well be normal female hormone correlates to the variations of normal female behavior.

"The main message of most of this work, both with animals and with humans," she added, "is that hormones before birth may have an organizing effect upon behavior that will appear only much later—that social environment is the mold in which basic tendencies, already present, will be shaped and formed. The idea is that testosterone, by its presence or absence, sets some kind of behavioral potential; and that postnatal experiences are actually acting upon a physiologically biased substrate."

One very strange factor emerging from Dr. Ehrhardt's study of the ten progestin-virilized girls was that their I.Q.'s were all unusually high. Six of them had I.Q.'s above 130; thus, in a random sample in which one would normally expect to see this elevated value in 2.2 percent of cases, it appeared in 60 percent. In an earlier study of seventy adrenogenital girls and boys carried out by Drs. Money and V. Lewis, the same peculiar incidence of high I.Q. was encountered. In a group where, it would have been expected, 25 percent of those tested would have I.Q.'s above 110, it was found that there was an actual observed frequency of 60 percent having I.Q.'s above that value.

"Does this make you think," I asked Dr. Ehrhardt, "that boys, who are normally exposed to more masculinizing hormones *in utero*, would be expected to be by that very fact brighter than girls?"

"I don't think boys are brighter," she answered quickly. "But again, female and male intelligences do tend to cluster, statistically, around different sets of abilities. Boys appear to do better in mathematics and more abstract kinds of intellectual functioning, while girls score much higher in verbal capabilities." She paused: "I would be willing to allow that chemical influences in prenatal life might increase the level of energy and activity; and that they might have some enhancing effect upon intellectual capacities."

In a recent British publication, "Antenatal Progesterone and Intelligence," by Dr. Katherina Dalton, the very same phenomenon appeared. Dr. Dalton studied a group of boys and girls whose mothers had been given progesterone during pregnancy. (Progesterone, a female hormone, is similar to the progestins, but has no masculinizing side effects.) All of the progesterone offspring studied by Dr. Dalton, both male and female, progressed better and faster than a comparison control group of children. They stood earlier, walked earlier, received significantly better grades in academic subjects, verbal reasoning, English, etc. Moreover, the more of the hormone their mothers had received, the earlier they walked and the better they did in school.

Thus, according to Dr. Ehrhardt, the intelligence-enhancing effect, if it proves to be definitely there, may have nothing to do with the masculinizing effect: "The kids in Dr. Dalton's study showed an increase in I.Q. without becoming virilized. So what we're seeing may just be due to some general chemical influence of these hormones. As far as I'm concerned, the whole question of the connection between intelligence and prenatal hormones is definitely a wide-open one."

1972

Brain Researcher José Delgado Asks

"What Kind of Humans Would We Like to Construct?"

We are going to talk about love and war and hate," begins the professor, Dr. José M.R. Delgado of the Yale University School of Medicine. The class is an undergraduate course at Yale. Although registration was limited to fifteen, the seminar room is crowded; every chair around the long table is filled, and some students are sitting on packing cases stored at one end, and some are on extra chairs near the door. "But we shall consider these subjects in a novel way: from the inside of the thinking brain. What is going on there, what is happening *in the nerve cells* while we talk, while we behave, while we feel?"

Delgado, an emotional speaker, pauses. A spare man in his midfifties, he leans forward on the table, resting his weight on both large hands. His eyes, restless and light in color, rove swiftly around the circle of staring faces. "We have a new way to study behavior, a new methodology which we have developed," he resumes in a voice that is low but as vibrant with promise as a preacher's. There is a stir, almost a sigh from the students; this is what they want to hear about, this "new methodology."

It is E.S.B: electrical stimulation of the brain. Delgado is one of the leading pioneers in its refinement and development. He is also the impassioned prophet of a new "psychocivilized" society whose members would influence and alter their own mental functions to create a "happier, less destructive and better balanced man."

A few days earlier, just before the start of classes, *The New York Times* ran a front-page story on Dr. Delgado that was picked up by newspapers across the country. It described his most recent accomplishment: the establishment of direct nonsensory communication between the computer and the brain of a chimp. This study was the latest in a series of experiments involving two-way radio-wave contact with the brains of freely interacting animals. Because it clearly demonstrates that behavior can be influenced by remote radio command, this research has

36

been seen by some as posing an ultimate threat to human freedom and integrity.

The morning that story appeared, it was raining mildly in New Haven. In Delgado's secretary's office, part of the cluttered wing his staff occupies on the second floor of the Sterling Hall of Medicine, the telephone started ringing early; it kept on and on. In the darkroom next door, Delgado was just finishing the photographing of some E.E.G. recordings, or "brain waves." He bustles back across the hall and into his own office, immaculate as a surgeon in his white laboratory coat. "What do you want me to tell you?" he asks shortly, sitting down at his desk. He runs an irritable hand over his short-cut, curly hair. "I don't want to talk about my wife, my family, my friends. That's not science." He glances, scowling, through the window at the large white square of the School of Public Health building next door, and his expression suddenly clears. He turns back, leans forward over his desk relaxedly in one of the rapid mood changes which one very quickly learns to expect.

"The human race," he says, "is at an evolutionary turning point. We're very close to having the power to construct our own mental functions, through a knowledge of genetics (which I think will be complete within the next twenty-five years); and through a knowledge of the cerebral mechanisms which underlie our behavior. The question is what sort of humans would we like, ideally, to construct?" He smiles. "Not only our cities are very badly planned; we as human beings are, too. The results in both cases are disastrous.

"I am an optimist," continues Delgado. "I don't accept Lorenz's 'cosmic slip.' I don't think we're condemned by our natural fate to violence and self-destruction. My thesis is that just as we've evolved in our understanding of material forces, so we can—through a combination of new technology and of intelligence—evolve in our understanding of the mind.

"Man once used his intelligence to achieve ecological liberation, so that he no longer had to be wet when it rained, or cold when the sun was hidden, or killed because predators were hungry. He can achieve mental liberation also. Through an understanding of the brain, the brain itself may act to reshape its own structures and functions intelligently. That we bring this about is most essential for the future of mankind."

Delgado glances at his watch: "Come, I will show you around. I must hurry; I'm leaving for Zurich in two days." He looks impatient and harried again.

We go across the hall, through the secretary's office, into a large room full of equipment. Here, the two electronics engineers on Delgado's staff are at work. "How are you coming along?" asks Delgado, falling into a rapid conversation about equipment that will be needed for an experiment going on in Bermuda, for a motion-recording study to be carried out in a psychiatric ward, for a monkey-colony investigation going on upstairs; also, he checks over drawings of an improved transdermal (under the skin) brain stimulator. The noise of the phone and the secretary's voice provide a constant backdrop: "Dr. Delgado?" she asks, hurrying in suddenly. "How would you like to be on television?"

"What?" he says distractedly, in his rapid Spanish accent. "I wouldn't like it at all."

"How would you like to be on the David Frost show?"

"What's that?" He taps his foot impatiently. She seems uncomfortable: "He doesn't know," she says, looking at the two engineers helplessly. But they both shake their heads and shrug; they don't know either. "What shall I say?" she asks.

"Say no," Delgado answers curtly, but then, more gently, adds: "Tell them I'm going to Zurich. Tell them to call me some other time. I'm sorry."

On the way up to the fourth-floor laboratory, he stops in his office to pick up a small plastic box which at first sight looks empty. "Here is something that's going to be fantastic, really exciting," he says, holding it up like a conjuror. "But I can't tell you what it is; it's too early, it wouldn't be scientific."

Wouldn't he be willing to explain what it is privately? He hesitates: "All right . . . " But then he hurries off, at a pace only a little short of a run. Staring at the box in his hand, I see that it does contain something—two tiny chemitrodes, that is, arrays of electrodes and fine chemical tubes that can be inserted into the brain. "When we know the mechanisms by which the brain operates," resumes Delgado, "then we will be able to control our reality. The predicament of mankind is not too different from that of the dinosaurs, who flourished on earth for some thirty million years. They had very little intelligence; and forty tons of flesh and bones. When the environment began to change, they lacked the intelligence to understand their situation, to adapt. Their fate—extinction.

"We, too, have developed disproportionate muscles and bones: missiles, guns, biological warfare. Our brains are not developed accordingly; they must become so or our own fate will be the same." We pass through a wide corridor. On either side are shining steel machines with bright plastic, electric leads coming out of them; it looks as cheery as a nursery school. In one room a monkey is calmly sitting in a plastic chair while his brain waves are recorded. He throws us a curious glance as we go by.

Delgado turns into a room at the left, the laboratory of his new young assistant, freshly arrived from Germany. They sit down together and the older man begins a careful explanation of how the chemitrodes are to be mounted. When he is finished, the new researcher blushes and stammers: "Please, I'm still not understanding too well . . . the English. Won't you repeat?" Delgado very patiently goes over the instructions. Then he stands up and excuses himself for a moment.

While he is gone, I ask the assistant what the new experiment will be. He explains haltingly that they are going to infuse a radioactive substance through the monkey's brain very slowly—"Stop, don't say anything!" cries Delgado, rushing back into the laboratory. "You mustn't tell her, she's dangerous. She's a journalist!"

"What, what?" demands the assistant, jumping back, frightened. And suddenly, inexplicably, the three of us burst out laughing.

In a small corridor off the end of the main hallway are the animal cages, full of rhesus monkeys and gibbons right now. Delgado goes into one room, opening the cage of a female rhesus named Linda (after his eight-year-old daughter). "Hello, hello, Linda," he says softly to the monkey, who scampers up onto the wire-mesh ceiling. "It's okay, it's okay, come down." He takes a piece of apple, holds it out to her. Linda comes down, grabs the apple; a moment later she throws it at Delgado. He laughs. "That's not nice Linda, come down." She consents at last, comes swiftly to sit in Delgado's arms and throws her own around his neck.

He parts the hair on her shoulder, revealing an almost invisible transdermal brain stimulator. "Linda has been wearing this for over a year now; it's very important in its implication for humans. One of the real difficulties with humans is the cosmetic one. This transdermal can be placed below the skin and sealed forever, so that there are no unsightly plugs or equipment showing. We're working now on another one that would be even smaller."

Delgado strokes Linda's fur; then he looks up. "I have a great respect for the human brain," he remarks with the air of a man who has had to

reiterate the statement often. "It distressed me greatly when I first came
to this country in the early fifties to see so many patients without frontal
lobes. Of course, much psychosurgery has now been replaced by drug
treatment, but there are still people with dangerous seizures that simply
do not respond to medication. In these cases, rather extensive portions
of the temporal lobe may be removed—and since brain tissue doesn't
regenerate, those functions that are lost are lost.

"Intracerebral electrodes offer a more conservative approach. Instead
of cutting down through cerebral tissue, we insert very fine stainless steel
wires. Then we can record the activity of various brain areas; in this way
it becomes possible to locate the disturbances with a good degree of
precision. After that, damaged areas can be treated by cauterization, or
by E.S.B. in a brain area which inhibits on-going activity. Or still
another possibility would be inducing electrical excitement in a
competing area. For instance, there is one epileptic patient who uses a
self-stimulator each time he feels a seizure coming on. By activating
another part of the brain, he stops the discharge from spreading; the fit
never develops."

In the past several years, electrode implantation has been used in the
diagnosis and treatment of involuntary movements and intractable
pain, as well as in epilepsy, some cases of schizophrenia and of excessive
anxiety. Delgado was one of a small group of brain researchers to
pioneer their clinical application. Implantation of electrodes, although
carried out only as an alternative to destructive surgery, is "like
installing a magic window through which one may look at the activity of
the conscious, behaving brain.

"We are," says Delgado, "only in the initial stages of our
understanding of E.S.B., but we know that it can delay a heartbeat,
move a finger, bring a word to memory, evoke a sensation."

Brain stimulation in humans has elicited diverse and curious
responses. It has stirred long hallucinations, such as hearing a piece of
music being played from beginning to end; it has produced peculiar
illusions of *déjà vu*—the intense feeling that the present moment has
been experienced in the past. Patients have also described the vivid
"reliving" of moments from their past, far more immediate than mere
recollection. All the sensations of the former experience seem to spring
to life—cars passing in the street outside, the sounds of children playing,
words said and forgotten long ago.

"There are basic mechanisms inside the brain, I believe," says Delgado, "that are responsible for all mental activities, including emotion. I think we are now on the threshold of understanding them. We must do so—and soon—if the precarious race between unchained atoms and intelligent brains is to be won."

José Manuel Rodriguez Delgado was born in Ronda, Spain, in 1915. The town, which stands high on a rocky cliff to the southwest of Granada, was one of the last strongholds of the Moors. Dr. Delgado is the son of Rafael Rodriguez Amerigo; on the paternal side he is directly descended from Amerigo Vespucci. (The name Delgado is his mother's maiden name: in Spain, where lineage is of paramount importance, a child takes the names of both grandparents as surname. Thus, Delgado's last name there is Rodriguez Delgado.)

José, the second of three boys (his older brother is a staff member of the United Nations), went directly from high school to the University of Madrid, taking his degree in medicine just before the outbreak of the Spanish Civil War. In 1938 he was drafted and joined the Spanish Republicans. "I fought with them until the triumph of Franco, then I was thrown into a concentration camp. Those few months had a great effect upon me; they shaped me."

In what way?

"Oh, well"—he shrugs slightly, his brows beetling in annoyance; he dislikes direct questions —"that all has nothing to do with my work." After his release in 1939, Delgado returned to the University of Madrid to take his M.D. once again (the old one was no longer valid). Then he lingered to take a Ph.D. in science at the Cajal Institute in Madrid. In 1950, he was invited to Yale by the famed neurophysiologist John Fulton. "And I never have left here," he concludes in a pleased voice.

In 1956, Delgado, in his early forties, met Caroline Stoddard, the pretty, twenty-two-year-old daughter of a Yale administrator; they were married within the year. They now have two children: Linda, eight, and José Carlos, eleven. After fourteen years of marriage, Caroline Delgado is quietly and passionately devoted to her husband's work, perhaps even a bit awed by it. (She sometimes refers to him, in a voice innocent of irony, as "the great Delgado.") "I go in to the lab with José pretty much every morning," she says cheerfully. She generally works in the same office, editing and typing papers. Does she mind the work? "Oh, no, I love it! It's nice being with someone who's always optimistic. And then it's a continuing circus; it's fun to see what's coming next. The brain is a relatively new field—there's a tremendous feeling of excitement."

The human brain—that most delicate, complex organ, the organ of selection and imagination—is a mass of about 10 billion neurons, or nerve cells, which are almost continually receiving, transmitting, and discharging electrical impulses. In the early nineteen-twenties, Hans Berger, a German psychiatrist, first recorded the electrical activity of the human brain. Berger's electroencephalograms (E.E.G's) were made by attaching electrodes to the outside of the scalp. They could convey only the crudest information, for the signals emanating from the "black box" of the brain were bewildering and manifold: It was like opening the door on a cocktail party where many conversations were going on at once. Some of the voices were persistent, some started and stopped; there was a great deal of background racket. Not for many years—and not until the advent of electronic computers—were researchers able to sort out the signals coming from various structures and areas of the brain.

Shortly after Berger first recorded brain waves, the Swiss neurophysiologist W. R. Hess implanted very fine, stainless-steel electrodes deep within the brain of a cat. The cat, once recovered from the anesthesia, could not feel the wires at all. For the brain, the most exquisite of sensory interpreters, actually has no receptors or nerve endings in its own tissue; it feels nothing. Hess introduced a mild electrical impulse, stimulating the central gray matter, and the cat suddenly behaved "as if threatened by a dog." Evidently, nerve cells associated with emotions of rage had been activated. "It spits, snorts or growls," wrote Hess," . . . its pupils widen . . . its ears lie back, or move back and forth to frighten the non-existing enemy."

Hess's experiment raised some excited speculations. It was known that certain areas of the brain controlled specific functions such as speech, sight, the flexing of arm and leg muscles. But emotions were not thought to be represented specifically—was it possible that there *were* areas or "centers" in the brain which corresponded to the different emotional states? E.S.B. seemed to offer a way to study the mechanisms of emotions experimentally, and yet, says Delgado, "When I came to this country some twenty years after Hess's early work, there were very few people—practically no one—working with brain stimulation."

Delgado had learned E.S.B. techniques while still in Spain, "mainly from reading about Hess's experiments. I was self-taught." Electrode implantation does not entail a large opening in the skull. Only a small burr hole is drilled, through which micromanipulators guide the electrode shafts—assemblies of very fine wires insulated with Teflon and scraped bare at the tips to permit the passage of current—down to their desired locations in the brain. The electrodes can be placed quite precisely with the aid of special (stereotaxic) maps of the brain and measuring instruments. Once they are in, the ends of the wires are soldered to a small exterior socket anchored to the skull.

After anesthesia wears off, plugging into the fully awake brain of cat, monkey or man is as simple as putting a lamp plug in a wall socket. There is no "awareness" of the electrodes, no ensuing damage to brain tissue. "There are chimps in our laboratory," Delgado says, "who have had up to one hundred contacts implanted for more than four years; there seems to be no limit to how long they may safely be left in."

Delgado's early work at Yale was done with cats, and then increasingly with the far more intelligent and interesting monkey. Under the influence of E.S.B., the animals performed like electrical toys. "By pushing the right 'button' we could make a monkey open or shut his eyes, turn his head, move his tongue, flex his limbs. He could be made to yawn, sneeze, hop." During one experiment, a cat began the motions of licking each time it was stimulated at a certain point in the cortex. If the animal happened to be sleeping, it licked in its sleep; if awake, however, the cat looked around for a milk bowl to lap at; if there was no bowl, it began licking its own fur. "The cat seemed determined"—Delgado smiles—"to make sense out of what he was doing."

E.S.B. can evoke not only simple but complicated behaviors which may be performed in sequence. Each time a monkey named Ludy was stimulated in the red nucleus (in the posterior part of the brain) she would stop what she was doing; change expression, turn her head to the right; stand up on two feet and circle to the right; climb a pole and then descend again; growl, threaten and often attack another monkey: then change attitude and approach the rest of the group in a friendly way. This "automatism" was repeated in the same order each time—through twenty thousand stimulations!

"Interestingly enough," remarks Delgado, "when Ludy was

stimulated at another point in the red nucleus only three millimeters away, she simply yawned."

Stimulation of certain brain areas has caused animals to increase the amount of food they eat by as much as 1,000 percent, while E.S.B. at hunger-inhibiting points will make starving monkeys and cats turn away from food. The tickling of a few electric volts can send a monkey into a deep sleep, or snap him awake. "By brain stimulations in the hypothalamic region we can adjust the size of a monkey's eye pupil, making it larger or smaller as easily as you would the lens of a camera," Delgado adds.

Sometimes it may happen that the voluntary impulse of an animal opposes an electrically evoked movement such as raising of a foreleg; in that case, the movement might not occur. "But," Delgado says, "by increasing the intensity of stimulation it is always possible to get the animal to respond as 'directed.'"

Similarly, human beings are unable to resist motor responses elicited by E.S.B.: Delgado describes a patient under treatment for psychomotor epilepsy who slowly clenched his hand into a fist each time he was stimulated through an electrode in the left parietal cortex. When asked to try to keep his fingers extended through the next stimulation, the man simply could not do it. "I guess, doctor," he commented ruefully, "that your electricity is stronger than my will."

One fascinating question, debated since the time of Hess, was whether the rage which could be induced in cats by E.S.B. was truly experienced by them emotionally. Were the hissing and spitting mere motor responses—or did the cat actually feel all the noxious sensations which accompany anger and fear? In 1954, Delgado, working with Warren Roberts and Neal Miller, the well-known psychologist, demonstrated that E.S.B. in certain brain areas which produce rage responses could act as a powerful punishment. Hungry cats who received E.S.B. at these points each time they began to eat quickly learned to avoid food. But cats being stimulated in other cerebral areas—though they might rear back from the bowl momentarily—never were motivated to learn to refuse food: they returned to eating as soon as the stimulation was over.

"The implication," explains Delgado, "was that there were places in the brain which corresponded to negative emotional states, to the cerebral perception of pain. If that were so, we could understand the mechanisms of suffering and block them at their source." Shortly after this experiment, doctors started to use brain stimulation for the relief of intractable pain.

A few months after the Delgado-Roberts-Miller study was published, a young Canadian, James Olds, began wondering . . . If there were "pain centers" in the brain, were there also areas devoted to the perception of pleasure? Olds, working at McGill University, implanted electrodes in the brains of a group of rats: He meant to probe an area just below the one that the Yale group had been studying, but in one rat an electrode went astray, landing a good deal above its target—it was an inspired mistake. For, as Olds soon realized, the rat found the stimulation rewarding; in fact it kept continually and dedicatedly returning for more.

Olds's subsequent large-scale studies of rats with electrodes in this "pleasureful area" found that they preferred E.S.B. above all else— including water, sex and food. Even when famished, they would run toward a stimulating lever faster than they would run toward food. They would remove obstacles, run mazes and even cross electrified grids in order to press the wonderful lever that provided self-stimulation. Sometimes ravenously hungry rats, ignoring nearby food, would stimulate themselves up to five thousand times an hour—persisting with manic singleness of purpose for more than a day running, until they keeled over on the floor in a faint!

Olds thought that the pleasure areas must contain nerve cells that would be excited by satisfaction of the basic drives—such as hunger and sex—but that somehow E.S.B. of them was even better. In a subsequent experiment he demonstrated that the delights of E.S.B. in certain brain areas could be abolished by castration; they could then be restored by injections of the sex hormone testosterone.

Delgado, among others, later confirmed the existence of "reward areas" in the brain of the monkey. "In humans also, during diagnostic procedures, states of arousal and pleasure have been evoked. We have seen this in our own experience. One patient of ours was a rather reserved thirty-year-old woman suffering from psychomotor epilepsy; she had electrodes implanted in her right temporal lobe. E.S.B. at one cerebral point made her suddenly confess her passionate regard for the therapist—whom she'd never seen before. She grabbed his hands and kissed them and told him how grateful she was for what he was doing for her.

"When stimulation was over, she was as poised and distant as ever; she remained so during E.S.B. through all other electrodes. But"—one of Delgado's eyebrows rises slightly—"the same thing happened when she was stimulated at the same point on another day."

There have been several studies of humans with implanted electrodes. One carried out by Dr. C. Sem-Jacobsen in Norway with a group of patients suffering from schizophrenia and Parkinson's disease describes E.S.B. at different cerebral points as producing moods which ranged from "feeling good," to "slight euphoria," to where "the euphoria was beyond normal limits" and the patients laughed hilariously. During another study, a man being treated for narcolepsy (irresistible sleep attacks) was given a small self-stimulator. He kept pushing one particular button which, he declared, made him feel as if he were building up to a sexual climax.

"Pleasure is not in the skin being caressed or in a full stomach," remarks Delgado. "It is somewhere inside the cranial vault."

And so, also, are anxiety, fear, aggression. Early in the sixties, Delgado wanted to study problems of aggression—and its inhibition— among rhesus monkey colonies in which some members were receiving E.S.B. which increased or decreased levels of hostility. But there were practical problems: the monkeys tended to become curious about trailing wires, and their destructive capabilities were legendary. Most researchers had to keep them separated and restrained in little plastic chairs.

The nineteen-fifties, however, had brought advances in electronic technology and miniaturization of components. Delgado, who is, in the words of a colleague, "a kind of nineteenth-century mad inventor, a real technological wizard," developed an instrument called a *stimoceiver*. This was, as its name implies, both a brain stimulator and brain-wave receiver; it could send stimulations by remote radio command on three channels and receive E.E.G. recordings on three channels. Weighing roughly just over an ounce, the stimoceiver was easily anchored to the animal's skull: it was monkey-proof.

A series of experiments was now carried out with monkeys who were freed of wires, interacting spontaneously and receiving E.S.B. by remote radio command. They demonstrated that while stimulation could increase the level of hostility experienced by an animal, whether or not he expressed his hostility against another monkey depended upon the social situation. Monkeys form hierarchical societies. If rage and aggression were evoked in a monkey at the bottom of the social scale, no threats would be directed against other monkeys. If, however, the animal were moved into another colony in which he held a higher rank, he would threaten or attack the animals below him. When the "boss monkey" of a colony was stimulated, his attacks were also carefully determined by the social situation: he attacked the male just below him in rank, never his favorite girl friend.

Thus, while E.S.B. could arouse aggressions in peaceful simian societies, these feelings were always expressed in socially intelligent ways. In one study a small female named Elsa learned to press a lever which activated a radio stimulator and inhibited the aggressiveness of the powerful, mean-tempered boss of the colony. "The old dream of an individual overpowering the strength of a dictator by remote control has come true," laughs Delgado. "At least, in our monkey colonies."

Two years after developing the stimoceiver he and his invention made world headlines when Delgado took part in a "bullfight" in Spain. Climbing into the ring at a farm near Cordova, this matador in sweater and slacks faced a brave bull—one of a species genetically bred for fierceness.

Delgado, standing in the sun, waved a heavy red cape in the air. The bull lowered his head and charged through the dust. But, as the animal bore down on him, Delgado pressed a small button on the radio transmitter in his hand: the bull braked to a halt.

When the professor pressed another button, the bull turned away and trotted docilely toward the high wooden barrier. The bull had, of course, had electrodes implanted shortly before. The radio stimulation had activated an inhibitory area deep in the bull's brain, thus halting it in mid-charge.

This disquieting demonstration of the power of brain stimulation aroused a flurry of speculation about the possibilities of remote-controlled behavior. "Since that time," Delgado says ruefully, "I've received mail each year from people who think I'm controlling their thoughts."

Crank letters are not likely to stop arriving after Delgado's recent announcement that he has established two-way, nonsensory communication between the brain and the computer. In the experiment a young chimp named Paddy (after an Irish research assistant) was equipped with 100 electrodes implanted in his brain and wired to a socket on top of his skull. Mounted over the socket was a stimoceiver, its tiny components encased in a Teflon box not much bigger than a cigarette lighter.

Paddy, in the company of three other chimpanzees, was left to roam about an artificial, moat-surrounded island at Holloman Air Force Base in New Mexico. As he ran, ate, sat and played, his brain waves and other activities were monitored twenty-four hours a day. During early testing, it was found that E.S.B. in the central gray—the emotionally "negative" area explored by Hess and then Delgado—was obnoxious and disturbing for Paddy.

In the meanwhile, a computer standing nearby was programed to receive radio signals which were broadcasts of electrical activity from the chimp's brain and to respond to certain waves called *spindles*. The spindles, coming from the amygdala, a structure deep in the temporal lobe, are correlated with aggressiveness and excitement; they occur spontaneously about one thousand times an hour in the brain waves from the amygdala. In response to each spindle, the computer was instructed to deliver a radio stimulation to Paddy's central gray.

When the experiment began, each spindle produced by the amygdala was followed immediately by the punishing E.S.B. in the emotionally negative area—it was similar to the slapping of a child's hand each time he touches a forbidden object. Within two hours, spindling had diminished by 50 percent. A few days later, there were practically no spindles at all. One part of the brain (the central gray) had "talked to" the other: it had forced the amygdala to change its normally occurring electrical activity! Paddy's behavior changed also. He was less aggressive, his appetite waned, he sat around lazily with visitors or with the other chimps. "In this case, we were able to get one area of the brain to communicate with the other," Delgado says. "Soon, with the aid of the computer, we may have direct contact between two different brains—without the participation of the senses."

Paddy's changed behavior persisted for two weeks following the experiment. Then the amygdala resumed its spindling and the chimp returned to normal. "One of the implications of this study," explains

Delgado, "is that unwanted patterns of brain activity—for instance those correlated with assaultive or antisocial activity—could be recognized by the computer before they ever reached consciousness in order to trigger pacification of the subject.

"Another speculation is that the onset of epileptic attacks could be recognized and avoided by feedback." (Feedback occurs when the activities of an organism or machine are modified continuously by the interaction between its signals or output and the environment; thus, E.S.B. in the central gray made the amygdala suppress its spindling in much the same way that warmth rising in a room causes a thermostat to shut off the supply of heat.)

Delgado looks forward to a time "not very far in the future" when cerebral pacemakers, operating in much the same way that cardiac pacemakers now do, will treat illnesses such as Parkinson's disease, anxiety, fear, obsessions, violent behavior, by direct stimulation of the brain. The premise is that each of these illnesses has its own characteristic pattern of electrical activity. In the case of an epileptic, these would be the high voltage slow waves which represent the simultaneous "explosion" of groups of neurons. Long before the first muscle twitch of an epileptic fit is seen, the brain waves show this typical pattern. If they were being monitored by a computer, the machine could respond immediately by triggering radio stimulation to brain areas that would inhibit and contain the seizure.

This would all take place below the level of perception, without the person's conscious awareness. For instance, a man walking down a street, equipped with a subcutaneous stimulator, could avoid an epileptic seizure through interaction with a computer miles away—and never know it. Or, as seems quite feasible technologically, a minicomputer programed to respond to a specific type of electrical activity could be worn on the person's body. Thus, the "go-between" connecting two areas of the same brain might be situated either in the middle of a medical center or the middle of a shirt pocket.

Certain types of uncontrollably assaultive behavior might be treated without the computer, using carefully programed stimulation in inhibitory brain areas. According to Delgado, these could, over a period of time, cause a mellowing of aggressive reactions.

What is the choice? Does it lie on the one hand between spiraling violence and continuous outbreaks of aggression and war, and, on the other hand, the development of a race of electrical toys whose every antisocial impulse could be neatly nipped by the computer before it ever became realized in the form of behavior? In his intriguing, troubling book, *Physical Control of the Mind*, Delgado carefully explores the implications of E.S.B.:

"The possibility of scientific annihilation of personal identity, or even worse, its purposeful control, has sometimes been considered a future threat more awful than atomic holocaust," he writes. "The prospect of any degree of physical control of the mind provokes a variety of objections: theological objections because it affects free will, moral objections because it affects individual responsibility, ethical objections because it may block self-defense mechanisms, philosophical objections because it threatens personal identity."

However: " . . . it is not knowledge itself but its improper use which should be regulated. A knife is neither good nor bad; but it may be used by a surgeon or an assassin . . . Psychoanalysis, the use of drugs . . . insulin or electroshock . . . are all aimed at influencing the abnormal personality of the patient in order to change his undesirable mental characteristics."

Patients on drugs, he points out, are being controlled. Their behavior is modified, their systems are flooded and sometimes there are deleterious side effects; also, they are made lethargic and stupid. "And why? Because one little group of neurons keep misfiring. Is it destroying that patient's personal freedom to offer him precise, on-demand medication affecting only the area involved, so that none of his other mental processes are altered?

"Suppose that the onset of epileptic attacks could be recognized by the computer and avoided by feedback: would that threaten identity? Or if you think of patients displaying assaultive behavior due to abnormalities in brain functioning: do we preserve their individual integrity by keeping them locked up in wards for the criminally insane?"

E.S.B. is actually a rather crude technique based on the delivery of a monotonous train of messageless electrical pulses. Like the button which launches a rocket, it sets off a train of programed events: biochemical, thermal, enzymatic, electrical. "Nothing which is not already in the brain can be put there by E.S.B.," Delgado says. It cannot be used as a teaching tool [to impart knowledge]. "Since it doesn't carry specific thoughts it can certainly *not* be used to implant ideas or to order people about like robots—you couldn't use it to direct a person down to the mailbox to get the mail."

Brain stimulation does offer, however, an experimental method for the study of the neurophysiological basis of behavior. "True freedom," insists Delgado, "will come from an understanding of how the brain works; then we will be able to control our reality." A high-priority national goal ought to be an intensive study of cerebral processes for the purpose of establishing an educational system based on that knowledge: "We must first start with the realization that the mind, to all intents and purposes, does not exist at birth; in some brain areas as many as eighty to ninety percent of the neurons don't form until afterwards. Personal identity is not something we are born with. It is a combination of genetic bias, the sensory information we receive, our educational and cultural inheritance. In other words, the mind is not revealed as the child matures; it is constructed."

Genetic determination is like the blueprint of a beautiful house, Delgado contends: "But the house itself is not there; you can't sleep in a blueprint. The kind of building you eventually have will depend on the choice of which bricks, which wood, which glass are used—just as the virgin brain will be shaped by what is given to it from the environment. Now in order to give this newborn brain the best possible building materials, there are questions to which we need answers: What is the chronology of imprinting? At what ages are certain patterns fixed? What are the true sources of pleasure and accomplishment?—this question has not only a psychological but a neurophysiological component, since we know that pleasure is localized in certain areas of the brain."

Most important, according to Delgado, is the need to develop an educational system that is based on knowledge of our biological realities, an education that would attempt to: first, establish good "automatisms" in the child, and, second, as he matures, permit his thinking capability to evolve without being subjected to unknown forces and impulses which may overpower his rational intelligence.

Like many another prophet, Delgado is not always seen as such in his own country. Aside from the fantasy and fears aroused by his experiments, there are criticisms of the public stance he has adopted, as well as of his techniques and method. "There's something idiosyncratic about the way he works," remarks one Yale colleague. "He doesn't follow the ordinary rules. I mean one mustn't confuse technological elegance with methodological rigor: there must be the slow dogged part, the careful checking of observations, the randomization of experiments, the estimate of the probability that your findings weren't just due to chance . . .

"Delgado doesn't seem to have the patience to fool around with that. If he stimulates a monkey's brain and gets an expected reaction he gets bored. He gets a lot of things started, and then leaves other people to clean up after him. But let's face it, technologically the man's incredible; he's a real genius in a practical way—a sort of Thomas Edison of the brain."

Questions about the brain, says a young neurophysiologist, are extremely complex: "People like Delgado can talk about breakthroughs in this and that, but progress in knowledge is slow. It may be several centuries before we have any real understanding of what is going on . . . And besides there are different schools of thought. Some neurophysiologists think it's a waste of time to study groups of neurons and over-all behavior—that we'll learn more by figuring out what's happening in a single nerve cell. To a man with this approach, trying to understand the workings of the brain through gross stimulation appears silly—like using a hand lens to try and unlock the mysteries of the fine structure of a virus."

Nevertheless, if not the dogmatic experimentalist, Delgado, according to his research associates, more than makes up for it: "He's an inventor in the purest sense. You can't fault his creativity," says Dan Snyder, a Ph.D. in physiological psychology who has worked with Delgado for the past several years. "The man drops gems of ideas in his casual conversations the way some people shed bacteria. That's part of the problem: he hasn't time to beat an experiment to death because he's got so many good ideas that he more or less has to be in ten places at once.

"The truth is," adds Snyder, "he's opened up enough research potentials to keep several laboratories busy for a lifetime."

Speculations about the future implications of E.S.B.—medical and social—are still various and vague. According to Dr. Morton Reiser, chairman of the Yale psychiatry department (in which Delgado holds his appointment as professor of physiology), there are "probably some frightening potentials" in Delgado's work. "If you can use computer technology to send an unmanned space satellite to the moon, then it doesn't seem utterly impossible that one day our computers will be sophisticated enough to be used to put thoughts into people's heads." He pauses doubtfully. "At any rate, one could possibly exert some influence on gross emotional behavior. Suppose, for instance, there were someone with uncontrollable rage reactions which were due to something detectable in the nervous system. The computer could send back a stimulus to inhibit that response. I don't think *that's* science fiction. . . ."

Professor David Hamburg, chairman of the psychiatry department at Stanford and an expert on brain and behavior, says: "The stronger our scientific base, the better our position for making rational choices. Brain stimulation could lead to the relief of much human suffering, to new treatments for mental and neurological disorders; it could possibly help to solve some human problems and it may ultimately affect man's understanding and conception of himself.

"Of course," adds Hamburg, "the utilization of knowledge always presents certain problems. Any increase in understanding can be used in ways that are harmful or helpful. As with atomic research, as with our investigation into the chemistry of behavior, E.S.B. does open up possibilities for exploitation and harm. Any new technique for understanding how the brain mediates behavior could affect our lives for better or worse."

Certainly, mistrust and doubt are aroused on many sides by the suggestion that thought process can be rerouted and the mind physically controlled. According to one psychoanalyst, "The danger of this being abused is, I think, tremendous."

"I suppose," remarks Delgado, aware of the controversy his work inevitably stirs, "that to primitive man the idea of diverting the course of a river would have seemed irreligious."

1970

Hangover

The hangover, when it happens to strike me, comes as a complete surprise. The misery of the morning after, like an insult from a close friend, is not something I really expect to have happen. There is injustice inherent in the situation. I am, for one thing, a light and circumspect drinker; and, for another, my liquor consumption is altruistically motivated. Like Jackie Gleason, who once said, "I drink to remove warts and pimples from the people I'm looking at," I drink to render those I don't like likable, and those I do care for even more lovable than they naturally are. Why should such socially constructive behavior be punished, on occasion, by my awakening to the ravages of the four horsemen of the inner apocalypse—Headache, Heartburn, Thirst and Stomach Distress?

Why indeed? Early this month, with the season of wassail rapidly approaching, I decided to seek answers to this troubling and perennial riddle. My first question seemed simple enough: What causes hangovers, anyhow?

Unfortunately, no one seems to be certain. Among experts in the field of alcohol studies the subject appears to arouse a certain amount of controversy and disagreement. Some researchers link the Morning After syndrome to the individual's physical and mental state just prior to his partaking of alcohol, as well as to the social circumstances in which he happens to be doing his imbibing. Others tend to emphasize the purely physiological reactions which the drug is known to bring about. Still other experts stress the possible "placebo effects"—i.e., some people who drink may expect to have a hangover afterwards, and therefore get one—while yet others believe the hangover to be in the nature of a mild withdrawal phenomenon. (This latter suggestion was dismissed with a shrug by one pharmacologist I spoke to: "You can get a hangover the first time you ever drink alcohol," he observed. "It's hard to believe that any kind of physical dependence and withdrawal can be induced that fast.")

I asked Dr. Henry B. Murphree, professor of psychiatry and

pharmacology at the Rutgers Medical School, to define a hangover. "I would describe it," he answered carefully, "as a disagreeable feeling the morning after you've had something to drink the night before." Murphree hastened to add that he was being deliberately vague because a hangover can only be characterized in terms of a very loosely recognizable set of symptoms. "I suppose one can lump these together and call the whole thing a *syndrome*," he said with a shrug. "But in reality two people who describe themselves as having 'hangovers' can have quite different symptoms. And even if they have the same ones, the symptoms can still stem from different sources."

One individual, for instance, may awaken with dizziness and nausea (the nausea may be so severe as to cause vomiting). Another may have just a headache, or feel intensely thirsty, or experience heartburn. A third may arise with every one of these problems, or with none: This person may just be suffering from depression, with feelings of dullness and fatigue. In some cases the complaint may include diarrhea; in others, the hangover may consist of a general sense of jitteriness, which is an indirect effect of the diuresis, or overly large outpourings of urine, that is often brought on by drinking.

Diuresis tends to occur during that period of liquor intake when the drinker's blood alcohol level is rising. The urge to eliminate water comes about because the drug affects a chemical substance produced in the pituitary gland, a substance called *antidiuretic hormone*. As the name suggests, this hormone normally acts upon the kidney to inhibit the release, and promote the conservation of, water. What happens when a person imbibes alcohol is thus in the nature of a double negative: The drug suppresses release of the antidiuretic hormone, which in turn stops stopping the kidneys from letting go of water. "Booze makes the kidneys more prone to release urine," observes Murphree. "And they do."

This loss of water may, in turn, result in the excessive loss of magnesium. Ordinarily, mechanisms within the kidney act to conserve magnesium and other ions normally present in the body. However, along with the water loss which often results from the drinking of alcohol, there may be wastage of magnesium: "A person who is magnesium-depleted is going to get tremulous, irritable; he or she will have a lot of those edgy, jumpy feelings that people say they have when they are hung over. . . .And the point is, you know, that you do tend to end up with a magnesium loss every time you drink." This did not mean, continued Murphree, that the loss would affect *every* drinker—a person might have plenty of magnesium stored within his or her body, and therefore remain unaffected by elimination of magnesium ions usually conserved in the kidneys.

However, he added, the same symptoms—jumpiness, jitters, feelings of being spent—could still be present for totally different reasons. They could stem from the loss of REM ("rapid eye movement" or "dreaming") sleep. Alcohol is known to suppress normal REM sleep. "If," suggests Murphree, "the amount the individual has drunk has been small, then the alcohol can be metabolized during the night's sleep. However, since the REM-suppression has taken place during the first half of the night, the individual is going to get a sudden spate of dream activity during the latter part; he'll get that REM-rebound."

Thus, the carouser—who might have slept soddenly but well enough during the first half of the night—is likely to sleep restlessly, perhaps even horribly, toward morning. This unquiet slumber can in itself cause fatigue and grouchiness. If, on the other hand, a person has quaffed the cup so deeply that he remains REM-suppressed throughout the night, he is still likely to wake up with all of the standard, predictable symptoms of REM loss: irritability, anxiety and increased aggressiveness.

Chronic alcoholics who steadily ingest the drug do "adapt" to it: They eventually cease to suppress REM sleep, after an initial period of adjustment. But, whenever the alcohol is withdrawn (be it six weeks, six months or six years later), there is an attempt on the body's part to make up for the initial deficit. The resulting upshoot in dreaming activity serves to frighten many an alcoholic straight back to the bottle. There is currently some speculation that the hallucinations of delirium tremens—those well-known pink elephants— actually represent an intrusion of the long-suppressed "dream system" of sleep into the "wakefulness system" of conscious mental activity.

And what, I asked Murphree, is known about the cause of the Great Hangover Headache? Again, he replied, there may be quite different histories in different instances. In some cases the headache might come about as the result of vasodilation, or swelling of the blood vessels in the brain. "This is the same phenomenon as that which occurs in migraine," said Murphree. "The vessels expand, and there is just so much space for them to expand in—after all, the skull is there, enclosing the tissues. And so the inside of the head throbs and hurts. And every time you move, it seems as if there is a big drum bonging somewhere inside.

"There is another kind of headache as well," he went on remorselessly, "the tension kind. You feel a tight band across the brow or a tight band at the back of the skull, or both. That kind of headache is often related to an anxiety a person might be having about something he or she had done the night before—especially if it were in circumstances where misbehavior might be threatening. For example, suppose you'd been at a company cocktail party, and your drinking had gotten out of hand, and you'd told your boss all of the things you'd been wanting to say for the past several months. You might find yourself waking up the next morning and thinking: 'God, what have I done!'; and that in itself could be the source of a hell of a tension headache."

"Does smoking while one is drinking tend to enhance the magnitude of a hangover?" I asked, noting that many people (including some experts I had already spoken to) believed that it did.

"As far as the headache aspect of the hangover is concerned," Murphree said, "the smoking might—in some cases—be helpful. Nicotine is a vasoconstrictor; it shrinks the blood vessels. and if your headache happened to be the kind related to the vasodilation which is caused by alcohol, then the smoking could conceivably be having an antidoting effect."

On the other hand, both alcohol and nicotine cause release of epinephrine, one of the "stress" hormones prominently involved in the emergency "fight or flight" reaction. Epinephrine, in turn, produces an increase in blood-sugar production—and this may eventually result in a depletion of sugar in the blood (hypoglycemia). "This condition," said Murphree, "can cause symptoms like shakes and tremors."

Therefore, he said, the answer to the whole question of whether smoking amplifies hangovers is actually both yes and no: "My own opinion is that you are probably better off if you don't smoke—during drinking, or at any other time."

Our conversation turned, then, to nausea, stomach upset and heartburn—problems which all, it seems, can be traced to alcohol's irritant effect upon the mucous membrane lining of the stomach. To minimize any aftereffects which might stem from this source, therefore, Murphree suggests having food—preferably fatty proteins such as cheese or other milk products—inside the stomach before drinking. The food acts as a kind of blotter, soaking up the alcohol and reducing its impact on the stomach lining. "Another good thing to do is to be sure to sip your drink slowly. This gives the gastric tissues a chance to handle the alcohol in manageable doses. It will also minimize that 'jolt' you're likely to get if a lot of liquor is absorbed into the bloodstream and goes up to the brain very fast."

Development of a hangover may, however, noted Murphree, relate to none of the above-mentioned causes at all. "Becoming very drunk, and then feeling miserable the next day, may simply have to do with a person's expectations of what *ought* to happen. One finds that there are placebo effects arising from this kind of situation. For example, when I was in college I happened to be at a party where everybody was drinking Manhattans. One of the girls didn't drink; but she went around happily eating all the cherries from everyone else's Manhattan—and got roaring drunk. She even had a hangover the next morning. Now that wasn't pharmacology at work; she couldn't have had more than a couple of drops of alcohol. That was placebo effect—the power of belief."

Indeed, some fascinating studies of placebos have documented the way in which "expectations" can alter or override normal physiological functioning. In one study a nauseous patient was given a dose of syrup of ipecac, which usually induces retching and vomiting. However, the person was told that it was a fine new medicine that would be sure to cure his symptoms without delay. And, sure enough, the patient's symptoms all had disappeared within a quarter of an hour. Not only did he feel better subjectively, but objective recordings of his gastric activity demonstrated a complete return to normal functioning.

The relevance of placebo studies to hangover phenomena has to do with the many legends and folk-beliefs about the big drinking spree and its sickly sequel that we, as a culture, share. Everyone knows that the "high" of alcohol will be followed by the "low" of a hangover—and believing this to be true may have a great deal to do with actually bringing it about. The Morning After may be, in a great many cases, the ultimate self-fulfilling prophecy.

"A woman drove me to drink," W. C. Fields once confessed, "and I never even wrote to thank her." Fields always traveled with three trunks — one containing clothes, two containing liquor. He had this advice for fellow travelers: "Always carry a flagon of whisky in case of snakebite and furthermore always carry a small snake." Despite a lifetime spent in celebration of the joys of the bottle, Fields did, however, suffer through some of the epic hangovers of the twentieth century. On one occasion, the morning after some overindulgence in his favorite drink, the martini, his nerves were in such a tenuous condition that he objected to the fizzing noise an Alka-Seltzer made as it dissolved in a glass of water. "Can't anyone," he snarled, "do something about that racket?"

What is it that makes a hangover more severe, or less so? Is it the kind of liquor one drinks, the amount one consumes—or what? The search for some answers brought me to Rockville, Maryland, the site of the National Institute of Alcohol Abuse and Alcoholism Prevention. There I spoke to psychiatrist Morris E. Chafetz, director of the organization, and a person so eminent in the field of alcohol studies that I had heard him referred to as the King of Alcohol.

"The particular type of liquor you choose to drink won't have a determining effect on whether or not you develop a hangover afterwards," Chafetz told me. "But a highly congeneric drink will probably add something to the intensity of those symptoms, should they develop." The congeners in alcohol are small molecules—actually chemical agents other than ethyl alcohol—which are produced during the processes of fermentation, distillation and aging of liquors and wines. These "by-products," more complex alcohols, acids and oils for the most part, come primarily from the barrels in which alcohol is aged: "You tend to find them in your better whiskies—good bourbon, for example—because aging is one of the marks of fine whisky," he explained. "And, the longer that whisky is in the wood, the more of the congeners it is going to take on. They give the alcohol flavor: They give it that smoothness of taste which we associate with good liquor. But the suggestion remains, nevertheless, that there are minuscule after-effects from these congeners. They are toxic substances; if you had them in large doses, they would be absolutely deadly."

One kind of alcohol which is especially low in the congeners is vodka (particularly charcoal-filtered vodka); this liquor is simply a mixture of pure grain alcohol and distilled water. Whiskies that are stored, however, such as bourbon and Scotch, contain more of these other-than-ethyl-alcohol substances. Nevertheless, any liquor produced by the distilling process will contain less congeners than will those beverages produced by fermentation—which includes all wines. "I am not saying," stressed Chafetz, "that the congeners are in any sense of the word *causative* in bringing about hangover. But they probably do heighten the misery."

The volume of liquor one drinks, like the particular type one chooses to drink, will have something to do with the quality and severity of the Morning After syndrome. Again, however, the *amount* one drinks is not seen as being directly correlated with whether or not a hangover does develop. "I've seen people who have reported all the signs and symptoms of hangover after having partaken of very small doses of alcohol. And then, on the other hand, I've seen people who can put away a great deal of liquor which is high in the congeners, and still wake up feeling perfectly fit and able the following morning," he said.

Neither "type" nor "amount" of alcohol consumed serves, in his view, to truly explain the gruesome Morning After problem: The real key to understanding of the hangover lies in an understanding of the drug itself. Alcohol is an anesthetic. It is the pharmacological equivalent of drugs used in the operating room. Like ether, which is another central-nervous-system depressant, alcohol produces a second-stage excitement, or "high" (in the operating room, anesthesiologists use certain drugs to phase patients through the ether "high" very rapidly). "The reason we drink alcohol," pointed out the psychiatrist, "is, very frankly, in order to anesthetize certain parts of the brain. The parts where the liquor goes first are the 'newer,' phylogenetically speaking, areas of the cortex—those brain areas concerned with new learning, control, judgment, the regulation of behavior. And these become anesthetized; it's a release phenomenon. Many of the inhibitory factors—all of those patterns of response, those controlling factors which make it possible for us to comport ourselves adequately within a civilization—are put out of commission. And so it takes the edge off things, somehow; it's a relaxant."

By anesthetizing certain portions of the brain, however, we cut ourselves off from those inner stimuli which generally control our behavior: We stop responding to those signals which might make a person say to himself: "Hey, I'm getting tired," or "Hey, I'm overdoing things." We overstrain muscles, make unrealistic demands upon both our physical and mental supplies of energy. The result is crushing fatigue and/or bodily dysfunctioning, which begin to make themselves felt the following morning, once the masking effects of the alcohol have worn off.

What goes under the rubric of "The Morning After" is, according to Chafetz, largely the result of simple overexertion on a physical, psychological or social level (or some combination of these factors). If, he explained, an individual is tired or strained—either mentally or physically—before he takes alcohol, the drug will offer him temporary anesthesia and analgesia: He will be able to stop responding to the true state of his inner affairs. This may mean that, should he be physically exhausted, he will be able to stretch himself imprudently beyond his resources; or, should he be emotionally distressed, he will be able to avoid his problem by "killing the pain"—until it appears the following morning, in the guise of a hangover.

"And even if a person feels in good mental and physical shape before he begins his drinking," said the psychiatrist, "the particular social circumstances in which he partakes of the alcohol may have an enormous impact on the way the drug affects him. I'm not referring to circumstances which are necessarily psychological; they can even be physical. A lot of bodily tension (which you may not feel at the time, because you're anesthetizing those brain cells with alcohol) can result from the way you are forced to hold your body—I mean simply to *stand*—because you happen to be doing your drinking in a very crowded room."

"Then why is it," I asked, "that a person can go to a very small dinner party, drink very little, be somewhat bored, interact very little, and still wake up with a raging hangover the following morning?"

"I've just explained that to you," he replied. "I think that when you are bored, when you are at a place where you really can't stand being, you tend to hold yourself with a certain degree of tenseness. And, however much alcohol you happen to drink, it suppresses your own sense of that tension—for the time being. You do experience it later on, however, in the form of a hangover."

This "postponement model" of the hangover didn't quite, I suggested, explain why it was possible, on certain occasions, to drink a great deal, have a marvelous time at a splendid party, waken the next morning feeling completely on top of things—and then experience a massive slump in spirits and energy later on in the day. "It's the same fatigue phenomenon, simply hitting you belatedly." He shrugged. "We have all—at least everyone has, I hope—had those moments when things all seem to come together. It has to do with a special occasion, a face, a figure, a moment. Life seems as lovely as it is humanly possible for it to feel, and the use of the alcohol certainly enhances the experience. Every sensation is heightened: There's a special feeling of the whole struggle, you know, being past. And one might waken after such an evening with the sense that everything is wonderful and beautiful, that one is still somehow 'aloft'—but then, all of a sudden, find himself or herself simply and totally exhausted."

Once an individual has managed to achieve a hangover, is there any known "cure"?

"After the fact—no," said Chafetz. "There are, of course, thousands of placebo measures—and these may help somewhat because they contain that most powerful of ingredients, belief. And a shot of sauerkraut juice or a voodoo ritual certainly can't *hurt* a person. However, realistically speaking, the best friend of a hangover is really rest. And quiet . . . isolation . . . a dark room . . . patience. Some aspirins would also be useful; that is, if the individual's stomach can tolerate them."

But was rest alone the best thing he could suggest? "After the fact, yes," he said. "But before, there are preventative measures that can certainly be taken. For one thing, be sure to have food—protein—in your stomach before drinking. Don't drink water *before* alcohol; it will promote rapid absorption. Water is, however, a good mixer to have along with the alcohol; it's better than the fizzy carbonated beverages, which also hasten absorption (that's why champagne goes to your head so quickly). And then, relax or, if possible, nap before the party—and don't *take* that drink if you happen to be feeling physically exhausted, or perhaps distressed for some reason."

The latter suggestion was, I reflected, a wise one but thoroughly impracticable. I rolled my eyes heavenwards and then asked one last question: "What about a little of the old 'hair of the dog' as an antidote?"

"Well, again, you'd obtain some temporary relief because you would, of course, be anesthetizing those brain cells anew. And that might take care of some of the symptoms—for the moment. But it would be only for the moment, because the effects of that added dose would eventually become dissipated too. . . ." His voice trailed off, and Chafetz fell silent.

So did I, and began thinking about my New Year's resolutions.

1973

Oh, for a Decent Night's Sleep!

It was 11:15 P.M. Most of the electrodes had already been pasted into place. One was behind each of the patient's ears and one above each eye; two were on her chin and three on her forehead—these five were for measuring muscular tension. There was also a single electrode to the right of her nostrils, for measuring the rate of breathing. Now, Dr. Peter Hauri, director of the Dartmouth Sleep Laboratory at Hanover, New Hampshire, was positioning two more electrodes on the very top of the patient's head, just over the parietal lobes of the brain; these were for picking up and recording her brain waves. "You know," said the woman apprehensively, "I have an awful time getting to sleep ordinarily. I don't see how I'm ever going to sleep with all these wires coming out of my head."

"Oh, don't worry about trying too hard to sleep," Dr. Hauri said cheerfully. "You'll get off eventually; everybody does. *Everybody* sleeps in my lab." He placed an electrode under the patient's armpit and anchored it firmly with a strip of translucent tape; this one was for monitoring body temperature. A final electrode went on the middle of her back—for measuring heart rate. "Okay," he said, "now you're all ready for sleep."

Lifting the trail of wires like a bridal train, Dr. Hauri walked behind her, directing her out and into the hallway, then into the small, comfortable-looking sleeping room next door. There, helping her as she settled herself in the bed, he assured her that he would be available, via the intercom system, throughout the night: He would come to her immediately should she summon him. As he talked, he was carefully plugging the wires into jacks in a small panel just over the bed.

"Doctor, that big machine in your laboratory—I guess these wires here must connect up with it. And I was wondering—if one of the fuses shorted out or something like that, the electricity—it couldn't go into my head, could it?" She laughed slightly, as if embarrassed.

"You're not the only person who's been worried about that," he replied, his German-accented voice courteous and full of sympathy.

63

"But I assure you that it is really completely safe. Hundreds of sleep subjects have been tested on these machines and no one—*not one single person*—has ever been harmed in even the slightest way."

Back in the laboratory, Dr. Hauri began checking the polygraph recordings as they started to emerge from the electroencephalograph, or brain-wave recording machine. He was also monitoring heart-rate variability, body temperature, breathing rate and muscle tension as well. The patient was, at the moment, still tossing and turning; the needles tracing muscular tension were fluctuating wildly.

As he began to calibrate several of the dials, Dr. Hauri told me something about this woman's sleep history. She had had severe and chronic insomnia for thirty years. Now in her early fifties, she managed only about three hours of sleep a night—and only with the aid of heavy dosages of pills.

"At least," said Dr. Hauri, "she *thinks* the sleeping drug is the only thing that will get her any respite at all. The fact is, however, that if the medication has any effect in inducing sleep in this patient, it is at this point a purely psychological one. For, as has been shown in sleep study after sleep study, the hypnotics—I mean all sleeping pills—become ineffective after two or three, or at the very outside, four weeks of steady use. After that period of time, they simply don't work.

"You know, there is a very familiar pattern to all this, we see it time after time. An individual starts out by taking one of these sleep medications; he takes a single pill at night, and that's just fine. Then, perhaps after a week or two, he needs a couple of those pills to get the same results. And then, after a while, that doesn't have the same effect either—but he keeps on with the pills because, without them, he sleeps even worse. Well, what has happened in this situation is really quite commonplace: The person is not being helped by the pills at all anymore; meanwhile, he's gotten himself hooked on the drug.

"I'm not saying that the sleeping pills won't continue to have a psychological effect long after they've ceased to have a physiological one. In other words the individual may, because he *believes* the drug is putting him to sleep, actually be able to relax enough so that he can doze off. . . . But the pill itself isn't doing a thing. On the contrary, the pills are most probably going to disturb the pattern of his sleep, and his sleep is certainly going to be far more rotten because he's taken them."

As he spoke to me, Dr. Hauri was keeping an eye on the lines of data steadily being recorded on the machine. He pointed out the one denoting the patient's muscle tension: It had changed dramatically, and now looked smaller and as evenly drawn as a design. The patient's heart rate was steady, her breathing deep and uniform. The brain waves were in the alpha—"awake but resting"—phase. If her sleep pattern ran true to her descriptions of it, she would now, Dr. Hauri told me, lie awake for several hours doing something which she called "fidgeting." Then, toward two or three in the morning, she would resort to two capsules of her sleep medication. After that she would doze off for perhaps three to three-and-a-half hours, then lie awake again. "One thing that we do see all the time with insomniacs, is that they stay in bed without being asleep much more than other people do—much too long. They are there for hours before falling asleep; and the same thing happens when they awake in the morning as well."

Much to my surprise, however, before even so much as an hour passed, the patient began the slow descent into sleep. Muscular tension had diminished again: The "design" looked even more regular, the waves lower in amplitude. Her brain-wave pattern was showing the mixed-frequency, "half-awake, half-asleep," somewhat slower configuration of stage one, the lightest phase of sleep. A normal sleeper would have stayed at this level for no more than a few minutes. But in the patient's case it persisted for over half an hour.

Then she shuttled downward into stage two, the next level of sleep. Her brain-wave pattern altered again, and was punctuated with the characteristic "sleep spindles" of this phase—small bursts of electrical activity that look, on the recording paper, like tightly coiled little bedsprings. She was now, by all objective standards, definitely asleep.

The stage two level is considered a "medium" kind of sleep: Some researchers consider it no more than the prelude, the gateway, to the more profound—the restorative, recuperative—phases of sleep represented by stages three and four. These deeper stages are characterized by the appearance of "delta" waves on the E.E.G. recording: large, slow, rolling waves that are sometimes about five times the amplitude of the waking alpha rhythm. Delta waves have a satisfying appearance: They look like brain waves of deep slumber *ought* to look— lazy and easy and wide. The only real differentiation between stages three and four is that recordings made during the latter stage show a higher percentage of delta waves.

In this particular instance, however, the patient was unlikely to exhibit any of the deep-sleep pattern at all: "The sleeping pills have, most likely, knocked out all of her delta sleep," said Dr. Hauri. "And even though she hasn't had the pills so far this evening, the fact that she's been on them so long will mean that this kind of sleep is being pretty much obliterated."

In fact, she never did descend into the lower stages of healthy slumber, as a normal sleeper would have done. An individual with no sleep pathology would have gone downward to the stage three and four levels, then returned slowly upward, to enter into a first REM—or "rapid eye movement" period, when the eyeballs dart vigorously under closed eyelids—some ninety minutes after the onset of sleep. This patient, however, went directly from stage two sleep into REM.

REM sleep, sometimes called "paradoxical sleep"—because breathing becomes irregular, heart rate is elevated and brain-wave patterns resemble those of waking life—is that phase of sleep which has been shown to be correlated with dreaming activity. Roughly speaking, some 80 percent of sleepers—four out of five—will report a dream if they are awakened during a REM period. REM sleep is characterized by a rise in the amount of adrenal hormones circulating in the bloodstream. For males of every age, there is some degree of penile erection during REM sleep (and if there is none, or very little, the sleep volunteer almost invariably reports an anxiety dream). There is a comparable reaction in female erectile tissue as well. Everyone, during a normal six to eight hours of healthy sleep, will have four or five REM periods, occurring some ninety minutes apart. The first REM, or "dreaming-phase," of the night—the one which completes the first sleep cycle—generally lasts some five minutes.

Dr. Hauri's patient, however, displayed a very lengthy REM period. Her elevated heart rate, irregular breathing and "wakeful" brain-wave pattern continued for almost half an hour. Then, abruptly, she woke up.

Nocturnal awakenings, Dr. Hauri told me, are nothing out of the ordinary even for normal sleepers; adults generally awaken some three to five times during a healthy night's sleep. Most people, however, return to sleep at once and retain no memory of these brief awakenings. The individual with a sleep disorder, on the other hand, tends to wake up more frequently; and, once awake, finds getting back to sleep either difficult or impossible.

This was indeed what happened. The patient lay in her bed, tossing and "fidgeting," until close to three in the morning; then she took two sleeping capsules. Shortly afterward, she fell into a long stage one sleep, and then spent a briefer time in stage two. This time she returned to stage one without having any REM period at all. The medication, now metabolizing through her system, was suppressing the dream phase of normal sleep. All sleeping pills, including even the mild, over-the-counter antihistamines, affect REM sleep profoundly; so do anti-anxiety drugs such as tranquilizers, and so do alcohol and amphetamines. Antidepressant drugs also act to inhibit or erase dreaming sleep.

One fascinating clue which did emerge from the night's sleep-recording session was the curious fact that the patient believed she had not slept until she took her pills at 3:00 A.M. In an interview with Dr. Hauri the following morning, she said that up until three o'clock she had lain awake "fidgeting." And yet, according to objective standards—the recorded E.E.G. readings—she had actually fallen asleep within an hour of retiring.

"Her own subjective experience is that she didn't sleep until she took the pills," Dr. Hauri told me, after he had spoken with her. "And this makes me suspect that she may be, in part, suffering from a condition called 'pseudo insomnia'—she's actually sleeping, but dreaming that she's awake. I've had such cases before: The worst was a student here at Dartmouth who used to get a full eight hours' sleep every night, but spent all his REM periods dreaming that he was awake. He was exhausted by morning."

As he talked, Dr. Hauri was beginning to write out instructions for the sleep technician who would be monitoring the same patient the following night. He planned to have the assistant speak to the woman during the time of night when the E.E.G. readings indicated that she was asleep, although she believed herself to be awake. "I'll have the technician simply *talk to her,* ask her if she thinks she's sleeping or not. And then, when we see what she answers, we'll know better what has been going on in her mind.

"We won't, by the way," he added, "come up with any magical solutions; not in the 'Eureka!' sense of the word. What we will come up with is, very likely, a reasonable hypothesis about what might be causing the sleep disturbance. . . . I mean, whether it is neurological in origin, or secondary to some medical or psychological problem, or something else. And this educated guess will be followed by a list of several recommendations about what that person then might do. Usually—in about seventy-five to eighty percent of our cases—one of these recommendations will work well, and we'll get a cure: The person will be able to sleep much better."

Informal estimates indicate that some 20 million Americans probably suffer from some form of sleep disturbance. A Department of Health, Education and Welfare report, covering the years 1952-63, stated that while sales of all drugs had increased 6.5 percent during this period, retail sales of hypnotics and tranquilizers had increased 535 percent. One can only imagine what the rise may have been in the decade just past — no hard statistics are available. And yet, despite the fact that a large untreated "sleep-patient" population patently does exist, there are only three formal sleep clinics—laboratories whose main function is to treat patients rather than to carry out sleep experiments (although some laboratories primarily oriented toward research do occasionally take a few private patients)—in the entire nation. One is, of course, the Dartmouth Laboratory. Another is located at Hershey, Pennsylvania. The third, and by far the largest, is in California at the Stanford University School of Medicine complex.

The Dartmouth Sleep Laboratory, although part of the Dartmouth-Hitchcock Medical Center, is very small. It is the Swiss-born Peter Hauri's own baby. A clinical psychologist with a Ph.D. from the University of Chicago, Dr. Hauri is assisted by a group of trained sleep technicians; he also works in close consultation with the varied medical specialists and psychiatric experts connected with the Dartmouth-Hitchcock Center.

If sleep clinics are few in number, and all fairly new, it is because the entire field of sleep research has just begun to consolidate—and to try to apply—what has been a virtual explosion of new information. Obviously, if sleep specialists were to offer counseling on specific disorders, they needed to have some basic understanding of the normal patterns of human sleep—otherwise, what was the standard against which they could make comparisons? How could one help a person with a problem unless one were fully aware of what constituted a normal night's sleep?

Such fundamental information has become available only recently.

Indeed, more has been learned about sleep in the past decade and a half than during the rest of human history. We know now that sleep is not a period of brain inactivity, illuminated from time to time by the brief flash of a random dream. To the contrary, it is a structured experience, following an orderly progression from phase to phase, as mentioned earlier.

Studies have demonstrated that normal sleepers, within roughly similar age-ranges, will show a remarkable consistency in the course and pattern of their sleep. Healthy sleepers are pretty much alike. For the sleep clinician it is the particular infrastructure, the form and shape of a patient's sleep (as it is recorded by sophisticated laboratory instrumentation) that is far more important than the length of that sleep. Indeed, analysis of the sleep of individuals with very long or short sleeping periods will sometimes reassure the patient with a "sleep problem" that there is, in fact, no problem at all.

"We had a seventy-year-old woman in here recently," remarked Dr. Hauri, "whose husband sent her because he thought she had a sleep disorder; she only slept four hours a night. She told me that she hadn't ever slept much more than four hours a night in her whole life—she thought it was peculiar, too.

"Well, we tested her in the laboratory, and there was nothing at all wrong. What she did have was a remarkably efficient sleep. She went very quickly into deep delta slumber, the stage three and four phases. And then, after about an hour-and-a-half of that, up she came: She went directly into a little REM dream period. After that, back down she went, came out once more: Then it was all over. And if she didn't have more than a tiny bit of the stage one or stage two intermediate stuff, it was because she didn't actually need more than the four hours of sleep. She was as sound as a bell."

Another patient, a physics professor in his early fifties, came to the sleep laboratory with the reverse problem: He needed fourteen hours of sleep a night. "We had him spend two nights here in the clinic; and we didn't find any disorder in his sleeping at all," says Dr. Hauri. "His pattern was perfectly normal; and it was right for him. He simply *had* to have that fourteen hours. If he only got twelve hours of sleep he was exhausted the whole next day."

Sleep disturbances fall into one of three broad categories: Problems relating to too little sleep (insomnia), to too much sleep (hypersomnia), and another, more or less wastebasket category which includes all the other disorders (dyssomnia). Included in this last group are such things as persistent nightmares, sleepwalking or sleeptalking.

Walking or talking in one's sleep are usually not related, as is commonly believed, to the "acting out" of the sleeper's dreams. Actually, it would be impossible for an individual to move around or to communicate during the REM, or dream phase, of sleeping. Despite the fact that the sleeper's body is in a physiological state comparable to fright or excitement in waking, and the brain is hyperalert—the sleeper's body musculature is flaccid. Indeed, many postural muscles are paralyzed during this episode of sleep. Some sleep scientists believe that our brains are behaving as if awake during REM, and giving commands to our muscles as usual, but that our bodies cannot respond to these messages, having become temporarily limp.

Although patients with every kind of sleep complaint turn up at the Dartmouth Clinic, the largest group Dr. Hauri sees are those with problems of insomnia. Among the chronic insomniacs, there are distinct subgroups. "We differentiate," Dr. Hauri says, "between the person with a sleep onset problem, and the guy who *can* get to sleep but has frequent awakenings during the night, and the person who does get to sleep all right, but then snaps wide awake in the early morning hours. This last pattern is, we find, often not primarily a sleep problem; it is frequently secondary to depression. You clear up the depression, and the sleep disturbance disappears."

In treating the three different kinds of insomniacs, Dr. Hauri says, his greatest successes are with the first group, the ones who have chronic difficulties getting to sleep.

"There might be one of a hundred things wrong with a person who can't fall asleep," Dr. Hauri says. "An individual might have some difficulty in metabolizing the serotonin in his brain. Serotonin is the 'sleep juice,' the brain chemical which is believed to be related to sleep. Or, perhaps the patient suffers from some chemical difficulty in making the serotonin out of tryptophane, a precursor to serotonin; trytophane is in foods like milk, cheese and meat. The tryptophane goes from the food into the blood, and then to the brain, where it's converted into serotonin. You know how you sometimes feel very groggy after a heavy meal? That's because you have, in a sense, eaten a sleeping pill. There's about a gram of tryptophane in an ordinary-sized steak; and that's enough to make a person quite drowsy."

This extraordinary piece of information prompted me to confess, on the spot, that every night just before going to bed I myself have a cup of hot milk, usually mixed with Ovaltine. He laughed: "Ovaltine has, in fact, been shown to be helpful in inducing sleep. A 1937 study, done by Nathaniel Kleitman—a distinguished sleep researcher who was one of the co-discoverers of REM sleep—demonstrated this." Another study, Dr. Hauri told me, which was more recent but equally respectable, demonstrated that the bedtime milk and cereal drink called Horlick's was also a "natural" hypnotic. "Warm milk at night is good, too, and not only because it smells like mother, but because there is tryptophane in the stuff. But the effects of these things are not, of course, all that strong. If we have somebody who is a real insomniac, neither of these warm-milk drinks is going to overcome that."

Treatment, for two patients presenting themselves at the sleep clinic with seemingly identical problems—for instance, an inability to fall asleep—may be radically different. This is because the therapy a person receives will always depend on an analysis of his sleeping pattern, and the clues that turn up regarding the possible causes of the disorder. The same kind of symptom—for example, sleep-onset disturbance—may stem from any one of a variety of conditions. The problem may be neurological in origin, and related to degeneration of nerve cells deep in the brain. Or it may be genetic, or may be caused by myoclonic seizures—those strange muscular jerks that most of us have experienced while falling asleep—which go on and on, waking the individual every time he is about to fall asleep. Or the disorder may be secondary to some organic difficulty—a persistent low-grade headache or minor pain which can be pushed from awareness during the day's activity, but which becomes more insistent during the stillness of the night. Or the problem may be psychological in origin.

Sometimes a sleep disturbance is even related to a difficulty long since worked through and solved. "This is something which we call a 'functionally autonomous' onset problem," says Dr. Hauri. "It's a situation in which there was, at one time, a reason why a person couldn't sleep. Maybe the reason was even medical; most likely, it was psychological. And so, for a period of time—maybe a month, maybe more—the individual was not able to fall asleep easily. After that, the person got himself into a cycle where he hated the night because he dreaded not being able to sleep, but he couldn't sleep because that dread got him too tensed up. In this kind of case the individual has, somewhere along the line, become conditioned to his bedtime environment. The pillow, the bed, the lamp, etc., are not cues for drowsiness but for increased alertness and arousal. And so he starts tossing and turning."

Even though the initial problem which originally caused such a person to lose sleep may be solved—indeed, may have been solved twenty years earlier—he is left with the sleep disturbance which began at that time. These people often sleep much better in very dissimilar kinds of environments; not infrequently, they go right off to sleep in the laboratory.

Patients treated for this kind of sleep-onset disorder may follow a regime (first developed by psychologist Richard R. Bootzin) that attempts to recondition them to the bedtime stimuli that have been serving as signals for tension and wakefulness. The patient is told that if he is not sleeping when he is in bed, then he is misusing the bed. The bed is only for sleeping. And he is forbidden to lie in it, tossing and turning— for that, as he is informed in no uncertain terms, is counterproductive.

The patient is enjoined not to lie in bed awake for more than about ten minutes; if he has not fallen asleep within this period, he must get up and leave the room. He is to do all his worrying, all his thinking about his shortcomings, away from the bedroom situation.

If after an hour, three hours (or sometimes twelve hours or more) the patient feels ready to sleep, he may return to the bed, hit the pillow and fall asleep. If, however, he fails to do so in the five to ten minutes allotted, he has to get up and go out again—he is misusing the bed. He must follow this regimen even if it means staying up throughout the entire night. There is one final admonition for the patient: He must not sleep late, even if he manages to fall asleep a mere five minutes before the time he should be awakening for the next day.

"On the first night of this treatment the patient usually won't sleep at all; he'll feel miserable the whole day after. But the following night, being tired, he'll get off to sleep somewhere about three or four in the morning. The night after that he stays awake for something like three hours. The next night, it might be two. And then the individual gets happy, because he sees that it's going to work. Within about two to three weeks, many chronic insomniacs can be retrained in this way so that they can just hit the pillow and fall asleep.

"But it does," Dr. Hauri acknowledges, "take a good deal of fortitude: At five in the morning, say, when a person still isn't sleeping, and he knows there's a full day's work ahead of him. And once again he has to get out of that bed because he is misusing it. Most often a patient will need someone behind him, some sleep or behavioral therapist, to hold his hand and tell him that he's doing fine and that things are sure to get better."

Serotonin is the neurochemical in the brain which is related, it appears, not only to falling asleep but to that profound delta sleep of the stage four phase. Another chemical in the brain, norepinephrine, is believed to mediate the REM or dreaming phases of our sleep. Any substance which affects delicate brain chemistry—most specifically, the norepinephrine and serotonin levels—will influence both our sleeping and dreaming patterns. Unfortunately, all known sleeping drugs *do* affect brain neurochemicals, and all distort or suppress one phase or another of normal sleep.

"I am not," Dr. Hauri assured me, "against sleeping pills for the guy or the woman with an occasional sleep problem. We all, in the course of events, get into some situation or another where we cannot sleep at night; I do too. The main thing is not to exaggerate the importance of losing a night's sleep. It might make a person *feel* bad but, as a number of studies have shown, it will have practically no effect upon his objective efficiency. It would take three or four nights of no sleep at all before his ability to perform actually went down.

"But if an individual is getting himself all uptight and into some sort of a bind about his inability to sleep; and if this should continue for a few nights running, then he might be moving into a vicious cycle—that 'functionally autonomous' sleep-onset problem. So for myself, if I start getting miserable, I'll take a sleeping pill and that will knock me out. I know, however, that the pill-induced sleep will be lousy, because hypnotic drugs suppress the dreaming phase of sleep. And then, the following night, I would expect something which is called the 'REM rebound': That is, in that next sleep period I'd be making up for the dreams that were suppressed the night before."

The "dream rebound" is what makes it so hard for people who are hooked on sleeping drugs to get off them. "The first night they try to make it without the pills they get this horrible sleep—it's virtually all REM, and full of anxiety dreams and nightmares," explained Dr. Hauri. "That's why you can't take people off the sleeping drugs 'cold

turkey'; REM rebound hits them, and they become terrified."
Withdrawal from the chronic use of sleep medications must always, he
cautions, be done very gradually—and if at all possible, under the
supervision of a doctor. If a habitual user suddenly ceases taking his
sleeping pills, he may suffer such serious effects as convulsions,
delirium, hallucinations, hypertension.

"To get a patient off drugs, I try to give him something else.
Something like progressive relaxation exercises that he can do by
himself, to relax his body muscles—and which will keep him from
feeling so utterly helpless. Or I may start him out with some form of
biofeedback: We've been trying that out recently, with good success.
Biofeedback involves, very simply, taking some parameter of the
patient's body—his brain waves or his muscle tension, something not
usually under his control—and measuring those brain waves or the
tension in those muscles, and then displaying that measure to the person
himself. When a patient can observe, say, his muscle tension, he can
begin to learn what it is that he unconsciously does that tends to increase
or decrease it. In this way he can eventually learn to control it."

The same relaxed state which is related to decreased muscle tension is
associated with "letting go," to decathexis from the environment—to
falling asleep. When a person has managed to get himself hooked on
sleeping medications, he has to start out by becoming adept either at the
relaxation exercises, or at some sort of biofeedback. Only then can he
begin cutting down on the pills.

"We literally do just that," Dr. Hauri explained, "cut off pieces of the
pill. We chisel off a very little bit at a time. Meanwhile, we are doing our
best to control the REM rebound, to reintroduce the dreaming sleep in
such a way that it won't get him too anxious or upset."

That long history of sleeping-drug involvement was going to be a
major stumbling block in treatment of the woman patient whose sleep
Dr. Hauri had monitored last night; that case would be, he said, "a
toughie." She was to sleep in the laboratory for another two nights; in
the meanwhile, she was undergoing extensive psychological and medical
testing. "Our work here is really a sophisticated diagnostic process,
which can often reveal quite a lot about the specific factors contributing
to a person's sleep problem," Dr. Hauri said.

If, for example, the disorder were related to neurological difficulties,
treatment—with appropriate drugs—would be worked out in close

consultation with a neurologist. Or if the insomnia appeared to stem from an imbalance of brain chemicals such as serotonin and norepinephrine, drugs that act to inhibit destruction of these substances might be recommended. If the problem seemed connected to some minor medical disorder, careful attention to the medical condition itself would be warranted. Or, if a sleep problem seemed to be caused by a depression which was psychological in origin, a regime of psychotherapy would be prescribed.

Treatments are, obviously, as varied as the sleep disorders themselves are. The best that one can say about "cures" in the sleep clinic is that they appear to be roughly similar to "cures" in medical and psychiatric practice: A few people get dramatically better, most are helped somewhat (and therefore feel and sleep better), and a percentage are not helped in the slightest. These latter patients, according to Dr. Hauri, comprise some 25 percent of his practice: "But many are still not sorry they came. Very often they arrive here believing they've got a condition far more serious than they actually have. And so they do find some comfort in knowing something more specific about what's really going on."

Because so many of the substances which depress REM sleep — like alcohol, tranquilizers and sleeping pills—are in common use, many sleep scientists and clinicians have puzzled over just why we seem to need the REM phase of sleep so urgently. What necessitates that striving to recoup lost dreaming time? During the first spate of dream research in the nineteen-fifties, some experiments carried out by Dr. William Dement (now director of the sleep clinic at the Stanford Medical Center) suggested that dreams, in some inexplicable way, served to maintain the individual's psychological equilibrium — and that loss of dreaming time led to personality disturbances. This is not, it now appears, invariably the case: For example, people suffering from psychological depressions often seem to do better without their REM sleep. And many individuals seem to function adequately over extended periods of time, even though tranquilizers and/or antidepressant medications are suppressing all or much of their REM sleep.

One current theory about REM sleep is that it may be related to the integration of new information into the mass of old information already stored in the brain. This notion seems to have been borne out by a number of recent studies, both with animals and human subjects. "The function of dreaming is, in a loose sense, I believe," said Dr. Hauri, "that of going over what happened during the day, especially those things we weren't able to make sense of, and those things we couldn't pay attention to. And then, we incorporate whatever has been acquired into the old stores of information, while throwing out the 'garbage,' getting rid of those things we don't really need to retain."

Another function of the REM phase of sleep appears to be the regulation of some generalized sort of impulse-control mechanism. This might explain why subjects in the Dement study—as well as people taking part in later dream-deprivation experiments — showed increased irritability and aggressiveness. Sometimes they experienced weight gains resulting from a sudden inability to control food intake.

The notion that REM sleep is somehow related to impulse control might also explain why depressives often appear to do better without it. The depressed individual frequently has problems connected to harsh overcontrol of his instinctual urges, thoughts and feelings.

Although these theories have done much to explain the function of REM sleep, the need for sleep itself seems puzzling. Why do people and animals sleep at all? Why is sleeping any different, for example, from simply closing one's eyes and resting?

"There is actually a great controversy going on at this moment among sleep scientists about this very problem," said Dr. Hauri when I asked him. "The fact is that nobody has been able to prove that anything basic happens during sleeping, anything which is that different from what happens when we merely lie down and relax. From a strictly neurological and physiological viewpoint, there is no objective proof that any restorative or recuperative processes get under way. And yet we all know, subjectively, that sleep makes us feel better—that we feel refreshed by a good night's sleep and feel miserable when we're sleepless."

At the present time, there appear to be two opposing theoretical camps among sleep researchers. One group believes that restorative physiological processes get underway during sleep—that there is resynthesis of brain tissue, for example.

The other side maintains that our need for sleep is no more than a behavioral adaptation—that the recurrent state of inertia and unresponsiveness which we call sleep has been programed into us specifically because it promotes survival. They argue that if we take our own species as an example, then it is clear that early man would have been ill-adapted to protecting himself while foraging for food during the dark hours of the night. If he had attempted to function during the darkness, he would have wasted energy uselessly and exposed himself to danger from night predators as well. Therefore, goes the theory, it was necessary for our early ancestors *not* to respond during certain hours of darkness. Sleep is, in this view, essentially a behavior-control mechanism. Dr. Wilse Webb of the University of Florida, the most eloquent spokesman for this theory, points out that the various sleeping patterns of different animal species do not seem to be linked to physiological processes such as the need to synthesize brain protein. There do seem to be, however, curious ties between the sleep and the safety needs of a species. Predators sleep much more than prey; they can afford to relax. The hare and the gazelle sleep little and lightly; the lion may spend up to sixteen hours a day in deep and heavy sleep.

"And yet," I protested to Hauri, "we all make so many distinctions between the qualities of our sleep—whether it's been good or bad, or light or heavy, or too short or long or full of dreams. We all feel so refreshed after a good night, and so destroyed after a night of wakefulness. It seems almost ridiculous to think that, possibly, nothing restorative is going on—that, from a physiological point of view, nothing at all may be happening."

"I know," he said. "It goes against all our common sense. And I, personally, don't believe it myself. But if you asked me to disprove that theory—to offer one shred of evidence to the contrary—I couldn't possibly do it."

"Isn't there some minimum amount of sleep that is necessary simply from the point of view of survival?"

Dr. Hauri shook his head. "There are two cases in the literature — well-documented—of people who just don't sleep at all. One is an Italian farmer; the other is a guy from Australia. These people have been tested in sleep labs, and it is true: They don't sleep. Now, if you compare sleeping to something like fluid intake, you see that there is a real difference—there is a minimum amount of liquid that is necessary for life; without it, a person will dry up and die. But there are individuals who can, apparently, make do without any sleep whatsoever. And they survive."

1973

Tuning Down with TM

I t was a Saturday morning, and I was going to get my mantra. "Does this handkerchief look absolutely fresh and like it's never been used before?" I asked, hurrying into the kitchen where my fifteen-year-old daughter, Susie, sat drinking coffee with her best friend, Patty.

"I don't know," said Susie with a shrug, looking at the starched white square. I already had my fruit—two big apples and a tangerine—wrapped in Saran Wrap and set aside. The only other thing that I needed was a bunch of fresh flowers—six, to be exact. I hastened out into the back garden to retrieve six of the last of the autumn's hardy chrysanthemums, which had all been laid flat by a violent rainstorm the night before. I brought the bouquet into the kitchen, picked off the brown petals of the flowers and wrapped the stems in foil.

"What is your mother *doing?*" my daughter's friend asked.

"She's going to get her mantra."

"Yes," I put in briskly. "It's my word. It's in Sanskrit. It's the thing, you know, that I'm supposed to say to myself when I'm meditating."

"Oh." Patty's face was expressionless; but a moment later, when I was in the hallway getting my coat, I heard her murmur something in a low voice. Both girls started laughing. I went out of the house, slamming the door behind me irritably.

I was feeling cranky—partly because I'd slept badly, from thinking about today's initiation ceremony. And then my husband had been ragging me about my interest in transcendental meditation. Just before bedtime, he'd asked me slyly: "What do you think your mantra will be? Will it be 'Ommmmmmmmmmm'?"

"No," I'd replied, "'Ommmmmmmmmm' is a mantra for mystics.*

"Well, what do you think yours will be?"

"A mantra for housewives, I imagine. Probably something like 'Blehhhhhhh.'"

"Are you going to tell me your mantra when you get it?"

"No, of course not. You can't tell anyone your mantra; you know that."

---

*The syllable "om" is a mantra representing the three component parts of the cosmos.

"Oh." He'd grinned at me. "Then you really do believe in it."

Did I "believe" in TM? As I parked my car in the lot behind Yale's Hendrie Hall, which houses both part of the Music School and the New Haven SIMS-IMS (Students' International Meditation Society-International Meditation Society) center, I wondered whether anything would indeed "happen." Would I, after today's instruction in meditation, experience some altered state of being—or at least new feelings, new sensations? Certainly a growing number of friends and acquaintances were reporting to me that *they* had. A respectably hard-headed Yale social scientist had told me that meditation was not only a pleasant experience in itself, but that it dissipated his tensions, made him feel far more relaxed in general and also seemed to give him added energy and alertness.

A senior editor in a New York publishing house had spoken of TM in terms of release of stress and had added that she often entered states of great exaltation as well. She had, however, to be careful not to meditate more than the prescribed forty minutes per day; otherwise she found herself experiencing mild hallucinations ("Not frightening ones; just flowers and birds and fountains. But I don't like having it happen"). A man I'd sat next to at a dinner party had said that, for some incomprehensible reason, meditating made him feel far less anxious. There had to be something to TM—or at least it had to be the best kind of snake oil ever.

In any event, if I could be seen as somewhat gullible, I had the consolation of being one among some 400,000 similarly gullible Americans. For, although the movement is worldwide, embracing some 60 countries, its largest following is in the United States. There are now 350 TM centers scattered throughout the nation, where roughly 10,000 new meditators—including businessmen, housewives, students, athletes, doctors, nurses—receive instruction each month. Since the late nineteen-sixties, TM has evolved from what was primarily a student movement into a far more establishment-oriented organization. Its sympathizers and followers include the director of training for the American Telephone & Telegraph Company, the vice president of the Crocker National Bank in San Francisco and the commandant of the U.S. Army War College.

At the same time, it remains highly visible on hundreds of college campuses, where courses on TM and on the "Science of Creative Intelligence" (this is, supposedly, a systematic, scientific analysis of the physical and mental phenomena associated with meditation) are or have been offered for credit. The TM organization itself operates three permanent teacher-training academies—two in California, one in New York State—and is in the final stages of purchasing the old Parsons College campus in Fairfield, Iowa, as the site of its own Maharishi International University.

The movement is, in other words, a thriving and growingly "respectable" one. What accounts for its success? What reservoir of inner needs are the TM leaders and teachers tapping—and what are they actually doing for the people who come to them and who do seem to find some kind of satisfaction? What, in short, is meditation all about?

Transcendental meditation is not a religious movement or practice, though it is often easy enough to mistake it for one. It may more aptly be described as a technique, a fairly simple sort of procedure. The technique derives, according to the Maharishi Mahesh Yogi, founder and leader of the TM movement, from certain aspects of the ancient Vedic tradition of India. Maharishi, whose exact age is uncertain—"A monk does not meditate upon his own life," he has said—imbibed the Vedic teachings during a thirteen-year sojourn in the Himalayan foothills. During this period, he apprenticed himself to the sage, Swami Brahmananda Saraswati Shankaracharya of Jyotir Math—now known to Maharishi's followers as the great teacher and "grandfather" of the movement, Guru Dev.

It was to Guru Dev, as a matter of fact, that my flowers, fruit and handkerchief were being brought. They were to be used in a "ceremony of gratitude" to him and to the other Vedic masters who had passed down knowledge of the ancient practice. (This was, as I and the rest of the people attending the lectures had been advised, a totally nonreligious event.)

The thanksgiving ceremony was in Sanskrit and took place in front of a makeshift altar above which hung a portrait of Guru Dev. While my initiator, John Lewis, murmured unintelligible phrases, I stood to one side, holding a flower and feeling silly. At the conclusion I was given my own mantra—a sound in Sanskrit, meaningless to me, but supposedly carefully chosen as suitable for my particular nervous system—and to my astonishment found the sound objectionable. The idea of disliking my own mantra struck me as funny. I felt myself on the verge of laughter. But my teacher was earnestly explaining the meditation procedure to me. (John Lewis is one of a handful of paid instructors working at the New Haven SIMS-IMS center; many of the workers there are Yale student volunteers, and the premises are occupied rent-free—because TM is a Yale student organization.) I managed to restrain my mirth sufficiently to listen to John and then to follow his directions. We meditated together for ten minutes.

Then he left the room and I meditated alone for ten minutes.

To my surprise, I began responding immediately. The hysterical urge to laugh receded; I started breathing deeply and began sinking into a restful, almost "floating" state. I wondered, even as I experienced a sort of calm emptiness, whether this could be a placebo reaction on my part. I felt funny, tingling sensations in my jaw, and this seemed an odd coincidence—my jaw is one place that usually gets taut when I feel generally tense. And there was a similar, small tingle in a particular back muscle, a muscle I had been aware of only twice before in my life—both occasions when it had knotted into a painful ball following upon an acutely stressful incident. Did this tingling represent, then, the "release of stress" that the TM people had said one was very likely to perceive physically? It was certainly strange that the tingling should occur in those particular places. . . . That first session ended with a huge yawn. I felt refreshed and relaxed.

I had been intrigued, ever since the first two "introductory" TM lectures, by the series of charts that depicted the alterations in body metabolism and in brain-wave patterns which meditating was purported to bring about. The charts, I had noticed, were reprinted from such impeccable sources as *The American Journal of Physiology*, the British medical magazine *Lancet* and *Scientific American*. One of the researchers who appeared to have been involved in the TM studies from the very outset was Herbert Benson, a cardiologist on the Harvard faculty. I telephoned Dr. Benson to ask whether I might come to talk with him but found him oddly reluctant. "I don't want to be involved in any article which will be either 'pro' or 'anti' transcendental meditation," he said.

I assured him that I was neither trying to sell, nor crusading against, the movement—and it was on this basis that he agreed to an interview.

Dr. Benson, who is in his late thirties, is an associate professor of medicine at Harvard and director of the hypertension section at Beth Israel Hospital in Boston. His interest in the bodily effects of meditation—an integrated set of physiological reactions he now subsumes under the term "relaxation response"—was awakened during the late sixties when he was studying the relationship between cardiovascular functioning and the emotions. "Of course, it was well-known at the time—and had been known for many years—that many of the problems that heart doctors encounter have been created by daily stresses and tensions—the cost, so to speak, of living at an often hectic pace in a highly complex society. But the particular question that I and the people working with me were interested in exploring was: 'How do factors that are psychological in nature come to exert these physical effects upon the heart, blood pressure and other aspects of circulatory-system function?' "

Benson and his colleagues embarked on a series of experiments, using monkeys as subjects, to ascertain whether or not high blood pressure (or "hypertension"; the two terms are interchangeable) could be induced in the animals by behavioral means. Using a technique which would "feed back" to the subjects information about the rise or fall of their own blood pressure, Benson and his collaborators trained the monkeys by systematic "rewards" and "punishments" to make their blood pressure move up or down. "We trained the animals, in other words, to control their own blood pressure. Not only could the high blood pressure be produced in the first place. We were able to teach them to lower it as well."

The effort to lower blood pressure by means of biofeedback and conditioning techniques was then repeated, this time with human beings as subjects. In the human studies, subjects were rewarded with scenic color slides (worth about a nickel apiece) which they "earned" by lowering their blood pressure. They, too, were able to learn to do so, but the puzzle was, just *how*? Unlike the monkeys, the people could be asked about this directly—and when they were, most of them seemed to feel that they did it by "thinking relaxing thoughts."

"This made me wonder," related Benson, "why we should be playing with the costly biofeedback equipment. I mean, if this were the case, why not go directly to the 'relaxing thoughts'?"

Even prior to the studies with humans, the transcendental meditation people, hearing of his research interests, had approached Benson and asked him to study them. They were confident, they said, that they were able to control their own blood pressure and were eager to demonstrate this in controlled scientific experimentation. "At first I didn't want to get involved with them," Benson said, smiling. "The whole thing seemed a bit far out, and somewhat peripheral to the traditional study of medicine. But they were persistent, and so finally I did agree to study them."

While Dr. Benson was beginning his preliminary studies of the physiological effects of meditation, a graduate student at U.C.L.A., Robert Keith Wallace, started doing very similar kinds of research while working toward a Ph.D. in physiology. Before long, the two scientists had become aware of their overlapping interests, and Wallace came to work with Benson at Harvard's Thorndike Memorial Laboratory. The first order of business was to establish that there *were* physiological responses to meditation which were distinct and different from the sort of bodily responses which might result from a person's simply sitting very quietly, for an extended period of time, with eyes closed.

In order to ascertain whether or not there was a measurable difference between what happened in these two conditions, the meditator-subjects were asked to sit quietly for a period of twenty to thirty minutes, then to practice meditation for another twenty to thirty minutes and then to sit quietly once again for the same period of time. Each meditator served, therefore, as his or her own "control." Devices for continuous measurement of heart rate, blood pressure, rectal temperature and skin resistance were attached to the subjects, as were electrodes for monitoring brain-wave activity.

The meditator was seated in a comfortable chair. After an initial thirty minutes to allow getting used to the instrumentation, measurements in the "pre," "during" and "post" meditative periods were taken. "What we found," said Benson, "was that during the meditation itself there were distinct changes. The essence of these changes could be, I think, summarized by saying that the whole body's metabolism slows down. And it slows down to a degree that would be seen otherwise only after several hours of sleep. In this case, however, the changes occur within a few minutes of starting what I now like to call the 'relaxation response.'"

During sleep, continued Benson, there is a drop-off in the rate of oxygen consumption, a drop-off which occurs at a very slow pace. During meditation, the same drop-off occurred, but within three minutes. This decline in oxygen consumption was nothing short of dramatic: Among a group of twenty subjects, average oxygen consumption fell from 251 cubic centimeters per minute to 211 cubic centimeters during the meditation period and afterward rose again to 242 cubic centimeters. These figures represent a decrease in oxygen consumption of some 16 percent—twice the reduction that is known to take place after five hours of sleep (or about 8 percent). "Now there are very few ways in which oxygen consumption can be voluntarily decreased so rapidly," noted Benson. "You can't do it by holding your breath and other such methods, because your tissues will continue to take up oxygen at the same rate—you'll then expel a great deal of carbon dioxide on the next outbreath and need to take in more air on the next inhalation. So you see that what this decreased need for oxygen reflected was an essentially involuntary reduction in the rate of body metabolism."

Generally speaking, it is true that the more effort one expends, the more oxygen one consumes. A person who is standing uses more oxygen than a person who is sitting; someone running uses more than someone who is walking. The respiration rate corresponds to the amount of "work" being performed. What was striking was the difference between the oxygen consumption of an individual who simply sat quietly, eyes open or closed, and of a person who was meditating or invoking the "relaxation response."

"In the latter case," according to Benson, "we saw not only the marked decline in respiration rate but a number of other distinct physiological changes as well. Skin resistance, for example, rose. This, too, is known to occur during sleep, but during meditation it increased by an amount and at a rate never seen in sleep. Actually, no one has an explanation for what's happening in skin resistance, except that it's measurable, and that a number of people have associated a decreased resistance with 'being more nervous.' The idea is that you sweat more when you're feeling upset, and so it's easier for an electric current to pass across your skin—whereas if you're feeling relaxed, your skin is drier and higher resistance is offered to the current."

Another and very striking physiological correlate of meditation was the decline in the level of blood lactate (a chemical which circulates in the arterial system), which tended to fall precipitously within the first ten minutes after the subject had begun to meditate. This was particularly significant because, as the work of psychiatrist Ferris Pitts Jr. and his colleagues at the University of Washington had demonstrated, patients hospitalized with anxiety neurosis show a large increase in lactate when they are exposed to stress. Injections of this blood chemical, moreover, can bring on anxiety attacks in such patients—and can cause anxiety symptoms in "normal" persons as well. Interestingly, people with hypertension show higher lactate levels when they are resting than do persons without hypertension when they, too, are at rest.

The words "at rest" are important here, because the concentration of lactate in the blood decreases when an individual is resting quietly in a comfortable position. But, during meditation, the rate of decline was more than three times faster than normal. And postmeditatively the blood lactate level tended to remain lower than it had been prior to the meditation session.

Brain-wave configurations as well were consistent with a state of deep and complete relaxation. E.E.G. readings tended to be in the alpha—9 to 12 cycles per second—"resting" range with rhythmical theta waves—6 to 7 cycles per second—occasionally appearing. (Such brain-wave patterns appear to correlate with subjective reports of "being relaxed," "peaceful," "floating," "feeling very pleasant," etc.) "The whole picture that emerged," Benson told me, "was that of a general quieting or damping down of the sympathetic nervous system."

"But could one achieve the same sort of effect through hypnosis?" I asked.

He shrugged briefly, then said this question was currently under investigation. "Naturally the hypnotic subject's physiological state will correspond to the emotional meaning of whatever is being suggested to him or her," Benson said. "If you tell a person that he's about to be assaulted, he'll show distinct 'fight or flight' responses. If you tell him that he's feeling peaceful and lolling on a beach in the Caribbean, you'll see physiological changes that correspond to that deeply relaxing set of circumstances. As a matter of fact, some work from other laboratories has indicated that the physiological changes seen in hypnosis when deep relaxation is suggested are akin to the changes seen during the elicitation of this wakeful resting state."

However, what Benson had been searching for at the outset—that is, a means of lowering blood pressure without pills—did not appear to be provided by meditation. For during the meditative period, the subjects displayed no appreciable changes in their blood pressure. "A question then arose," Benson said, "concerning what these people we were studying had been like *before* they started TM, because they were all long-term practitioners of meditation. And so a group of us set up an experiment in which the subjects were people who suffered from hypertension but had never practiced any form of meditation. We measured blood pressure in those subjects on a daily basis, both for a period of time before they learned TM, and for weeks and months afterward. And what we found was that, yes, there were decreases that took place in the blood pressure; but these had nothing to do with the meditation session per se. The blood pressure was simply lower across the board. There had been a carry-over from the meditation, which could be measured at any point during the day. The decrease wasn't, by the way, curative; pressure was simply somewhat lowered. And the fall was very clearly related to meditation. Because in cases where the person, for one reason or another, stopped the practice, his or her blood pressure began climbing again—and was usually right back where it had initially been within the space of three weeks."

In 1971, writing in *The American Journal of Physiology,* Benson, Wallace and a third colleague, Archie F. Wilson, suggested that the pattern of physiological responses generated by meditation could be seen as a "wakeful hypometabolic state" — that is, a bodily state which bore some resemblance to sleep inasmuch as there was a "tuning down" or quieting of the sympathetic nervous system, but which was different from sleep in that the individual remained conscious and aware of his or her surroundings. (A while later, Wallace was to go further and to suggest that the changes occurring during meditation actually imply the existence of a fourth state of consciousness — the others being waking, sleeping and dreaming.)

The following year, writing together in *Scientific American,* Benson and Wallace raised the hypothesis that the physiological changes generated by TM might be part of an integrated response mediated by the central nervous system. As such, it might perhaps be regarded as the direct opposite of the "fight or flight" response first described by physiologist Walter B. Cannon in 1914. This so-called "defense alarm" reaction is, of course, the complex set of visceral changes which ensue when a human being or lower animal perceives a situation of threat. These changes include an elevation in heart rate and blood pressure as more blood flows to the muscles of the arms and legs (to promote running or fighting), a rise in oxygen consumption as bodily metabolism moves into high gear to meet the emergency, the release of sugar stores into the bloodstream to provide extra energy, and the stepped-up secretion of adrenalin to help mobilize a host of other "crisis" resources as well. (For example, the spurt of adrenalin entering the bloodstream causes the pupils of the eyes to dilate; an individual can literally see better when under stress.) These elaborate physiological changes, elicited virtually instantaneously by situations which are seen as menacing to the organism's integrity—situations which, in human terms, can range anywhere from an insult from one's mother-in-law to circumstances involving genuine physical danger—are brought about through an arousal of the sympathetic nervous system.

The pattern of changes generated by meditation, suggested researchers Benson and Wallace, represented an equally interrelated, though diametrically opposed, set of responses. The "fight or flight" situation mediated a hyperactivation of the sympathetic nervous system; meditation caused a quieting, a tuning down. A crucial difference between the two physiological reactions was, however, to be noted: While the "emergency response" could be and was elicited spontaneously in a wide variety of situations, the "relaxation response" needed cultivation. It had to be consciously and conscientiously elicited.

At this point, the thinking of Benson and Wallace began to diverge markedly. Wallace, already deeply committed to the transcendental-meditation movement, was convinced that Maharishi's method—which involved the use of a mantra* which the meditator was enjoined never to reveal to anyone—was the one method capable of evoking the "wakeful hypometabolic state." As Benson saw it, however, the mantra was a good enough device for meditation, but it could not be seen as being more useful than any other sound, word or phrase used in the same fashion. He could not concur in the TM people's assertion that

---

*The basis on which an individual mantra is deemed "appropriate" for a particular person is one of the well-kept secrets of the TM movement. No one knows how many of the ancient mantras in existence are used by TM initiators, or the method they use in assigning them. There has been some suggestion that the choice is based on a simple formula combining factors like age and sex. But as a fellow meditator remarked to me, age couldn't be a real factor since the mantra is meant to serve the individual for a lifetime. This person, who taught his wife to meditate with an invented mantra, is convinced that all mantras are simply nonsense words, combining vowels and soft consonants. His mantra, he told me daringly, begins with the "sh" sound; mine, I confessed, begins with an "h." Both of our mantras end in "m" and both consist of two syllables. Similar mantras might be sounds like "rash-shom" or "shah-rahn."

meditating with a sound other than one's "appropriate" mantra might have disorganizing effects upon, and cause damage to, the central nervous system.

And, while the TM procedure constituted a valid means of eliciting the deeply restful "relaxation response," it was by no means the only procedure capable of doing so.

Transcendental meditation is, clearly, only one among a variety of meditative techniques. There are a multitude of Eastern religions and daily practices—including Zen and Yoga, with their many variants—which can evoke similar states of profound physiological relaxation. Some, quite similar to the TM method, employ the repetition of a sound or word or phrase; others use exercises or rhythmic breathing to exclude meaningful thought and banish distractions. One Zen Buddhist practice, Zazen, combines two of these approaches: Inhalations and exhalations are coupled with rhythmic counting. In time, the meditator ceases counting to "follow the breath" to achieve a state of no thought, no feeling, of being in "nothingness."

In the Western world, meditative practices have been associated with religious practice—most commonly with mystical trends within the major religions. A fourteenth-century Christian treatise, for example, counsels the reader that in order to attain union with God, all distractions and physical activities, all worldly things (including thoughts) must be eliminated. As a means of "beating down thought" it is suggested that a single-syllable word, such as "God" or "love," be repeated over and over again. "After that," writes the anonymous author, "if any thoughts should press upon you . . . answer . . . with this word only and with no other words."

Another Christian meditative practice, developed within the Byzantine church, was known as Hesychasm. This involved a method in which breathing out gently was to be combined with the repetition of the prayer "Lord Jesus Christ, have mercy on me." The meditator using this method of prayer was instructed to ". . . say it, moving your lips gently, or simply say it in your mind. Try to put all other thoughts aside. Be calm, be patient, and repeat the process very frequently. . . ."

In Judaism, similar practices date back to the earliest forms of Jewish mysticism and became an important part of the cabalistic tradition. In the thirteenth century A.D., when the Rabbi Abulifia published his major works, he described a mystical system in which he methodically contemplated the letters of the Hebrew alphabet which form God's name: (YHWH). The purpose of this prayerful contemplation was that of passing beyond normal sensory and emotional experience to a transcendent state of consciousness.

Similarly, the basic elements necessary for eliciting the altered internal state are found in the Shinto religion of Japan, in one of the traditional religions of China—Taoism—and in Islamic mysticism or Sufism. According to Dr. Benson, meditational practices are found in practically every culture of man, and they have been developed within secular contexts as well. "We see the same sort of things in the writings of the so-called nature mystics," he observed. "Wordsworth believed that anyone could deliberately induce a 'happy stillness of the mind' through a deliberate relaxation of the will. Tennyson, as his son later revealed, was able to induce altered states of consciousness through a steady repetition of his own name."

The instructions given to the TM novitiate were not, Benson noticed, basically very different from those used in many other meditative procedures. Most techniques appeared to include four essential ingredients: A quiet, calm environment in which to elicit the response; a passive attitude, which involved not trying to "force" anything to happen; a comfortable position, so that one's muscular activity would be reduced to a minimum; and a mental device. This could be a single-syllable word or sound, which was repeated over and over again, either silently or in a low, gentle tone. (The purpose of the repetition was that of halting meaningful mental activity.) All that was necessary in order to evoke the deeply restful "relaxation response" was, he speculated, to position oneself in these ways and to meditate upon the word of one's choice.

To test this supposition, Bensen drew up a simple set of laboratory instructions. He wanted to see if, simply by following these rules, naive subjects would be able to elicit the restful "wakeful hypometabolic state." The instruction list, which he later described as a "simple, mental, noncultic procedure," reads as follows:

In a quiet environment, sit in a comfortable position.
Deeply relax all your muscles, beginning at your feet and progressing up to your face—feet, calves, thighs, lower torso, chest, shoulders,

neck, head. Allow them to remain deeply relaxed.

Breathe through your nose. Become aware of your breathing. As you breathe out, say the word "one" silently to yourself. Thus: breathe in . . . breathe out, with "one." In . . . out, with "one". . . .

Continue this practice for ten to twenty minutes. You may open your eyes to check the time, but do not use an alarm. When you finish, sit quietly for several minutes, at first with your eyes closed and later with eyes open.

These instructions, though not identical to those received during training in transcendental meditation, are quite similar to them.* Benson's guidance sheet contains additional tips: "Remember not to worry about whether you are successful in achieving a deep level of relaxation . . . permit relaxation to occur at its own pace. When distracting thoughts occur, ignore them and continue to repeat 'one' as you breathe. The technique should be practiced twice daily, and not within two hours after any meal, since the digestive processes seem to interfere with the elicitation of the expected changes." An arresting footnote is the comment that "people who are undergoing psychoanalysis for at least two sessions a week experience difficulty in eliciting the response."

The efficacy of his laboratory procedure was tested in a controlled study of seventeen healthy subjects, and Dr. Benson published his findings last spring in the journal *Psychosomatic Medicine*. In this experiment, the subjects—people who had never practiced any kind of relaxation technique—were given the instruction sheet and allowed an hour to familiarize themselves with the method and practice it. Each individual was then studied for five consecutive periods of twelve minutes each.

During three of the periods, the subject sat quietly and read material selected for its emotional neutrality—excerpts from the book *Navajo Wildlands*. During the fourth period, the subject was instructed merely to sit with eyes closed. During the fifth period, the subject was asked to follow the instructions for the relaxation technique. (These experimental periods did not follow this order in every case but were organized in different sequences.)

"What we found," said Benson, "was that, using the number 'one'

---

*The only tangible difference between the two techniques is that in TM one is not asked to pay attention to one's breathing. One simply "thinks" the mantra. If thoughts drift elsewhere, one is advised simply to let them return to the mantra effortlessly.

instead of the mantra, we could produce essentially the same physiological changes that were produced during transcendental meditation. For example, the mean oxygen consumption when the subject sat quietly and read *Navajo Wildlands*—which is to say, during the control period—was 258.9 milliliters per minute. When the same individual sat quietly with his or her eyes closed, there was no significant change from that control value. But during the time when the relaxation technique was being practiced, oxygen consumption fell to 225.4 milliliters per minute—a decrease of 13 percent." The respiratory rate decreased 4.6 breaths below what the control values had been.

Benson's current feeling about transcendental meditation is that it is quite as good as any other relaxation technique, including his own laboratory method—and that it may be better for individuals who need personal instruction to get themselves started, post-instruction "meditation checks" to keep themselves going, and the support of an organized group. What the TM movement has done essentially, he believes, is to isolate and attractively package for the modern consumer a practice available throughout the ages but more traditionally within a religious context. "What we have done, as a society, is to turn our backs on these traditional modes of achieving states of relaxation," he remarked. "At the same time, the stress of living in a complicated society, with a multitude of anxieties and pressures, involves the frequent elicitation of 'fight or flight' responses. Since, very often, there's no way for the individual to discharge that physiological-arousal state (because it is socially unacceptable to do so), there may be a chronic rise in blood pressure—that is, hypertension. And high blood pressure is an important, if not the most important, predisposing factor to heart attack and stroke."

This is among the many reasons why Dr. Benson believes most of us should be practicing one relaxation method or another as part of our daily routine. He cautioned, however, against the use of TM or his own laboratory procedure as self-treatment for chronically high blood pressure. Decreases in blood pressure must be effected under the careful supervision of a physician. "I'm frightened," he said, "of people starting to elicit the 'relaxation response' and then getting the idea that it's all right to throw their medications away on that basis."

There appears to be little threat of other dangers or undesirable side effects from the regular practice of meditation or self-relaxation—

unless one evokes the response beyond the suggested two brief periods a day. "Overmeditating" in this fashion is considered unwise.

"If done excessively for weeks on end," Dr. Benson observed, "it can lead to hallucinatory or dissociative states." Dr. Benson's ideas and researches in this entire area are more fully presented in his book *The Relaxation Response.*

It is now about a month and a half since I began the practice of transcendental meditation. I reserve forty minutes daily, twenty in the morning, twenty in the evening before dinner, for meditating. On occasion, I also invoke my mantra if I'm too wakeful at bedtime; I find it a highly effective sleeping pill. (Using one's mantra for sleep is, by the way, frowned on by the TM people; they insist that one should meditate for energy and activity.)

My husband also meditates regularly; he uses the Benson laboratory method, which he says is quite effective. I wonder occasionally how long the two of us will keep it up. Will we, a year or so from now, still be scrupulously setting aside time for meditation amid the demands of the busy day? A number of people have warned me that, though they themselves began as avid meditators, they found it easy to drift off from the practice. One acquaintance said she had stopped meditating shortly after moving to New Haven: She found life there so much less stressful than in New York. "And besides," she added, "I'd only started to meditate because of the excruciating lower-back pains that I suffered— and meditation had already cured them. In fact, it was the strangest thing; I'd begin to meditate and then, around ten minutes into the period, I'd feel all those tense muscles go 'blop'."

My own responses to meditation have changed and intensified somewhat since that first training session. I now rarely experience those strange, tingling sensations, but I do find that, some fifteen minutes after the start of the twenty-minute session, tears start to trickle down my cheeks. These tears are not accompanied by feelings of sadness; they are like the tears one weeps when slicing onions. Each session still ends with one or more enormous yawns. The most notable change resulting from these relaxation periods is that I feel much less wound up, much calmer. If I were an oven, I would say that my temperature had been turned down from 500 to 375 degrees.

My only problem with TM is trying to explain it to friends and acquaintances. Those of more mystical and religious inclination insist that I cannot divorce meditation from its theological and metaphysical origins. They look shocked when I reply that to me it's no more than a terrific aspirin, a wonderful kind of bromide. My more rationalist, outer-reality-oriented friends seem to think, on the other hand, that I've adopted some strange set of beliefs and now imagine myself to be experiencing "physiological reactions" for that reason. With these people I hear myself sounding embarrassed and apologetic.

Recently, I was quizzed very closely about exactly what I had *paid* for. Was it the instruction or the mantra? Exactly what had I gotten for my money? "I suppose," I admitted, feeling my cheeks redden, "that, looked at with hindsight, it was simply my mantra that I bought." This was met with a silence, so I laughed and added: "I guess it sounds pretty silly, doesn't it, paying one hundred twenty-five dollars for a nonsense word?"

But to my surprise my questioner shook her head in disagreement: "Not at all; I think it's a bargain. Look at me. I've been in analysis four days a week, at fifty dollars a time, for the past year. And my therapist still hasn't come up with *my* nonsense word!"

1975

Goodall and Chimpanzees at Yale

The large auditorium of Yale's Sterling Law School was darkened; a film on chimpanzee behavior in the wild was in progress. Off to one side of the movie screen, her fair hair and green dress illumined by the glow, the noted animal behaviorist Jane Goodall narrated: "Of course we do know that the chimpanzee is man's nearest living relative, that anatomically and biochemically he resembles us more closely than does any other primate species. We know that the circuitry of his brain is remarkably similar to that of *our* brains. And yet," she observed, her voice quiet, her accent proper and very much that of the English girls' boarding school, "when one views the very striking similarities between certain chimp and human behaviors, one simply *is* astonished. There is something rather funny about it; it seems like caricature. One has the feeling that one is looking, not so much at animals living in their natural habitat—one is looking at one's long-lost cousins."

And indeed, even for those of us in the audience who were already familiar with Jane Goodall's work and her book on chimpanzee life, *In the Shadow of Man*, there were sequences in the movie—a remarkable film, shot and edited by Goodall's husband, Hugo Van Lawick—which were startling. Here, for example, were two female chimpanzees meeting after a separation: They threw their arms around one another, hugging excitedly, their behavior indistinguishable from that of their human counterparts in a similar situation. Here was another oddly "human" greeting incident: A mature female, happening upon one of the dominant males of the troop (again, after a period of separation), came up to him and kissed him upon the lips. And here, as well, was some curiously familiar play behavior: three juvenile chimp siblings chasing each other endlessly around the great trunk of a tree. Their mother, an aging female to whom Goodall had given the name Flo, sat nearby watching, a new infant in her arms. (Later in the movie there were scenes of the whole family—including Flo and the baby, now grown up enough to join in the play—chasing each other around the tree.)

One of the film's strangest sights, at least as far as I was concerned, was that of a young chimp female, coming down a path and twirling round and round, her arms outstretched, looking for all the world like a little human girl trying to make herself dizzy. This drew an amused laugh from the audience. A much more hilarious reaction greeted a sequence in which a group of males approached what Goodall called a "desirable food source"—the bananas she and her husband put out regularly to lure the chimps into their Gombe Stream camp. The males communicated their heightened excitement by means of a ferocious "charging display." At first, one could see their heads, then their bodies, as they emerged from clumps of trees at the top of a long hill. They paused momentarily. Then they began swaying, rocking, drumming on tree trunks. The hair on their bodies became erect; they drew up their shoulders to give their bodies a huge, powerful rounded shape—the exaggeratedly supermale appearance of football players. At last they came charging down upon the camp, pulling up branches and hurling rocks as they entered the clearing. It was all such marvelous nonsense: such sheer masculine bluff and threat. The entire audience burst into laughter and I heard the student beside me saying incredulously: "I don't believe it. I just don't *believe* it."

Jane Goodall was scheduled to give four lectures during her stay at Yale. After the first one, the word got around fairly quickly. On the second day of the talks, arriving at the auditorium forty-five minutes early, I found most of the seats already taken. The next day it was even more crowded; the aisles were choked with student and faculty members who were sitting on the floor, and the high window ledges of Sterling Law auditorium were crammed with latecomers who had scaled the walls and come in from the outside. At the fourth and final lecture— "Chimpanzee and Human Behavior: Some Similarities and Differences"—the situation was a fire marshal's nightmare: every inch of space downstairs and in the balcony was occupied, doorways and window ledges were jammed and scores of people were turned away. Afterward I ran into a friend, a Law School faculty member. "This is pretty astonishing," he said, looking around with a smile. "With these blasé kids, you know, it's hard to get any sort of a turnout. We can't even fill up this auditorium when there's a porno movie." Yet the whole of Yale College, or so it seemed, had come to hear Jane Goodall talk about her life among the wild chimpanzees of the Gombe Stream Reserve—

and at the end of her lectures gave her a clamorous standing ovation.

What is the explanation for Goodall's widespread appeal? She has, without doubt, made an important contribution to our scientific knowledge of chimpanzee behavior. But that is not, one suspects, the sole reason for the upsurge of popular interest in her work.

One part of the enthusiasm may stem from the excited speculations generated by the wave of primate studies begun in the late nineteen-fifties—Irven DeVore's work on the baboon, George Schaller's study of the gorilla, Phyllis Jay's observations of a langur colony in India, and others. These studies made it abundantly clear that primates other than man live in structured social groups of fairly complex organization which exist within pretty well-defined geographical territories or "home ranges." Whereas laboratory work with primates had concentrated on the animals' "human" capabilities—Yale's great pioneer primatologist, Robert M. Yerkes, had demonstrated the chimp's capacity for learning through trial-and-error and had even taught some of his animals to eat together at a table like well-behaved children—the field studies suggested that scientists might profitably try the opposite approach: Instead of exploring the limits of the primates' ability to learn "human" behavior, science might learn something about *humans* by observing our anthropoid relatives. (It had become increasingly obvious that such observations had to be made in the animals' natural habitat. In captivity a male baboon often showed fairly brutal behavior toward the females and juveniles with which he shared the cage. In the wild, male baboons almost never displayed such brutality; their aggression was turned toward predators and other outside threats. Just as one could not generalize about male humans by observing prisoners in San Quentin, one could not study natural primate behavior under the abnormal conditions of capitivity.)

The major primate field studies of the past decade—and Goodall's ongoing chimp study is the most extensive—have underlined the notion that a good deal of what has been considered uniquely "human" in our behavior may in fact be rooted in our evolutionary history; that, just as we and other primate species share a common biological inheritance in terms of physiology, so we share a common heritage of behavioral tendencies as well.

This kind of supposition assuredly accounts for much of the stir that Goodall and her work have been creating. Another, and wholly nonscientific cause for her popularity probably lies in her personal story, a wonderful mixture of jungle fantasy and scientific fairytale. In recounting it, one has the temptation to begin with "Once upon a time . . ."

In the nineteen-fifties a young English secretary named Jane Goodall, who was working at a documentary film studio in London, was invited out to Kenya to visit an old school friend. Miss Goodall had always wanted to visit Africa, for she was fascinated by animals and animal behavior. (Even as a child, as she recounts in her book, she was so curious about animals that she once spent an entire day in a stuffy henhouse waiting to see a hen lay her eggs.)

Jane Goodall had been in Africa about a month when a friend suggested that if she liked animals so much she ought to look up Dr. Louis Leakey. Leakey, the late, eminent prehistorian, was at that time curator of what has since become the Museum of Natural History in Nairobi. Goodall went to see him and was hired on the spot with the rank of an assistant secretary—although she had no academic credentials, no scientific qualifications and indeed no university training whatsoever. (Leakey's penchant for hiring completely inexperienced people—and giving them responsible posts—was legendary. He tended to minimize the need for academic expertise, insisting that an untrained individual with a sympathetic understanding of animal behavior was often the better observer.)

For Jane Goodall Dr. Leakey proved to be a kind of good genie or fairy godfather. It was he who first called her attention to a group of chimpanzees living on the shores of Lake Tanganyika in Tanzania, suggesting that if she would attempt an intensive, long-range study of the chimp (a study no one had yet succeeded in making), he would try to raise the necessary funds to support the project. It was Leakey who, while his protégée was working alone at her camp in the African bush, sent out the young Dutch photographer, Baron Hugo Van Lawick, to assist her (at the same time writing Miss Goodall's mother that he had "found someone just right as a husband for Jane . . . "). The young couple did fall in love and did marry; they now have a young son. And later in the nineteen-fifties, Leakey arranged for Miss Goodall to enter Cambridge University, where she transformed a bulging satchel of observational notes into a Ph.D. thesis on chimpanzee behavior.

The tale of Goodall's early days at Gombe is partly a jungle idyll, partly the story of endless frustration and grueling work. She spent fourteen discouraging months tracking the frightened and elusive chimps in an effort to make contact with them. Out of this ultimately successful preliminary work, however, and out of the months of painstaking observations that followed, there emerged a fascinating, even astonishing portrait of man's closest primate relative, the chimpanzee.

Here, then, was an animal whose behavior, in a wide variety of situations, bore a striking resemblance to the human behavior which might occur in the same situations. Not only did chimpanzees greet one another after separations in strangely familiar ways—with hugs, embraces, sometimes kisses—but much of their "reassurance" behavior was uncannily similar to our own. For example, a chimpanzee, in instances of alarm or upset, often reached out to touch another chimp or to take its hand. In situations where deference was to be shown, the subordinate animal might bow, bob or crouch submissively in front of the dominant one. In cases of aggression—threat or intimidation—the close parallel between chimp and human behavior was equally striking (as attested by the Yale audience's howl of laughter which followed the male chimps' charging display). Chimps engaged in slapping—more commonly seen among females— foot stamping and "glaring." One threat behavior typical among males was something Goodall named the "bipedal swagger." This was a slow, rhythmic shifting from foot to foot, while the chimp's shoulders were hunched upward and slightly rounded, its arms held stiffly away from the body. Anyone who has ever seen a John Wayne movie can readily visualize this intimidating posture.

The picture which Goodall drew of the chimpanzee was, in brief, that of a highly intelligent, quite social animal, well able to communicate with its fellow creatures through expressive gestures, postures, facial expressions and sounds which included meaningful calls, cries and screams. This was an animal that could also make skillful use of objects in the environment—it could use rocks as weapons, leaves for wiping away feces, etc. It could even *construct* a needed tool on occasion.

A striking example of such "tool-making" occurred in connection with the hunt for termites, a favorite chimpanzee delicacy. The chimp would carefully select a sturdy stem, twig or bark fiber and deliberately fashion it into a suitable "hunting pole." Then the chimp would select a promising-looking termite mound, thrust the pole down into the earth and "fish up" and devour the termites. Such a protracted sequence of behavior—the preparation of the tool, the choice of termite nest and the patient extraction of the termites—suggests at least a rudimentary ability to carry out a "plan." Equally surprising—indeed unique among primates save for man—the male chimpanzees would occasionally hunt and kill small prey cooperatively, and the hunters (only the males hunted) would share their food in response to begging gestures of females and other males.

Goodall's work has led many scientists to reassess the "great gulf" which has been believed to separate the animal and human worlds. As Harvard's Professor Irven DeVore, one of this country's leading primatologists, explains: "The behavior of the chimpanzee displays many of the rudiments of those sorts of behavior which became terribly important in the development of the human line—behaviors such as tool-use, the relatively efficient hunting of animals, the sharing of food (which in chimps occurs only in special circumstances: when the males have made a kill). In the chimp we also find a very prolonged and dependent infancy—longer than in any other nonhuman primate—and an elaboration of greetings and gestures which make it possible for relative strangers to get on with one another. In fact it's remarkable how *many* traits that we would have assumed came relatively late in the human line are in fact already present in the chimp."

Goodall's data, according to DeVore, strongly suggest that the gradation between what might have been our chimplike ancestors and a very early hominid, or true human, represents a small step rather than a great leap. At the same time, recent fossil finds have indicated that the human species is much older—surely more than 3 million years older— than scientists had believed only a few years ago. "The point is," says DeVore, "that the chimps have moved forward in the scale, in terms of their tool-use and other complex behaviors that they show. And the time scale of our own line now appears to extend back much further." The bold, sharp line which seemed to divide man from the rest of the animal world, DeVore remarks, is at present "a good deal *less* clear than one would ever have expected."

I was to interview Jane Goodall just before her third public lecture at Yale. She is a low-keyed, handsome woman in her mid-thirties who combines a slight shyness suggestive of a Victorian schoolgirl with an air of authority and control. I found her looking somewhat fatigued. She admitted that she was "just exhausted"; she had been on a round of meetings with students and faculty, giving some classroom lectures in addition to her major addresses. We agreed, therefore, to limit our conversation to no more than an hour. Here are some portions of that talk.

SCARF: *I think that many people have the somewhat romantic notion that when we look at the chimp we are somehow looking at man prior to culture. And yet, assuming some common ancestor from which both our species branched off at some unknown point in time, we also have to assume that not only humans but chimps as well continued evolving. So we really can't take it for granted, can we, that when we see a certain behavior in the chimp, this is the very behavior our own precultural ancestors would have shown? Because we don't know for sure, do we?*

GOODALL: That's so; but we can look at it another way. We can say that there are multiple similarities of behavior in man and chimp, some of them very striking; particularly those relating to nonverbal communication. Now if a pattern is common to modern man and modern chimpanzee, it's then probable—at the very least, probable—that it will have occurred in the common ancestor. And therefore in our own early ancestors.

The most one can really say is that anyone who is interested in theories of behavior in early man—and in the ways human behavior might have been molded during the evolutionary process—can't afford to ignore chimp behavior. It happens to be the best model we have; and it isn't perfect, and we know it isn't. I certainly appreciate that the chimp has evolved; nevertheless, this model is just about the closest we can come.

SCARF: *How far do you think this work can be carried? More specifically, how much do you think that scientific studies of chimp behavior can ultimately tell us about human behavior?*

GOODALL: Well, I think it is quite significant to study the chimp in his own right, as man's closest relative—to study his behavior in the natural habitat before it's too late, before his species disappears. And then I do think understanding his behavior may help us understand human behavior.

Now, by that I don't mean that because a chimp does something a certain way, we will do it in the very same way. What I mean is: The chimpanzee—although he lives in a complex society, although he is in fact a complex creature—is far less complicated than even the most simple human being. He acts out his emotional feelings with very little masking of his responses. Therefore it's probably easier to tease apart the biological basis of something like aggression in the chimp than could ever be done in man. And having looked at aggressive behavior in the chimp, it may be worthwhile to come back to man and look at the same behavior and ask: Are the same factors involved?

SCARF: *Which, of the many chimp behaviors you have described in your book and in your lectures, do you happen to find most interesting? As far as our common behaviors are concerned, which ones would you want to come back to and study in humans, after having observed them in chimps?*

GOODALL: I personally think that among the patterns we share, the most fascinating are related to things like embracing, patting, kissing . . . contact behaviors. But those aren't the things I would want to come back to and look at in man. I think the kind of thing we're hoping to examine at Gombe—and at the new laboratory now being set up at Stanford University—are behaviors like chimp aggression. Particularly at Stanford, we would do well to look at certain things inside the body— correlations between hormones and aggressive patterns. That's the kind of area where you want to tease some of these things apart and then look at aggression in man and see if the same kind of thing is involved.

SCARF: *How would you go about doing that?*

GOODALL: I think that's going to have to wait; we're in too early a stage of research. We haven't really begun it yet. That's something for the future.

SCARF: *One thing that quite intrigued me in your book and your talks— and which is, of course, related to an issue of our times—was the submissive role of the female within the chimp community. The female adolescent was, for example, submissive not only to older females and adult males; she was submissive to male juveniles as well. Older females would also be observed to "present" to juvenile males. ["Presenting," a turning of the rump toward the dominant individual, is an acknowledgment of inferior status and a gesture of submission.] It certainly looks as though the female is definitely submissive to the male in that society. Do you believe there is some biological basis for the female's behavior?*

GOODALL: Well, yes I do think so. For one thing the male is larger, stronger and heavier: he has much more dramatic aggression patterns, especially his charging displays. His more violent attack patterns—the stamping, dragging, slamming up and down—are typically male patterns. And it would be extremely nonadaptive, biologically, for the female to indulge in that kind of behavior because she has a little baby which she has to carry around and protect. And if she did all those things, she'd tend to damage her child.

SCARF: *So you're suggesting that for the chimp female it is adaptive to be so submissive?*

GOODALL: Well yes. (She smiles.) A student came up to me the other day and said he had an awful problem. He said he belonged to a certain group—I'm not quite sure what his group was—but at any rate he told me: "I'm the only one of my group who's been looking into primate behavior. And I've been looking at the social structures in all different kinds of primates. And I have the feeling that primates live in male-dominated groups. And my group, the group I belong to, *doesn't like it.* . . . " And all I could say to him was that I really couldn't help him because it just happens to be true. Primates live in male-dominated groups. (We both laugh.)

SCARF: *I suppose, for some people, this might lead to a direct inference or belief that the human female is necessarily subordinate to the male. But that would be terribly facile thinking, it seems to me; we don't subsist on a diet which is mainly fruit and leaves, either, as the other primates do.*

GOODALL: Well, the best I could do for my young friend was to tell him that if he were looking for Women's Lib in the animal world he would have to go to the hyena, where there is a real sexual dimorphism which favors the female. The female is the aggressive individual in that species; and hyena society is female-dominated. Very much so.

SCARF: *But it isn't a very flattering model, is it?*

GOODALL: The hyena is interesting, actually. If one is interested in the problem of aggression, then one wants to ask: "If aggression exists, *why* does it exist?" The hyena has given me a whole new perspective on aggression. Because, you see, if you are a primate female, you can't afford to be aggressive; biologically it would be wrong because you'd risk losing your infant. But if you're a hyena female, you have a very unique pattern of child-raising, and a fairly unique social structure too, inasmuch as the female is dominant.

Hyena females don't take their babies to the kill, as lions do; nor do they bring food to the babies, as lions or wild dogs or jackals do. Instead, the baby depends on the mother's milk for a very long time—until it's eighteen months old. This is fantastically long when you think that for other carnivores it's usually six weeks. . . . But the point is that the growth and health of the cub depends on the nutritive qualities of the mother's milk. So in this case, aggression is extremely adaptive: the female's got to be able to fight for a big enough share of the clan kill to get her milk rich enough to nurse her cubs for eighteen months. And it turns out that two cubs belonging to a high-ranking dominant female hyena will grow just about twice as fast as one pup belonging to a low-ranking female of this species.

SCARF: *What is the male hyena up to meanwhile?*

GOODALL: Oh, he just toddles around. He doesn't seem to do much good, as far as I can see, except to mate with the female.

SCARF: *Returning to the chimp—don't you think it rather striking that one of the most clearcut and important submissive postures, which is to say this "presenting" or turning of the rump toward the dominant individual, is also the very same posture which the female assumes during copulation?*

GOODALL: Well, there is an obvious way in which one might explain this; but there are alternative theories as well. And you must remember that it isn't only the female who presents submissively; it's also the male. In fact in young males it is the most common submissive pattern (although neither for male nor female is it the only submissive pattern, by any manner of means).

But a very common posture which a chimp takes when he solicits social grooming ["grooming" involves the picking out of foreign matter, usually flakes of dried skin, from the animal's fur] is also to stand with his rump toward the chimp whom he is asking for grooming. And it's also the position the "loser" animal takes after an aggressive encounter, when he is asking for a reassurance pat or touch from the dominant individual. So it may be that this particular submissive position derives not from sex-related behaviors but from behaviors involving the request for friendly physical contact, for reassurance.

SCARF: *But then one is struck as well by the fact that "threat behavior" in the male—such as glaring, shaking branches and so on—is also "courting behavior."*

GOODALL: I think it's the other way around; the courting behavior is threat behavior. Because when you are courting somebody, you want to have them come to you; and typically, if you're a primate and you want someone subordinate to you to do something, you threaten them. In hamadryad baboons, for example, the male simply attacks the female and bites her neck; that means to follow him. It's exactly the same pattern as that of the male chimp: If the female won't follow him and he wants to go off with her, he attacks her and she follows him.

SCARF: *I'd like to talk a little about the chimp's use of tools. You appeared to be very excited, in your book, about "man's closest relative" using objects for specific purposes. But there are certainly other animal species which use tools—the sea otter uses stones to break open mollusks; that strange bird, the Galápagos woodpecker-finch, uses a cactus spine held in its beak to probe its insect food out of the bark. And so if we do see tool-using in other animals, aren't we anthropomorphizing if we say that this is something very special and unique simply because it happens to occur in a species so closely related to our own?*

GOODALL: Actually, we're not. I think the point here is that if you look at animals like the sea otter and the woodpecker-finch—and even insects (there are insects that use tools), you find that with many of these animals the use of tools turns out to be a major way of getting their food. You can really consider it a behavior adaptation which matches a structural adaptation in other species. An ordinary woodpecker uses his long beak and his long tongue; the woodpecker-finch didn't have one, and he uses a spine . . . which is fascinating.

But as far as I'm concerned, if you're interested in something which relates to human tool-use, the things which become significant are (1) if a species can use a wide variety of different objects for a wide variety of purposes and in a number of different contexts, and (2) if the individual of that species can meet a new environmental challenge by using an object or a tool for solving problems that he hasn't encountered before.

SCARF: *You're saying, then, that the chimp's behavior is much more elastic. Can you give me some examples of this?*

GOODALL: I'm saying that the behavior is much more elaborate, that the chimp shows tool-use to a far greater extent than any other animal save man. The chimp can also modify objects and make them suitable, and so shows tool-making. To give you an example of the way in which an object can suddenly be used: When Mike, who became dominant male during our time at Gombe, was still scared of people, we held out a banana to him one day. He didn't dare take it because it was in our hand. He stared at it for a bit, and made a threat movement. Then he grabbed a handful of grass and shook it at us, which is another threat pattern.

As it happened, a piece of the long grass touched the banana. It was instantaneous, his realization of what he had done. Immediately he dropped the grass and picked up a long piece of straw; but he didn't bother to try that. He chucked it down, and picked up a stick. Then he hit the banana out of the human hand.

Now here was a novel problem: he'd never encountered it before, and it didn't take him more than a quarter of a minute to hit on a solution and get that banana. Then we held out another banana, and immediately he picked up a stick and hit the banana out of the hand.

SCARF: *You also appeared, in your book, to be quite excited to find that chimps occasionally hunted small prey and ate meat. Why were you so intrigued by that discovery?*

GOODALL: I suppose partly because chimps have always been supposed to be strictly vegetarian, and it was interesting to find that they weren't. . . . But I think the real excitement is in finding that they show this terrific cooperation when they are hunting, and in the food-sharing that results from the eating of meat.

SCARF: *Could you say a little more about the meaning of food-sharing? I believe that food-sharing doesn't exist among other nonhuman primates, among baboons, for example.*

GOODALL: No, baboons don't share food. The chimps are the only nonhuman primates that have been reported to share food amongst adults in the wild. Of course, man is characterized by his ability to share food; so are the carnivores, mind you. You know, a lion makes a kill and shares it with the others.

Primates tend to be more selfish, presumably because normally they don't need to share. They each forage for themselves. And so if you develop a species in a kind of evolutionary way that forages for itself, then it requires a new mechanism—which may be something to do with intellect—to change that into a sudden ability to share a unique food.

SCARF: *As far as the chimp is concerned, what would be the utility of sharing food?*

GOODALL: Well, I don't think that it really is terribly utilitarian for chimps. Because meat isn't really a major portion of their diet. What it means is that other chimps get the taste of meat, and the tradition can be passed on in that way to the hunting tradition. This would be very significant if for some reason the chimps were pressured into hunting more.

It could be significant in human evolution. You see, it's hard to think how man could have evolved into a hunting creature who needed to share food if there weren't some kind of precursor to food-sharing.

SCARF: *One thing that rather astonished me in your book was the behavior of the female chimp Ollie, just after the death of her four-month-old son. I mean the way in which she flung the limp body over her shoulder as if knowing her baby was dead; and then her dazed behavior, and the way she went off alone and sat staring into space. Do you think she "understood" what had happened?*

GOODALL: I suspect that Ollie, who was an old female, had had a previous infant that had died. Because when her baby stopped responding, reacting, behaving—whatever you like to call it—she seemed to realize it. There was a sudden and complete change in her handling of her infant. In the case of a younger, less experienced mother whom I'd previously watched handling her dead infant, there seemed to be no realization of what had happened. In that instance, a full day after the baby's death, the mother continued to cradle it against her breast as if it were alive.

But whether this means that Ollie, because of a possible previous experience, had a "concept of death," I really don't know. It doesn't really matter. But you know that is the only way I can interpret it.

SCARF: *You didn't see anything in her that could actually be labeled "mourning behavior"? Or did you?*

GOODALL: Oh yes. I certainly think there is some kind of stress response which is probably very similar to human grief. She had this glassy expression and her behavior was quite aimless. She went off up a mountain and sat there, and came down again, and didn't eat, and generally didn't behave in a very purposeful kind of way. She had a vacant look in her eyes, an empty staring ahead—the same look that has been associated with grief in orphans.

SCARF: *I have heard that several months ago the other old female chimp whom you talked about a great deal in your book —Flo—died. And that her youngest surviving offspring, the adolescent male Flint, had what appeared to be an intense reaction to his mother's death. And that shortly afterwards Flint had died too.*

GOODALL: Yes, that's right. Flo lay down on a rock, toward the side of a stream and simply expired. She was quite old. Flint stayed near her corpse; he groomed one of her arms and tried to pull her up by the hand. The night of her death he slept close to the body, and, by the following morning, he showed signs of extreme depression.

After that, no matter where he might wander off to, he kept returning to his mother's body. It was the maggots which, at last, drove him away; he'd try to shake the maggots off her and they would swarm onto him.

Finally, he stopped coming back. But he did remain in an area comprising about fifty square yards; and he wouldn't move any further away from the place where Flo had died. And in ten days he had lost about a third of his body weight. He also developed a strange, glazed look.

At last Flint died too; he died very close to the spot where his mother had died. In fact, the day before he had returned to sit on the very rock where Flo had lain down (by then we had removed her body and had buried her).

SCARF: *Is it true that you've had a post mortem done on Flint's remains to find out whether he might have had some sort of a disease?*

GOODALL: The results of that have been negative. They indicated that although he had a certain parasite load and one or two bugs, there was nothing sufficient in itself to cause death. And so the major cause of death had to be grief.

SCARF: *But that's very strange—it's weird to think of a nonhuman animal having such an intense mourning reaction that he could literally die of grief.*

GOODALL: Yes it is. It really is.

At this point, Goodall, who had been drinking coffee throughout most of our interview, put down her empty cup and leaned back in her leather armchair with a sigh. A wave of fatigue must have come over her, for she suddenly looked quite pale. "I'm so sorry, I won't be able to go on much longer; I'm just so bone-weary and tired," she confessed. Then she smiled slightly: "I never—no matter *how* hard I may be driving myself— ever get this tired when I'm out in the jungle. . . . "

1973

Human Attachment

A Psychoanalyst Looks at Old Questions in New Ways

Although psychoanalysts have held varying views on the nature of the child's tie to the mother, all seem in agreement on the one point: it is the foundation stone of the personality. On what basis then, does this relationship form? The most widely accepted model is that the bond arises during the feeding experience. Recently, however, Dr. John Bowlby of London's Tavistock Centre, advanced a novel and biologically based formulation of the infant-mother tie. Bowlby's work leans heavily on the science of ethology—the study of animal behavior in the wild.

Bowlby's argument, presented in his book *Attachment*, is that the human infant, in common with many of the lower forms of animal life, possesses behavioral patterns which led to survival during the evolutionary eras. These patterns, or sets of genetic instructions, revolve around the need for food, the need to reproduce, the need for protection from predators. In the human baby, with his prolonged period of helplessness, the instinctual behavior patterns are keyed to keeping the mother close by. The need for her protection mediates what Bowlby calls "attachment behavior": the biological tendency for the child to form a strong bond with the mother. This in-built pattern of behavior, he maintains, was an adaptive response of the human species during our evolution in the wild.

"It would be hard," says Bowlby, whose bearing has a brisk suggestion of the military, "to understand the behavior of an animal except by reference to the environment in which it evolved. Now suppose a child is frightened; what will he do? He'll run to his mother. Why does he choose to do that particular thing? Because in the primitive environment, that behavior was adaptive; it promoted survival. We can see similar things in our physiology; when it's hot out, for example, we sweat. We don't sit down and think about why we're doing it, we just do it. But sweating is a physiological adaptation which has the effect of keeping the body temperature constant.

"Much of human behavior has the effect of ensuring protection; it's a notion we tend to lose sight of in our safe Western civilizations. But if we're to make any attempt to understand why we do certain irrelevant-seeming things, we can't leave out the idea of predation."

Bowlby, in his early sixties, is trim and white-haired, with shaggy V-shaped eyebrows. His eyes are a bright sharp blue. "The fact is that in the natural habitat, the need for protection is paramount. You can wait till tomorrow for food, if necessary. You can wait six months for sex. But if a predator threatens, the top priority is protection—or you won't *be* there tomorrow."

A great deal of behavior in the wild, Bowlby points out, does serve a protective function. A rabbit scampers to his burrow when threatened; in that species getting to a safe place is the adaptive strategy. In some species, however, "togetherness" has more survival value. A number of bird species maintain proximity: a falcon will not attack them in a flock but will attack the stray bird. "A lamb without its mother is, as every shepherd knows, the easiest target for the fox or eagle."

Dr. Bowlby is chairman of the staff committee of the School of Family Psychiatry and Community Mental Health, affiliated with the Tavistock Clinic; it is London's most famous teaching clinic. Built on the site of a bombed-out cancer hospital, the sprawling Tavistock Centre comprises not only outpatient clinics and classrooms, but also the Tavistock Institute of Human Relations—an array of autonomous groups doing research and consultation on social problems. The "Tavi" takes its name from Tavistock Square in central London, where some fifty years ago its founders occupied a small suite of offices. Now, hugely grown, the center is located in Hampstead, a northwest area of the city.

Bowlby spends three days a week at the clinic, dividing his time between administrative duties and seeing patients; the other two weekdays he works at home on his book *Separation* (Volume II of *Attachment and Loss*). "It was the effects of early separation that first made me wonder what processes in the infant were at work. As an environmental pathogen, loss of the mother could be identified and pointed to without doubt. I believed that in this lay very important implications for personality development which hadn't been recognized, let alone worked out."

Bowlby's interest in problems related to separation began early in his career. It arose "partly from a certain impatience with the psychoanalytic theories current in the late thirties. They showed a tendency to push things back to very speculative happenings in early infancy, such as 'rage at weaning.' But I had the notion that there were very real specific experiences which, if they took place in the early years, could be singled out as causes of later pathology."

In 1944, while serving as a lieutenant colonel in the British army, Bowlby published *Forty-four Juvenile Thieves: Their Characters and Home-Life.* This slim volume was based on work he had done at the London Child Clinic. In it Bowlby pointed to the disproportionately high incidence of early separation experiences in the life histories of forty-four thieves, comparing them with forty-four children referred to the clinic who did not steal. He also designated a group which he called the Affectionless Children; they were highly represented among the thieves, but there were none in the control group. In all but two cases the affectionless thieves, unstable and maladapted by age ten, had undergone prolonged separation from their mothers. Bowlby suggested that loss of the mother-figure might be a specific and very frequent cause of chronic delinquency. (Subsequent studies have confirmed this.)

"I came to the Tavistock just after World War II. The first thing I did was to organize the Department of Children and Parents; I was its chairman. Then in 1949, the World Health Organization (W.H.O.) asked me to write a report on the mental health of homeless children . . . All during 1950 I traveled around, visiting child-care centers both on the continent and in the States; at the same time I gathered all the material I could find, studies that had been done here, there and everywhere. What emerged from all of this was a rather clear-cut picture."

Bowlby's report, entitled *Maternal Care and Mental Health*, was published in 1951. The book's message was plain: Young children deprived of a mother's care are almost always retarded physically, intellectually and socially; often they develop symptoms of physical or mental illness. There was something much worse than a neglectful mother in a dirty home—and that was no mother in a clean institution. The institution infant, even from a few weeks of age, showed the effects of maternal deprivation. He might fail to smile at a human face or respond to a human voice; he often ate and slept badly, and if he did eat showed poor weight gain. No matter how modern and well-run an institution might be, it could not satisfy the infant's need to attach himself to a single, relatively stable mother-figure. And the young child who failed to make this attachment could be irreversibly damaged by the age of three.

"One must beware of a vested interest in the institutional care of children!" concluded Bowlby's report. He stressed prevention: keeping mother and child together wherever at all possible, providing adequate foster care or family-type living arrangements where it was not. (In 1953 the book was published in a shorter Penguin edition called *Child Care and the Growth of Love*; it has since been reprinted ten times, revised once, and is a minor classic.)

When Bowlby's report first appeared, it raised, as he recalls, "quite a stir. Most social workers were of course already aware of what I was saying: that early loss of the mother or frequent changes of mother-figure could cause irreparable harm. Most child psychiatrists agreed too; but to my great annoyance a number of analysts said it couldn't be true, this wasn't the way things happened." Bowlby laughs briefly. "It didn't fit in with their theories.

"Also, there were allegations that I thought separation and loss to be the be-all and end-all of psychopathology. But that was rather like accusing someone who's studying T.B. of thinking that all physical illiness is due to T.B. I didn't imagine that all mental illness was due to maternal deprivation."

The report addressed itself mainly to the problems of long-term separation. From 1948 onward, however, Bowlby and his Tavistock colleagues had been studying what happens to children during brief separations—while in the hospital or in a residential nursery. Out of these studies emerged what is—two decades later—still the definitive description of a child in a separation experience. "We saw three very distinct phases," says Bowlby, "which seemed to merge inexorably, one into the other. The first was Protest: the child would cry, shake his bed, make frantic attempts to rejoin the mother; at the same time he seemed to expect her at any moment and would refuse all comfort. This lasted anywhere from a few hours to a week or more. Next came Despair; he became quieter and (though he might cry from time to time) increasingly hopeless; he resembled an adult in a deep state of mourning. Last of all came Detachment, which the nurses often welcomed as a sign of recovery, of the child's 'settling in.' During this phase he became more sociable, took an interest in his surroundings. But all was not really well: you could see this when the mother visited. Instead of showing the attachment behavior normal for this age, he was remote and apathetic. He didn't cling to her; he turned away listlessly. He seemed to have lost all interest in her.

"I have been struck," remarks Bowlby soberly, "by how much this detachment resembles the more or less permanent detachment of the affectionless child. Fortunately, after a brief separation, this state seems to reverse itself . . . it's followed by a period of intense, desperate clinging."

Shortly after the appearance of *Maternal Care and Mental Health*, a psychiatric social worker at the Tavistock, James Robertson, filmed a child during a brief separation. Robertson's sensitive movie recorded what happened to a little two-year-old girl, Laura, who had gone into the hospital for an insignificant operation; the film was harrowing. The combined effect of written document and filmed evidence was to initiate a major shift in British social practices. This trend, says Bowlby, his naturally high color deepening slightly, "has continued, I'm glad to say, for the last twenty years. We're turning away from the big institution, trying to seek more familylike arrangements, to give the homeless child some person he can become attached to. And in hospitals, there have been major changes too. In the late forties when we started work, there was very restricted visiting, if any. Now, in most hospitals unlimited visits are permitted; many of them even allow mothers to enter and stay with their children."

Understanding of the things that happened to children during separation had greatly increased; no one, however, understood why they happened. "This was one valid criticism that was made of my work. I couldn't offer any coherent account of why separation caused such suffering, why it could have such grave consequences. The children weren't starving; they weren't ill-treated. But they had reacted to this experience with the utmost intensity; the need for mothering seemed to exist independently of any other circumstance. Why? What were the psychological processes involved? I didn't have time to concern myself with these questions while writing the report; I had only a few months in which to do it. Besides," admits Bowlby, "I didn't know the answers."

During the summer which followed the publication of *Maternal Care and Mental Health*, the Bowlbys vacationed in the western highlands of Scotland. One of their neighbors was Sir Julian Huxley, a friend of Ursula Bowlby's family. Huxley, a biologist, was greatly interested in the study of animal behavior; he was well acquainted with Konrad Lorenz and Niko Tinbergen, both leading ethologists. "I knew just enough to get along in a conversation with Huxley," confesses Bowlby.

"But he encouraged me. He gave me Tinbergen's book, which had been published in 1950. He also let me borrow Lorenz's book *King Solomon's Ring*, which he had in page proofs; he was writing the introduction."

Bowlby was fascinated. "Here was a body of biologists studying the behavior of wild animals," he wrote afterwards, "who were not only using concepts such as instinct, conflict, and defense mechanisms, extraordinarily like those which are used in one's day-to-day clinical work, but who made beautifully detailed descriptions and had devised an experimental technique to subject their hypotheses to test. . . ."

That winter John Bowlby read "all the ethology I could get hold of." The ethologists were studying the development of social behavior and especially family relationships in the lower species: ". . . and these things are the stuff of psychoanalysis." During a speech delivered to a group of psychologists several years later he remarked: "Ethology gives us new spectacles with which to look at things."

Both ethologists and psychoanalysts were interested in what are called "critical" or "sensitive" periods of early growth; periods during which many adult characteristics, which may include sexual behavior, are said to be determined. "Ethological studies demonstrated that there were, in the lower species, such critical phases," says Bowlby. "The young chick, for instance, who usually shows an instinctive pecking response after one day, never does at all if it's kept in darkness for its first fourteen days. The strong tendency of the mallard duckling to follow a moving object—which in nature, of course, is usually the mother— never appears if the bird sees no object within its first forty hours.

"As Lorenz's work on 'imprinting' showed, a young gosling will follow the first moving object it sees during the sensitive phase. But soon it reaches a point where it doesn't follow anything else: and the moving object can be something ridiculous, a human being or even a moving dog-kennel!" Thus, in lower species, natural capacities and patterns could be turned awry by the environment. Bowlby, seeing the human infant's attachment through his "new spectacles," had already begun to conceive of it as a natural and biologically rooted behavioral sequence. "Looked at this way, one could understand why disturbing the sequence might have such enormous implications for future development."

Bowlby's belief that ethology might provide a solid base for psychoanalytic theorizing was at first, he acknowledges, "a simple act of faith." Nevertheless, the two fields seemed complementary to one another. Where the study of instinct was concerned, they seemed actually to overlap. Psychoanalysts had written a good deal about instinct: "They looked at it as something mystical, something that couldn't be studied. Ethologists, on the other hand, *were* studying it experimentally, and were framing some highly explanatory concepts.

"For instance, the difference between function and causation. That is, distinguishing the long-range survival value of a certain kind of behavior from what makes the behavior actually commence. An example would be eating: the function of eating is nourishment; what generally makes an animal start eating is a drop in the level of the blood sugar which signals to the brain that he's hungry."

It was in their studies of what made certain forms of behavior commence that the ethologists made an important discovery: Some instinctual behavior patterns are activated by "signs" or simple stimuli in the environment. "For the young herring gull such a sign would be the sight of a red spot—he gapes for food when he sees it, because it resembles the red spot on the beak of the adult gull. The male robin reacts to the sight of red feathers in his territory; he shows the attack response, since they look like those on the breast of a rival male."

In dozens of species, Bowlby explains, behavior initiating courtship, mating, feeding of young is triggered off by simple environmental stimuli such as the color of a beak, the spread of a tail, or a song or a call. Since these "signs" bring about social interaction, they are called "social releasers."

It is Bowlby's belief that the human infant's smile is a social releaser, that is, an instinctual response to a stimulus (the human face) to which our species is innately sensitive. "Babies' smiles are powerful things; they have an effect on the mother which makes her more attentive, which enchants and enslaves her. They evoke instinctual responses in her."

But does the six-week-old infant, smiling up at his mother, perceive her as another human being, or is he simply responding to a "sign pattern" in the environment? According to Bowlby, there have been numerous studies of smiling in young infants. One of them, carried out in 1946, demonstrated that when babies were presented with different masks they smiled at those which had the visual configuration of the human face. The babies would not smile at a mask—or at a human face—in profile.

"In the human infant sucking and crying are the earliest manifested behavioral responses", says Bowlby, adding that in his opinion sucking and orality are given far too important a role in psychoanalytic theorizing. "In some species of our nearest relations, the primates, clinging appears before sucking. A newborn chimpanzee climbs up, or is placed by his mother, on her stomach. Once there he clings for hours; it's only after some time that he finds the nipple and begins to suck. Interestingly enough, the human baby, who is far less mature at birth, does retain vestiges of a powerful gripping response. If you place a stick in the newborn baby's grasp, he can hang on and support his own weight.

"Clinging, sucking, following when able; these are all part of the baby's instinctual repertoire. Of course the responses mature and develop at different times; the point is they have what you might call a set goal: to keep the mother close by, to bind her to the child. Crying and smiling cause her to respond—it's not exactly chance that what makes a baby smile most is the sight of a human face."

In the course of the first year, says Bowlby, the infant's instinctual responses become integrated and focused on the mother. The baby then displays the full range of "attachment behavior": behavior directed toward keeping the mother in close proximity. "He protests when she goes away, greets her when she returns, follows her whenever able, clings when frightened. Much of his behavior resembles that of his monkey and ape cousins; studies of infant primates in the wild show that they too stay close to their mothers and rush to her side at the least sign of alarm.

"The intense need to keep the mother nearby is based on a biologically rooted behavioral pattern. It's my belief," says Bowlby, "that proximity is in itself a satisfying thing; it's an end result, ensuring safety, especially from the danger of predators. . . . That's an odd new idea in psychoanalysis and psychology." He smiles. "In ethology it's old hat."

On the two days a week that Bowlby works at home he sits in a large, book-lined, sunny room. Even dressed in a baggy blue sweater and shapeless trousers, he looks very much the British gentleman. Bowlby is the fourth child of an English baronet; his father was president of the Royal College of Surgeons. Ursula Bowlby, born Longworth, is an explorer's daughter; she studied modern languages at the University of Edinburgh before her marriage. She has somewhat the shy manner of an English schoolgirl.

The large, rambling Bowlby house borders on Hampstead Heath. They don't know how many rooms there are: "I've never counted them," says Mrs. Bowlby. "We rent out part of the house as a flat. Then our daughter lives on the third floor with her husband and son. She's married to a Spanish national; we call them the Spaniards."

In the house next door, on land that was formerly a tennis court, their son Richard lives with his wife and two children. "She's part Russian," says Ursula Bowlby, with her quietly impish smile. "We call them the Russians." The Bowlbys' oldest daughter Mary is on her way back from Germany with her family; their youngest son Robert is working in a mission in Tanzania.

Bowlby has two older sisters, both unmarried; his brother, thirteen months his senior, is an industrialist who bears the family title. He has a younger brother and a younger sister. "Mine was a very stable background," says Bowlby definitively.

Reactions to him and to his work have been diverse. "Some people think he's arrogant," remarked a London psychiatrist recently. "But if he is, he's got a right to be. He's head and shoulders over any other British psychoanalyst."

A child analyst, Dr. Susanna Isaacs, is less convinced. "An infant can't follow its mother; it isn't a duckling. The human baby is very helpless for a prolonged period of time. And during this period it forms an internal image of the mother; this would be a mixture of memory, of fantasies, of the baby's response to the actual reality of the mother."

Dr. Isaacs, who is director of the child psychiatric services at St. Mary's Hospital in London, is a tall lean woman with white-streaked hair, steel-rimmed glasses and a breezy, straightforward manner. "Babies," she says, "are very capable of perpetuating a distorted view of the mother, of introjecting a 'bad mother' where none exists. It's their helplessness; helplessness and fantasy go together. And even the most perfect mother will frustrate the baby once in awhile, keep him waiting. This makes the baby angry, and the emotions of infants are terribly intense—it's so difficult for them to assess what's happening to them."

Some babies, Dr. Isaacs maintains, have an inborn capacity to make a better adjustment, to tolerate knowledge of themselves in relation to other people. "Some can introject a good internal picture when they haven't had a mother at all—just different people looking after them.

I'm not suggesting that it isn't best for the mother herself to look after the infant; just that there's a quality of adoration that's an important part of being a baby. If your mother doesn't adore you or positively dislikes you, you might be better off with a substitute.

"Speaking of early infancy, I'd place real emphasis on what picture the infant is internalizing. For instance, you can look at a family background and wonder how anyone could emerge normal. One would have to suppose an infancy where the child had managed to introject a good-enough image of the mother."

The trouble with Bowlby's approach, she feels, is that it ignores a whole range of intrapsychic processes. In reviewing his book *Attachment* for the British *Journal of Psychiatric Social Work*, she complained: "If one looks up love or anger in the index one will not find them there, nor fantasy or feeling or thought. Leopard, Lion, Loss are there."

Dr. Isaacs explains, "Science is measurement, and there are some things you can't measure. He's very rigorous, very careful in his use of language. But he undervalues feeling and emotion; he overvalues the similarities between humans and other animals, the ethological aspects. I think this is much more limited than the psychoanalytical approach; it doesn't explain the *differences* . . . Who's denying that we're animals? Of course we are."

But Dr. Kenneth Soddy, a well-known child psychiatrist, is enthusiastic about Bowlby's work. "I'm predilected in his favor," he says. "I'm a sitting duck for the sorts of things he does. I think that psychoanalysts have looked deep within themselves but haven't stopped to look into biology. I mean, the physical question is there: What can the baby, from a neuropsychological point of view, actually do? What can he perceive, and at what point is he able to connect his perceptions with the mother? When you assume aggression and fantasy directed at her from these early ages, you're assuming a lot of sophistication in the infant.

"It seems far more likely," says Soddy, "that these inborn attachment reflexes, which Bowlby suggests, do exist. That the baby is 'programed' in certain ways that have the effect of opening and maintaining communication with the mother. From a developmental point of view, this is much closer to what one would imagine the infant is actually capable of doing."

Bowlby is not clear as to what the research and clinical applications of the ethological approach will be. "In science it's always legitimate for theory to outrun data." But the picture of attachment behavior which he has sketched is, he says, helpful in clarifying certain situations which are recognizably harmful. "Aside from the starkest one, separation, there is the one which involves a mother's threatening to send a young child away as a punishment. Another is the disturbed parent who threatens suicide; this creates intolerable anxiety in a child. Even the mother who complains that her child makes her sick when he misbehaves . . . " Bowlby shakes his head, shrugs.

He hopes that it will be possible to link psychoanalytical phenomena with the rest of biology in much the way that physics and chemistry have been linked. "What we've got to do is to take some methods and concepts that are useful in ethology and apply them to the study of human behavior." These methods would include many more closely detailed observations of infants and young children in a variety of situations, studies of infant-mother relationships among primitive peoples, comparisons of instinctual behavioral sequences in our own and in allied or lower species. "The point is, to order the material you've got to have a theory; you can't do a damn thing without a theory."

Bowlby's attachment theory is a new view of the developmental process. It argues that the genetic makeup of a human child is such that it requires a special type of parental care. The idea, seen in the context of adaptiveness and the ancient need for protection, seems to be that we all drag along with us traits that stemmed from precultural times. Now, both psychoanalysts with an ethological bent and the growing number of young ethologists interested in the study of human behavior are, as Bowlby says, "starting to have a crack at it.

"The early years are the stock in trade of psychoanalysis," he adds. "And if they are important, we'd better get our heads clear about what happens during them."

Part 2

Alfred Adler

His Ideas Are Everywhere

D
o you think," Alfred Adler once demanded of Freud, "that it is such a great pleasure for me to stand in your shadow for the whole of my life?" If Adler were alive today, he might well reiterate the question: it is chiefly as one of the great early Freudians that he is remembered. And yet he always insisted that he was not a disciple; he had never been psychoanalyzed by Freud nor attended his lectures. Indeed, Adler became so radically opposed to the basic tenets of Freudian theory that the two men severed all connections in 1911 and remained bitter enemies for the rest of their lives.

Adler's school was the first major deviation from the psychoanalytical movement. The name he gave it—"Individual Psychology"—was meant to imply that man's mind is not, as Freud had suggested, locked in a struggle between conscious and unconscious forces, but that each individual represents a unified and self-consistent whole, striving toward a goal which floats before him. No man, Adler believed, could be understood without reference to his (usually unconscious) goal, much as a drama could be understood only in the light of its finale. The goal a person shaped for himself, and the characteristic ways he struggled to reach it were what Adler termed his "style of life."

February 1971 marked the close of Alfred Adler's centennial year, and the flurry of celebratory articles and tributes not only reawakened interest in him but also evoked a certain astonished recognition. For Adler's fate has been paradoxical: while his personal fame has declined, his ideas are everywhere. His early book on organ inferiorities, with its insistence on the unity of body and mind, was a precursor of psychosomatic medicine; many of his concepts, such as the inferiority complex, compensation, overcompensation and the significance of the child's birth order in the family, are now crucial to the thinking of most psychotherapists. Individual Psychology, with its stress upon the creative power of the individual—who is seen as the "novelist" of his own character—anticipated today's self-realization personality theorists; the late Abraham Maslow remarked, "For me Alfred Adler becomes more correct year by year." Similarly, the movement of existential psychiatry toward viewing a person as the sum of his choices, or what Sartre calls his "projections" (projected goals), is much the same as seeing him in terms of his "style of life." And, as Freud predicted they might, Adler's ideas have had great impact upon psychoanalysis.

Adler believed that neurosis sprang from the individual's attempts to adapt to the environment—which in human terms is always the social environment. Freud, who thought neurosis was caused by warring demands within the personality itself, denounced Adler's approach as oversimplified: " . . . it concerns surface phenomena, that is, ego psychology." The subsequent movement of psychoanalytic theory has, however, been toward an emphasis on the needs of the ego. Indeed, the very phrase "ego psychology," which Freud used so scathingly, has lost its unpleasant connotations and become the dominant trend in modern psychoanalysis.

Nevertheless, Adler himself has received curiously little credit. As Henri Ellenberger points out in his massive history of dynamic psychiatry, *The Discovery of the Unconscious*: "It would not be easy to find another author from whom so much has been borrowed from all sides without acknowledgment as Alfred Adler. His teaching has become, to use a French idiom, an 'open quarry' . . . that is, a place where anyone may come and draw anything without compunction."

Adler was born in the Viennese suburb of Penzing on February 7, 1870. Like Freud, he was the son of a middle-class Jewish merchant; but, while Freud was raised in the ghettolike section called Leopoldstadt and remained forever conscious of his membership in a minority group, Adler took his background lightly. There were few other Jewish children in the area where he grew up, and his accent and general outlook remained more Viennese than Jewish. Nowhere in his writings was he ever to refer to anti-Semitism; Freud did so frequently.

There were other differences between these two men of similar class and stock: Freud was the darling eldest son of an adoring young mother; Alfred was his mother's second son—and she was rather cold in personality, and seems to have preferred her eldest. Adler's childhood was unhappy, embittered by jealousy of his older brother, despite the fact that four younger children were born to the family. "One of my earliest recollections," he once reminisced, "is of sitting on a bench, bandaged up on account of rickets, with my healthy brother sitting opposite me. He could run, jump and move about quite effortlessly, while for me movement of any sort was a strain and an effort. . . . "

Adler placed this early memory of disadvantage at somewhere around age two. As he grew older, his health improved, but not his ease in the family: "I did not enjoy staying at home." Whenever at all possible, he ran to play on the large grassy lot next to his house, where the local children gathered every day. Here the young Alfred, short, stocky and not particularly good-looking, was a popular figure: lively, and always in good spirits, he gained among his companions the sense of equality and self-esteem which he had not found at home. The hours spent playing on this field were one day to flower into Adler's notions of human interrelatedness, that vision of a shared community of feelings and values which he called *Gemeinschaftsgefühl*, social interest.

During the period of Adler's growth into manhood, Vienna was a rich, enlightened city, at the height of her Habsburg power. When, at eighteen, Alfred entered the University of Vienna, it was one of the great European medical centers—and around it surged the life of the theater, of music and of the yeasty Socialist opinion which earned the city her nickname, Red Vienna. During his student years, Adler took part in it all; at one of the Socialist meetings he regularly attended he met the girl he was to marry. In 1895 he graduated, and began practice as an ophthalmologist in a run-down section of the city. He then shifted to general medicine, then to neurology; and by the time he became associated with Freud, had already found his career in psychiatry.

It was in the fall of 1902 that Freud sent Adler a postcard asking him to join a small group that was to meet Wednesdays "to discuss problems of neurosis." No one is now sure what prompted this invitation: the two men had never met. One legend has it that a nasty review of Freud's *The Interpretation of Dreams* appeared in Vienna's powerful daily *Neue Freie Presse*, and that Adler sent in a letter defending the book. But recent researches have turned up the fact that Freud's work (which sold barely 100 copies when it was published) was never even reviewed in that newspaper. Whatever event did lead him to seek out Adler remains mysterious.

At any rate, Freud's card initiated a nine-year working relationship which, though never intimate, was at first fruitful, then painful, and ultimately impossible. It was during Adler's time within the Freudian circle that his first major work appeared: a slim book about the effects of "organ inferiorities"—that is, congenitally weak or poorly functioning organs—on personality development.

There was, of course, nothing novel in the idea that the organism tries to repair its own weaknesses: clinicians had long been aware that where one kidney, for example, functioned poorly the other would become overdeveloped and attempt to do the work of two. But Adler's suggestion was that this process of compensation could also proceed in the psychological sphere; in that case the individual experienced powerful *mental* urges toward repairing his weakness, and concentrated his entire attention on the weak organ. If, for instance, the person had weak eyesight, he would lavish intensive care upon the whole process of seeing. The result, claimed Adler, was that often by psychological means an overcompensation was brought about; the function of the organ became not just adequate but superior. Where the adaptive struggle was successful, it could lead to striking accomplishments: Beethoven, who suffered from congenital ear disease; numerous sculptors and painters with defective eyesight; Demosthenes, a childhood stutterer who became one of the greatest orators. On the other hand, where nature failed to produce a correction, pathological processes might be set in motion: "Inability, neurosis, psychological disease . . . may appear in this event." The discouraged individual might withdraw from the demands of life to seek the greater security of isolation.

Freud approved of the *Study of Organ Inferiority and its Psychical Compensation*. It was a maverick work to be sure, but though independent of psychoanalytic theory in its approach, it could stand beside it quite comfortably. The following year, however, Adler advanced a theory which Freud found outrageous: he suggested that there was in man an innate instinctive aggressivity which spurred him onward. "Fighting, wrestling, beating, biting and cruelties show the aggression drive in its pure form," wrote Adler. "Its refinement and specialization lead to sports, competition, dueling, thirst for dominance, and religious, social, national and race struggles. . . . When the aggression drive turns [back] upon the subject, we find traits of humility, submission and devotion, flagellantism and masochism . . . the extreme is suicide."

Adler suggested that people with strong aggressive instincts were attracted to certain professions. These included—aside from the obvious examples of the revolutionary hero and the criminal—those of the judge, policeman, teacher, minister and physician. "Charity, sympathy, altruism and sensitive interest in misery represent new satisfactions on which the drive, which originally tended toward cruelty, feeds. If this seems strange, it is nevertheless easy to recognize that a real understanding for suffering and pain can only come from an original interest in the world of torment."

Freud indignantly denied that there was such a thing as a special aggressive instinct which stood alongside "the familiar instincts of self-preservation and sex, and on an equal footing with them." Like all great innovators, he took a defiantly protective attitude toward his newborn system; the idea that behavior might be motivated by aggressive as well as libidinal forces threatened the very integrity of his model. Nevertheless some fourteen years later, Freud reversed himself on this issue. He conceded that he was now "obliged to assert the existence of an aggressive instinct, but it is different from Adler's. I prefer to call it the 'destructive' or 'death instinct.' "

In formulating the death instinct, Freud borrowed from biology the notion that there is in all living things a tendency to revert to the inorganic state—that is, to die. He suggested that there was in human nature a trend or drive toward return to the inanimate, the so-called "death wish." Thus, a person's aggressive, destructive strivings (which existed alongside his life-enhancing libidinal strivings) represented his instinctual desire to reach a state of nonfeeling, the absolute zero of death. Curiously enough, Adler, too, reversed his position: he later came to believe that man had no instinctual tendencies toward aggression at all. "I enriched psychoanalysis by the aggressive drive," he once remarked. "I gladly make them a present of it."

By 1910, Adler and Freud had been associated for some eight years. During that busy period the new discipline which Freud called "psychoanalysis," although still the joke of Vienna, began achieving some international recognition. His "small group" had grown from five members to thirty-five; it was now the Vienna Psycho-Analytical Society and far too large to continue meeting in the waiting room of his office. That year, Adler was president of the society, coeditor of the

Zentralblatt für Psychoanalyse—and an increasingly noisy critic of Freudian psychoanalysis.

"I am having an atrocious time with Adler . . .," Freud complained in a letter written that fall. "I have been hoping that it would come to a clean separation, but it drags on and despite my opinion that nothing is to be done."

Adler had never subscribed to Freud's belief that it was sexual material, repressed into the unconscious during early childhood, that lay at the core of neurosis. According to Freud, sexual libido was the great dynamic force in psychic life: now Adler made the shocking move of suggesting an entirely different motive force, which he called the "masculine protest." This was—in a society which valued masculinity and devalued the feminine—the child's striving to become big, to take power, to dominate others; in short, "to be a real man." The masculine protest, which could be present in both men and women, was a strategy adopted in early childhood as a means of compensating for subjective feelings of weakness and disadvantage. The child who failed to adapt to his environment thus became the neurotic who sought to dominate it. Seen from this vantage, the neurotic symptom represented not an unresolvable sexual dilemma but a misguided attempt at compensating for feelings of inferiority.

Such views could not be tolerated within the Freudian orbit. In January of 1911, Adler was asked to present before the society a comprehensive report on his own evolving theories. A storm of protests followed. For Adler described sexuality as merely an expression of personality, not its fundamental motivator; while sexual maladjustment was often present in neurosis, he insisted that it was not its cause. The important biological fact, in Adler's terms, was not the child's instinctive sexual behavior but his smallness and helplessness in relation to the "giants" surrounding him. In his early adaptive attempts the child might settle upon faulty methods of gaining significance and self-esteem; he might see "success" in terms of wielding power over others. Adler pointed to the curious "social returns" of neurosis—the ability to screen oneself from the demands of life, and to dominate others by exploiting one's own symptoms and weaknesses. The neurotic's tyranny over his close circle was a theme to which Adler returned continually: "I have taken forty years to make my psychology simple," he often remarked later in his life. "I might have made it more simple by saying, 'All neurosis is vanity'—but this might not be understood."

Adler's January talks, his postulation of the masculine protest, following on the heels of the aggression drive, all led to his final explosive break with Freud early in 1911. That same year, Hans Vaihinger's celebrated book, *The Philosophy of "As If,"* appeared; it had a profound effect upon Adler. The theme of Vaihinger's book was that man, in order to avoid drowning in a sea of facts, creates systems or ways of looking at things which he then assumes are "true." The fixing of the zero point would be an example; we determine the zero on a Fahrenheit scale and then behave "as if" it actually existed. We draw meridionals and parallels on the face of the globe, and then proceed "as if" these lines had a counterpart in reality. While they do not, said Vaihinger, they are useful fictions—our lives, to say nothing of our sanity, often depend upon our behaving *as if* our fictions were true.

Adler found in Vaihinger's theories a conceptual framework for his own ideas. In his most important book, *The Neurotic Constitution,* Adler suggested that all human behavior, thought and feeling proceeds along the lines of "as if." In other words, in earliest childhood each person—as part of his striving to adapt to the environment and overcome his weaknesses—creates for himself an idealized goal of perfect adaptation, and then struggles toward it *as if* this goal alone represented success, security and happiness. "The human mind," wrote Adler, "shows an urge to capture into fixed forms . . . that is, fictions, that which is chaotic, always in flux and incomprehensible. Serving this urge, the child quite generally uses a schema in order to act and find his way . . . " In developing the schema, the child projects before him his goal, his unique vision of that thing which would overcome all obstacles and bring him perfect security. With the ideal in front, a line of direction is established: from then on, everything the individual chooses to see, and the ways he feels about those things, falls into place accordingly. Adler believed that the child's schema was fixed by the age of four or five (i.e., that his personality was more or less programed); this was the prototype which became the individual's "style of life."

According to Adler, the key to a man's behavior is that hidden purpose toward which all his strivings are directed: "Causes, powers . . . and the like cannot serve as explanatory principles. The final goal alone can. Experiences, traumata, sexual development mechanisms cannot yield an explanation; but the perspective in which these are regarded, the individual way of seeing them . . . can do so." In explaining this, he remarked: "It has the same effect on me whether a poisonous snake is actually approaching my foot or whether I merely believe that it is a poisonous snake." Similarly, if a man believed that his mother had been a monster and blamed all his later failures on that fact, it mattered little whether she was objectively monstrous or not—the effect was the same, for in that individual's schema, she *was*.

Adler's central idea was that life is always essentially a movement toward better adaptation to the environment, and that in man—the first animal in nature with the ability to form goals and purposes—adaptation assumes a psychological aspect. That is, by struggling forward to achieve our imaginary goals, we lift ourselves, as Adler said, "by our own bootstraps." He believed the great force motivating all human acts to be "a striving from a felt minus toward a felt plus situation, from a feeling of inferiority toward superiority, perfection, totality."

Neurosis was, in Adler's view, a species of maladaptation. The great issue in neurotic illness, he maintained, was not what had happened in the past to cause it, but where it was heading—what particular goal the patient was achieving with his symptoms. "The most important question of the healthy and diseased mental life is not 'Whence?' but 'Whither?'" he declared. "In this 'Whither?' the cause is contained."

The Neurotic Constitution was published in 1912. "With this book," wrote Adler to a friend, "I have founded the school of Individual Psychology." He submitted the book to the Vienna Medical School as a thesis, and applied for a position as lecturer.

He had to wait three years for a reply; and when it arrived, it came as an affront which rankled for the rest of his life. His candidature had been refused unanimously. (Recently, the report on Adler's work which was submitted to the medical faculty has come to light. Its author complains that, while Adler's ideas are often "ingenious," they are far too speculative, and are even occasionally as "grotesque as those of Freud.")

Meanwhile, World War I had broken out, and there were other worries. Adler's wife, Raissa, had gone with their four children to visit her family's home in Russia. When the assassination at Sarajevo took place, Adler telegraphed her to return immediately. "Shall wait," replied Raissa tartly—and then was caught there by the war for the better part of a year.

The Adler marriage does not seem to have been happy (the children all vastly preferred their ebullient, outgoing father to their sternly political mother). Raissa Adler was a radical and a feminist when she married, and Alfred's subsequent lack of interest in Socialist politics deeply disappointed her. Adler was, however, a sympathetic supporter of the feminist cause. Unlike Freud, who considered woman's inferior social role to stem from her innate physical and psychological inferiority, Adler felt that women were depreciated by a male-oriented culture. He believed that only resentment and resistance could result from their being forced to subordinate themselves to their husbands—or to man in society—and predicted that women would one day rebel. Still, as one of Adler's biographers noted drily:" . . . fighting for the emancipation of women and living with an emancipated woman are two wholly different things."

At the close of World War I, Adler was forty-eight years old. He had served for several years as a physician and psychiatrist with the Austrian Army. The peace, and the fragmentation of the Austro-Hungarian Empire, brought a period of utmost suffering to Vienna. Food supplies were low, and there was virtually no fuel in the city. Nevertheless, in the midst of this general deprivation, the new Social Democratic Government asked Adler to organize a program of psychological counseling for problem children. It was in these unpromising circumstances that the famous Vienna child-guidance clinics were launched.

Adler's clinics were a pioneer effort in the direction of what is now called community psychiatry. All were attached to the public school system; any child who behaved in a disturbed way in the classroom could be brought to the nearest guidance center for help and treatment. Although they were successful from the very start and grew rapidly in number, the clinics came in for a certain amount of criticism—especially from the psychoanalysts.

The Freudians were particularly scornful of the public therapy sessions which Adler, as part of his program, held every fortnight. To these sessions he invited audiences of schoolteachers, for he wanted to "teach the teachers"—one of his favorite phrases—concepts of mental hygiene.

Each session began with the teacher of the particular "problem child" reading out his notes on the pupil. Adler then discussed these case notes with both teacher and audience, after which the child was invited to come in. This was always a moment of high drama: Adler had a way of predicting, merely from hearing the notes and without having set eyes on the child, what his physical habits and appearance would be—even down to the most startling details. Thus, the child's entrance enchanted the audience, like the conclusion of a successful conjuring trick.

Adler warned the teachers to notice particularly the child's physical behavior as he entered: whether he went to lean against something or stood alone, if he held out his hand or shrank back, whether he met the therapist's eye or scowled and hung his head. For these were what Adler called "organ jargon," modes of communicating without the use of words.

Adler himself, a short, sturdy man with a black mustache and piercing eyes, always shook hands warmly with the patient and treated him as a contemporary and an equal. His first question usually aimed straight for the core of the problem: "Do you help your mother very much?" he might ask a child whose problems centered around his being spoiled, self-centered and anxiously demanding. The opening remark was generally followed by a long, absolutely silent pause, which Adler never interrupted; a friend once described him as a "past master in the art of the pause."

Adler's second daughter, Alexandra, now a well-known New York psychiatrist, recalls these clinic sessions well. "Children really loved my father and wanted to talk to him because he was absolutely nonaggressive. Once, when I was helping out at a demonstration, a child refused to speak or even look at him. To establish rapport, my father softly asked him, 'What do you think, how old am I?' The child turned to my father right away and answered."

Adler's method of therapy was essentially a gentle manipulation of both the patient and his environment. First, he would engage the child in a friendly, encouraging conversation. Its aim was to guide the child subtly toward understanding the real goal of his behavior and toward discovering how that goal determined his painful attitudes and thoughts. As the English novelist Phyllis Bottome, Adler's patient and biographer, has written: " . . . every child reacted differently to the treatment, [but] I never once saw a child either distressed or bored by it. The invariable effect . . . seemed to be relief and interest."

After his initial talk with the child, Adler generally asked the parents, and sometimes other family members, into the lecture hall to join the discussion; the patient's teacher and members of the audience would also participate. Together, the group consulted on ways both child and family might "try something a little different" to see what effect alternative approaches might have on everyone concerned. Adler's methods, pragmatic and eminently workable, won him the affection and respect of the city's schoolteachers; to this day, his reputation remains highest among professionals "on the firing line," such as teachers, counselors and social workers.

Viewed with hindsight, the Vienna clinics stand out as a remarkable early attempt to treat the individual within a group setting, and as a functioning part of his social milieu. The notions that not only the doctor but lay people could aid in the healing process, and that the patient must be seen in the context of his family group are, of course, both current in today's milieu therapy and in the entire therapeutic community approach.

Adler was the only member of depth psychology's "first triumvirate" (Freud, Adler, Jung) to spend considerable time in the United States. He first visited here in 1926, and after that, sojourned for longer and longer periods of teaching, lecturing and practice; soon he was spending only his summers in Vienna. With the rise of Hitler, he foresaw a coming catastrophe and believed that if his psychology were to survive anywhere it would be in America. There were now Individual Psychology groups all over the world, including Germany. (Adler, when invited to speak to the Berlin society and offered protection during his stay, asked the messenger to "tell them I laughed.") In 1934, the Fascist government in Austria suppressed the child-guidance clinics. Shortly afterward, Adler managed to sell his family's home and left Vienna for good.

He had already accepted the chair of medical psychology at Long Island College of Medicine and was becoming a widely known popular lecturer. "Once," recalls his daughter Alexandra, "I arrived with him at a building where he was to give a talk, but the place was so crowded that they wouldn't admit us. My father tried to tell them he was the lecturer, but the ushers said others had already tried *that* silly trick on them. It took quite a bit of talking until we were finally allowed to go in."

Adler always spoke without written notes; he felt that in this way he reached his listeners more directly. He had a style that was at once informal, serious and personal, and he had the born lecturer's knack for dealing easily with the unexpected. Once, at the meeting of a medical society in England, the chairman introduced him with some remarks that were so hostile that the audience sat staring in amazement. Adler, saying nothing, rose to his feet with a benevolent smile. Before starting his talk he walked over and patted the chairman gently on the shoulder. The entire group burst into applause.

Adler's teaching and thought were moving increasingly in a direction that had far-ranging appeal: they were becoming a curious blend of psychology, sociology and ethics. His ever-growing emphasis on *Gemeinschaftsgefühl*, social feeling, gave to Individual Psychology a quasi-religious air; his critics said sourly that Adler was no longer teaching but preaching. Fellow professionals looked askance at his habit of becoming friendly with his patients (something Freud carefully avoided) and then expecting them to become missionaries of his psychology. His carelessly organized writings were simply dismissed by many as mere "surface psychology"—a psychology, as one detractor remarked, for traveling salesmen.

Adler's new emphasis on social feeling was only half understood by many and often considered a mere mouthing of platitudes about "adjustment." He had, in fact, become convinced that each individual must be seen as part of his larger social whole—that life is first and foremost social life. "No psychologist," he insisted, "is able to determine the meaning of any experience if he fails to consider it in its . . . relation to society."

In Adler's view, true contact with others counteracted a person's tendency to form the kind of irrational fictitious goal which would lead to his isolation and estrangement. The neurotic, in his fruitless striving for self-esteem, mistakenly exploited those around him. The therapist's role, maintained Adler, was to perform what is rightly the function of the mother: to give the patient experience of a loving contact with another person, and then help him to transfer this awakened social feeling to others. The prime effort was to bring the patient's private goal into agreement with general human interests—for when a man operated on "private logic" he became ill and useless. "All failures in life— neurotics, psychotics, criminals, drunkards, problem children, suicides, perverts and prostitutes—are failures because they are lacking in social interest. They approach the problems of occupation, friendship and sex without the confidence that they can be solved by cooperation. The meaning they give to life is a private meaning . . . their interest stops short at their own person."

Adler's system of psychotherapy stressed—as Individual Psychological treatment continues to do—the importance of early recollections. Adler believed the memory was biased and that an individual retained only that which was central to his main problems and preoccupations. He also worked with the patient's dream material—but an Adlerian dream interpretation was far different from a Freudian one. For instance, in a dream of flying up and then suddenly falling a psychoanalyst would probably see sexual symbolism related to impotence; an Adlerian would view the same dream as related to a fear of failure in any one of a variety of daily activities, such as work, social relations or, indeed, sexuality. Adler saw no universal sexual symbolism in the dream: he thought each dream a unique creation which had to be interpreted in the light of the patient's line of movement, and often as a signpost pointing the direction he unconsciously was preparing to take.

As Dr. Kurt Adler, Adler's son and a leader in the current Individual Psychological movement, explains: "Our methods of therapy revolve around, first, helping the patient to understand his mistaken life style and the real nature of his goal by slowly elaborating upon these topics and gently elevating them into conscious knowledge. Then, in helping him to use this insight in his everyday life; we do this by discussing with him his successes and failures. But the crucial part of the process is his learning to relate to the therapist, and subsequently becoming able to extend that feeling outwards, to increase his feeling of belonging, of his humanity . . . so that he's able to begin to cooperate.

"What I'm speaking of is essentially a process of socialization that the patient goes through during therapy. It's something he has failed to learn sufficiently during his development; he's held on so anxiously to his self-protective devices. What the patient must learn is to give, to share, and eventually—a point my father considered vital—he must come to see that his self-interest is really best served if his behavior benefits others as well as himself."

In 1937 Adler, whose personal appearances were in growing demand, embarked on a heavy speaking tour in Europe. Just as he was leaving he learned that the eldest of his four children, Valentina, who had fled the

Nazis and gone to Russia with her husband, had been arrested by the Russian authorities.* He began making frantic attempts to get news of her and to send a message. In Holland, he suffered a minor heart attack. He continued on to England, and then to Scotland. On the fourth day of his tour he collapsed on a sidewalk and died on the way to the hospital.

Shortly after the funeral, which took place in Edinburgh, Freud received a letter from the German writer Arnold Zweig. Zweig mentioned how moved and saddened he had been by the news of Adler's sudden death. But the enmity of almost thirty years persisted, and Freud replied coldly: "I don't understand your sympathy for Adler. For a Jewish boy out of a Viennese suburb a death in Aberdeen is an unheard-of career in itself and a proof of how far he had got on. The world really rewarded him richly for his service in having contradicted psychoanalysis."

Epilogue

Adler's reputation sagged after his death. A number of Adlerian clinics closed down, *The International Journal of Individual Psychology* was discontinued, as were the activities of most of his European followers. Dr. Rudolf Dreikurs, now a prominent Chicago psychiatrist, recalls how in the late nineteen-thirties he was warned against revealing his identity as an Adlerian "for fear of professional discrimination."

Nevertheless, in the years just after the war, Individual Psychology began a steady return to life: New societies were formed; tired old groups experienced a spurt in growth; new periodicals were started and training centers established. Now, according to Dreikurs, the movement is growing at an astonishing rate, especially in the United States. "To gauge its influence is utterly impossible," he says. ". . . Any statement made at one moment is outdated in the next."

There are now Individual Psychological associations all over the world, including places as unlikely as Crete and Cyprus. In New York City, the Alfred Adler Mental Hygiene Clinic is directed by a daughter, Dr. Alexandra Adler, with the assistance of Dr. Kurt Adler, a son. There are some 250 Adlerian psychiatrists in the city, including the well-known Dr. Danica Deutsch and Drs. Ernst and Helene Papanek.

1971

---

*Eventually, the family learned, through the intercession of their friend Albert Einstein, that Valentina had died in a Soviet concentration camp sometime during the war.

Models of Sanity and Madness

What Do We Mean by the Word "Normal"?

During his 1969 trial for having led the Mylai massacre of more than three hundred helpless and unarmed civilians the lawyers defending Lieutenant William L. Calley raised the question of his "mental state" at the time of the assault. While they never asserted that Calley had been totally insane when he ordered the slaughter of the town's inhabitants—mostly old men, women and children—they suggested that his mental responsibility had been impaired; he had been overwhelmed, psychologically, by the fears and stresses of a combat sweep through a hamlet that he had been told was a Vietcong stronghold. One psychiatric expert, testifying on Calley's behalf, contended that the young serviceman had "behaved like a robot" when carrying out orders supposedly received from his company commander and "father image," Captain Ernest Medina; Calley's behavior had, the doctor suggested, been determined by powerful unconscious motives. A sanity board was convened to study the question; and for four weeks, Calley underwent extensive psychiatric testing. A panel of psychiatrists found him to be "normal in every respect."

A number of people interested in the case, and mystified by Calley's deeds, insisted that the man who committed them must, somehow, be sick. Could a person capable of lining up women, children and old men, and then systematically annihilating them, be considered to be normal in every respect? Was it the wartime context that rendered Calley's acts rational? What do we mean by the word *normal*? And on what grounds do we decide whether or not a person must bear full responsibility for his deeds; that is, whether or not he is sane?

In criminal procedure the legal test for sanity—at least in the majority of United States jurisdictions—is the much reviled, much criticized, and yet amazingly persistent M'Naghten rule. According to this rule a man is, quite simply, to be considered sane unless it can be proven that at the time he committed a criminal act " . . . he was laboring under such a

137

defect of reason, from disease of the mind, as not to know the nature and
quality of the act he was doing; or if he did know it, that the act was
wrong."

The "right-wrong" test, with its emphasis on rational awareness, arose
from a case which created a furor in England in the eighteen-forties.
Daniel M'Naghten had shot to death the secretary of Sir Robert Peel, in
the mistaken belief that he was killing the Prime Minister himself.
Suffering from paranoid delusions, M'Naghten believed that Peel was
pursuing him because he had voted against the Prime Minister in the last
election; and also that Peel had devised the Corn Laws with the express
purpose of ruining M'Naghten financially. It was the verdict in the
M'Naghten case—"Not guilty on account of insanity"—which outraged
both the public and Queen Victoria. In an angry note to Peel the Queen
demanded: "What did the jury mean by saying he was *not guilty*! I will
never believe that anyone could be not guilty who wanted to *murder* a
conservative Prime Minister!"

And she insisted that everyone was morally convinced that the
assassin had been perfectly conscious and aware of what he was doing.
The House of Lords then retired to consider the grounds for legal
madness: the new rule which resulted conferred a strange immortality
on the name of M'Naghten. (He, despite his acquittal, spent the
remaining twenty-two years of his life in an institution for the criminally
insane.)

The M'Naghten test, with its clear-cut standard ("Is the defendant
suffering from a mental disease so severe that he cannot distinguish right
from wrong?") has proven an exceedingly blunt tool in the difficult task
of trying to separate the "bad" from the "sick." Psychiatrists complain
that when they are asked to testify about whether a defendant knows
right from wrong they are being asked for an ethical, not a medical
judgment; there is no diagnostic category called "inability to know right
from wrong." The covert question being posed by M'Naghten, they
insist, is: "Should this man be considered responsible for his acts?"—and
that is, manifestly, a legal question. A psychiatrist who says flatly that a
particular offender is capable of distinguishing right from wrong may, in
expressing his medical opinion, be in fact acting as judge and jury at
once. And furthermore as Dr. Gregory Zilboorg pointed out some years
ago in *Mind, Medicine and Man*: " . . . except for totally deteriorated,
drooling, hopeless psychotics of long standing, and congenital idiots—

who seldom commit murder or have the opportunity to commit murder—the great majority and perhaps all murderers know what they are doing, the nature and quality of their act, and the consequences thereof, and they are therefore 'legally sane' regardless of the opinion of any psychiatrist."

How should the word *know* be understood? When does a criminal know what he is doing? Does "knowing" imply intellectual awareness alone, or does it mean fuller emotional knowledge as well? For example, a man who was delusional and murdered his wife because "God told me to do it" might be well aware that murder was a wrongful act; and yet he might also lack the full emotional appreciation of what he had done. In the same way if a child of three hit a baby with a hammer and killed him, he would not be held legally responsible: while the three-year-old might "know" in some sense that he could kill the baby, he would not be viewed as possessing the emotional understanding necessary to form a criminal intent.

"In order to have a crime in the classical sense," explains Abraham S. Goldstein, Dean of the Yale School, "you need not only an illegal act performed, but a culpable state of mind on the part of the doer. For instance if a man committed a crime while sleepwalking, or in the course of an epileptic fit, he'd ordinarily be seen as lacking in what is called *mens rea*, that 'intent' which is a necessary component of a crime."

Dean Goldstein, a tall quiet-spoken man in his mid-forties, is the author of *The Insanity Defense*, which has been called the definitive contemporary work on insanity proceedings. "The criminal law," he points out, "operates on the assumption that you have a person capable of responding to its signals, to its threats, to its sanctions. It assumes that a man may rationally calculate the consequences of an offense—and hopefully, be prevented from committing it. Now if that's our working model, we have to ask whether a particular person accused of a crime is capable of making those calculations: does he have the mental equipment necessary? We're all troubled by the idea of punishing a man who may be so ill and so disordered that he understands neither what was expected of him, nor what his punishment is about."

In its struggle to weed out those who cannot be held responsible from those who are blameworthy, the ill from the evil, the criminal law encounters problem after problem with M'Naghten. Not only *know* is difficult to interpret; so is the word *wrong*. Do we mean wrong according to law or according to prevailing moral standards? The courts have split on this issue. And furthermore, what is a "disease of the mind" which might make a man incapable of knowing right from wrong, thus exempting him from criminal responsibility? Would it include cases in which the inidvidual's judgment was thoroughly distorted by alcohol or by drugs?

There seems to be no clear definition of what is meant by mental disease under the M'Naghten ruling. In practice, most lawyers and psychiatrists assume that *mental disease* refers to something very serious indeed—either a severe psychosis with symptoms of delusion and/or hallucination, or an extreme form of mental defect. According to Goldstein, this is a mistaken supposition: it is not the rule itself, he says, but the conventions around it which make it seem to cover such a narrow range of mental conditions.

At any rate, where drug addiction or drunkenness are involved, the trend of judicial decisions under M'Naghten seems clear. The law rejects efforts to plead insanity in these instances, even if it is evident that the defendant was hopelessly intoxicated or stoned at the time of his crime—unless he can prove that his use of drugs or alcohol was linked to a previous and long-standing mental illness.

In some eighteen states and in the federal system, the M'Naghten test is supplemented by another known as the *irresistible impulse* rule. "This is used," explains Goldstein, "in identifying those people who, while they may know that an act they're engaging in is wrong, are simply lacking in the ability to control their conduct. That is, individuals who because of emotional illness, are driven into what appears to be an irresistible "acting out" of inner conflicts.

"I don't like the name *irresistible impulse*," remarks Goldstein parenthetically. "I think it's misleading. Rules about the individual's capacity for retaining self-control (there is more than one version of this rule) ought to be simply called the *control* rules.

"But a control or irresistible impulse rule does not supply, I believe, virtually all that's missing from M'Naghten. Taken together and construed in their broad sense, the two tests do cover the ground of mental states."

Still, "irresistible impulse," like "ability to know right from wrong," has been criticized as an artificial and arbitrary test for mental illness. Psychiatrists maintain that there is no scientific dividing line, no magic method to aid them in distinguishing uncontrollable behavior from that which is merely uncontrolled. And the phrase *irresistible impulse* serves, in itself, to compound the already existing confusion.

Some courts, in attempting to demonstrate that an accused was sane enough to have resisted a criminal impulse, employ such gambits as the "policeman at the elbow" test. This is a question which demands that the defendant answer yes or no as to whether he would have committed the same act if a policeman had been at his elbow. In most cases it is clear that he would not—and that his impulse was therefore not irresistible. And yet more than one critic has remarked that even the strongest and craziest criminal urges can probably be inhibited temporarily while the individual knows he is being watched.

Moreover, how is the word *impulse* to be interpreted? It certainly suggests an act which is unpremeditated and sudden. But as Professor Henry Weihofen has noted in *The Urge to Punish*, ". . . the melancholic patient . . . experiences a change in mood which alters his whole existence. He may believe that a future of such misery awaits both him and his family that death for all is the best way out. The criminal act, in such circumstances, may be the reverse of impulsive. It may be carefully and coolly prepared; yet it is still the act of a madman. . . ." Thus, a very sick person might fall between two stools. He might be sane according to M'Naghten because he knew what he was doing; and sane according to "irresistible impulse" because he had brooded over and planned his crime.

Some twenty years ago an attempt was made to reformulate the insanity defense in a way that would render it less rigid and would permit a wider range of psychiatric testimony. This was the Durham rule, handed down in 1954 by Judge David L. Bazelon of the United States Court of Appeals for the District of Columbia. In reviewing the appeal of a former mental patient and convicted housebreaker named Monte Durham, Judge Bazelon stated that "an accused is not criminally responsible if his unlawful act was the product of mental disease or defect."

The Durham ruling was hailed loudly by the psychiatric community: at one stroke it seemed to sweep away old, boxed-in standards of "reason" and "control," leaving the definition of mental disease as an open space to be filled in with the latest medical knowledge. It was anticipated that Durham would be rapidly adopted by courts across the country; and that it would usher in a time of harmony between psychiatry and the law. "In 1954, when the Durham decision was written," recalls Judge Bazelon, who is at present Chief Judge of the United States Court of Appeals, "the M'Naghten rule had an encrusted quality. It's a very rationalistic approach; after all, it predated Freud by half a century. But with the rise of psychoanalytic psychology, people had begun to understand that madness wasn't just a defect of reason— that it involved distorted feelings and emotions as well.

"And M'Naghten often operated, as it still does, without any recognition of these new scientific understandings," continues Bazelon. "For example, a horrible but not atypical case—and I could cite a number of them—was that of an eighteen-year-old college freshman who stabbed his father to death. This boy was termed schizophrenic by examining psychiatrists; one of his delusional motives for the murder was apparently to avoid taking final exams. But the doctors' diagnosis was questioned by the prosecuting attorney, along a traditional line. He asked the psychiatrist *if* the boy knew he had a knife in his hand and not a toothbrush; and *if*, when he hitched a ride home on the night of the murder, he'd realized he was heading for Elmira, New York, and not Timbuktu, and so on. . . . Of course the psychiatrist replied that the student did know; but he also kept trying to point out that his motivations had been psychotic. That testimony was stricken.

"In this case, the defendant was found guilty of murder in the first degree; he knew what he was doing. The New York Court of Appeals upheld the ruling; and a very sick young person received the death penalty. Now psychiatrists have been very loud in their condemnation of this sort of thing, and I don't blame them," remarks Bazelon.

But Judge Bazelon's Durham rule has not succeeded in replacing the old "right-wrong" test. Instead, Durham has touched off almost two decades of angry legal and psychiatric controversy. Court after court has rejected the new test, insisting that it is "ambiguous" and perhaps even dangerous. For any serious crime could, in itself, be seen as evidence of mental illness; and some psychiatrists maintain that all offenders are, in some sense, "sick." And if, for example, every murderer or rapist is sick, is any murderer or rapist responsible? The problems of defining mental disease have proven every bit as complicated under Durham as they were under M'Naghten.

"In the early fifties" —Bazelon sighs—"the psychiatrists were all entreating: 'Let us be honest men. We're scientists. Don't ask us ethical questions about right and wrong; let us testify about what we know.'

"But the fact is, when we tried to give them the chance, they *didn't* know—or at least they couldn't communicate their information in a courtroom. Are all the labels and jargon necessary? A psychiatrist can get up on the stand and by using a word—schizophrenia, psychosis, psychopathy—cover up a world of ignorance about that particular defendant. We can't seem to get them to understand what we want: it's just an educated guess. What, in the simplest terms possible, is the nature of the defendant's disease? What are the probabilities, on balance, that his crime was the product of his disordered condition?

"But many psychiatrists can't seem to understand this; they get upset when they're cross-examined. I think," adds Judge Bazelon with a quick smile, "they must feel insecure with their information."

Since the time of the Durham rule, the insanity defense has once again— in 1972—been reformulated (in the rules of the American Law Institute). The new rule dictates that a person is not responsible for a criminal act if, as a result of a mental disease or defect, he lacks substantial capacity either to appreciate the wrongfulness of his conduct or to conform his conduct to law. But the difficulties remain; and so does some legal ire over the failure of psychiatry to provide a clear and modern definition of what *mental disease* actually is. "As far as I'm concerned," says Professor Alan Dershowitz of the Harvard Law School, "we've placed an undue reliance on psychiatrists: The emperor of psychiatry seems to have far fewer clothes on than we once thought."

Dershowitz, who is in his late thirties, was formerly a law clerk to Judge Bazelon. "The insanity defense," he remarks, "does raise the most fundamental question of criminal law. And that is: Who should be held responsible? I'm not sure psychiatrists can provide us with the answers to our questions. They sound awfully scientific, but the information on which they base their judgments is relatively fuzzy.

"All of the different rules on insanity have been attempts to close and fix the question of responsibility," he continues. "And yet, I don't believe it can ever be resolved once and for all: it can only be settled for a given moment in time, in the context of a given society.

"It's certainly tempting to believe that certain kinds of people, like a

Hitler or a Calley, are crazy. It'd be a great luxury to say that anyone who behaves brutally is crazy, or that everyone is crazy, or that no one is crazy—then it's all so easy. But we can't do that without trying to decide who's *relevantly* crazy; I mean, relevant to the purposes of the law. In other words, which men are responsible?

"A trial like Calley's is far different from a case in ordinary criminal law. You get into the complicated questions of what constitutes sanity in extreme situations. Here was a not-too-bright fellow, fighting thousands of miles away from home, for people he didn't understand, against people he didn't understand, about issues he didn't understand. What he *did* see was that his friends were being killed. And given the war situation, and the whole process of dehumanizing the enemy, I think he'd come to see the Vietnamese as something other than people: they were the 'them' against whom all his fears and his rage were mounting." Dershowitz pauses. "And the upshot must have been his getting permission to do what he felt was in some way expected of him.

"I'm not trying to justify his barbarous conduct, just to understand it. I don't think his behavior was so far beyond the range of what could be called normality that he can be viewed as insane and thus not responsible."

The word *sanity* is, technically, a purely legal term. It refers to a person's capacity for assessing reality, making choices about what he does, and taking responsibility for his acts; nothing in psychiatry quite corresponds to this concept. Psychiatrists are more concerned with the strictly "medical" constructs of mental illness and health, normality and abnormality. But what, precisely, does it mean to be "normal"? Psychiatrists have had as much trouble in defining this ambiguous state as lawyers have had with the notion of sanity.

The *Random House Dictionary of the English Language* describes normalcy as: " . . . conforming to the standard or common type . . . usual; not abnormal; regular . . . approximately average in any psychological trait . . ." In other words what is common to most people, what occurs in most cases, is what is "normal." But this does not really define normality psychiatrically. For what is most ordinary, or average, does not inevitably coincide with what is normal in the clinical sense. As the psychiatrist F.C. Redlich points out in a 1952 paper "On the Concept of Normality": " . . . Kinsey found that approximately 40 percent of married males masturbate . . . (but) . . . this activity cannot be considered an adjusted form of sexual behavior. From a statistical point of view it is normal; from a clinical viewpoint abnormal." And, as other clinicians have noted, mild phobias—such as fear of snakes, of heights, of dentists—are widespread among large portions of the population. If frequency were the criterion for normality, these phobias would have to be seen as normal.

Some psychiatrists have attempted to define normality another way; that is, in terms of adaptation. They view the mentally healthy individual as one with the capacity for finding personal happiness and satisfaction within the context of his social environment. Normality, in this framework, is equated with adjustment: the ideally well integrated person is one whose behavior leads to success rather than failure, to social praise rather than punishment. Using this definition, however, a Nazi storm trooper might serve as our model "normal man." . . . The trouble with the "adjustment" approach is that it implies that conformity is a prerequisite for mental health. If an individual living in a totalitarian country protested and were sent to prison, would one want to define him as mentally ill?

Neither the adaptive nor the statistical definition really isolates the meaning of normality in a scientifically valid way. There have been numerous other attempts to define the word: one is "the absence of mental disease." But what, precisely, is mental disease? According to Dr. Alan F. Stone, an analyst on the Harvard faculty, "Psychiatrists have been unable to phrase clearly what is meant by such general propositions as mental health and mental illness. Nevertheless I can say," he adds, "that we are able to diagnose serious mental diseases— and understand them within limits—with a good degree of reliability."

Dr. Stone, a large burly man with a pleasantly calm manner, is an expert on psychiatry and the law: he lectures in both departments at Harvard. "The classical types of mental illness, such as schizophrenia, have been with us for centuries," he explains. "Symptoms of this disease—delusions, hallucinations—have appeared in every culture. They are familiar syndromes."

The question of who is "sick," says Stone, is easiest to answer when the character of the illness fits into one of the well-known syndromes. "For instance, take a case of paranoid schizophrenia: the classic example might begin with a young man beginning to worry about his masculinity. Let's say he's a college student: he starts thinking that the guy in back of him is whispering about it to the other people in the class. Before long he decides there's some sort of conspiracy to attack his masculinity; by now he's frankly hallucinating and hearing voices criticizing him. Everything he sees and hears in actuality becomes twisted to fit into his conspiratorial premise: soon, the situation becomes intolerable. He'll reach the point where he wants to kill himself, or where he's potentially dangerous to others.

"This would be a characteristic paranoid schizophrenic episode in a young person," continues the psychoanalyst. "Now, a number of people might object to this diagnosis by saying that there are *lots* of adolescents who worry about being homosexual; and that you can have hallucinations from drugs, or sleep deprivation, or sensory deprivation. And also, that many people think about killing themselves. So why should I attach the label *paranoid schizophrenic* to this fellow?

"The point is, each of these elements might, certainly, be compared to something you'd find in an individual who wasn't mentally ill. But together they add up to more than the sum of their parts: they form a classical syndrome of paranoid schizophrenia—a disease that can be recognized *and treated* with drugs that are now widely available."

The psychoses—schizophrenia, paranoia, manic-depressive psychosis—are the severest and perhaps most recognizable forms of mental disorder; all of them represent a divorce from reality. Psychiatrists typically distinguish two other categories of mental dysfunctioning: the neuroses, which are characterized by anxiety, obsessions, compulsions; and the character disorders, such as the "explosive personality," the "antisocial or psychopathic personality," and the like. But within the wide, gray, somewhat indistinct area represented by these two major categories, psychiatric diagnosis is, says Stone, "often virtually meaningless.

"Most doctors start out with the proposition that no one is in perfect mental health anyway. Interviews with random samples of the population have led some mental-health workers to believe there's a quite high incidence of psychological disturbance within the general community . . . so when a psychiatrist is asked to make a judgment about whether a certain person is sick, it's not always clear whom that individual ought to be measured against."

Even when the presence of psychosis is suspected it is not always simple to determine the moment at which deviant or different behavior ought to be termed abnormal. For example, where is the line between excessive daydreaming, fantasy and hallucination? And when does a firm conviction come to be called a delusion? Suppose a man insists on the reality of a strange idea, such as a belief that the world is ending, or that a group of conspirators is secretly controlling the government. "In the case of a man preoccupied with conspiracies," remarks Stone, "there are certain critical questions I would ask.

"Is he also having hallucinations? Has this conspiratorial point of view begun to affect the way he looks at the behavior of all the important people around him? Because the critical element in mental illness is that it becomes the central premise in all interpersonal relations. To the extent that he does make a distinction between his private life and what's going on at the State Department—to that extent, he's not mentally ill. I'd also want to know if he were experiencing the overwhelming panic and anxiety which accompany a true schizophrenic breakdown."

One powerful determinant of whether or not we view a person's behavior as normal or abnormal is the social context in which that behavior happens to occur. A new mother who felt she couldn't support her baby and therefore put it out in the back yard to perish would, in our culture, probably be seen as sick; and yet there are South Sea Island cultures in which exposure of new infants is a routine and acceptable method for controlling family size. Similarly, to return to the Calley example, his behavior in a wartime situation is viewed as fundamentally different from the way it would be seen if he had done the same deed in a village in rural Iowa; in the latter case, some sort of psychotic motivation would be assumed. Social situations and sets of shared beliefs have, in other words, a great deal to do with how we interpret an individual's behavior—and with whether or not we decide that he or she is "crazy."

A striking example of this is reported by Dr. Jay Katz, Professor of Psychiatry and Law at Yale. "Just after World War II," says Katz, "I was working as a psychiatrist in the Air Force; and I had three Jesus Christs on my ward. They had practically identical symptoms, and all were schizophrenic. When it came time to discharge them, two were sent to veterans' hospitals; their families felt they couldn't care for them. But in the third case, that of a boy from the hills of West Virginia, the mother insisted that there would be no difficulty at all. Her son was considered a lay preacher in his own subculture; he 'spoke in tongues'; and his behavior was completely normal and tolerable within that particular social setting."

The problem of cultural values is one that has plagued all efforts to define mental illness. In some societies the attaining of mystical states is seen as a form of madness; in others, it may be a part of normal behavior. In our culture an adolescent boy might be thoroughly shaken if approached by a homosexual, and start to fear that there was something wrong with him; yet there are cultures in which the very *absence* of an approach might make such a boy believe something was wrong. "What is seen as healthy or unhealthy has a greal deal to do with the judgments of a particular group," points out Katz. "It is the shared beliefs and values of the society that determine what things are considered normal."

Professor Katz is, like Alan Stone, an authority on psychiatry and the law: he is also one of a growing number of psychiatrists who are irritated by the unreal demands placed upon them by the law. For if psychiatry cannot provide definitive answers to the questions of who is normal and who is sick, the reason is, says Katz, that no scientifically valid—that is, value-free and objective—answers are possible. The judgments depend upon the viewers as well as the viewed. "Lawyers groan about the role psychiatrists have played in the legal process, and I'll agree that we have not been able to serve in that arena with distinction. But what is it about law that permits such sorry spectacles to occur? I'm personally convinced that because lawyers have been unable to think through their own problems, they've been using psychiatrists to bail them out. At the same time they have the sadistic satisfaction of expressing their disgust with the unsatisfactory answers they receive from psychiatry—when they themselves are posing the unsatisfactory questions."

Katz smiles wryly. "As far as I'm concerned," he says, "the insanity defense is to the criminal law what the dream is to sleep. It's a way of protecting it, of draining off all its irrationality. That way, the criminal process can continue to function and to retain its so-called sanity."

Normality Is a Four-sided Triangle or a Square Circle

At the State University's Upstate Medical Center at Syracuse, New York, a routine diagnostic interview is in progress. The patient, a dowdy woman in her late fifties, had been referred for psychiatric evaluation after complaining persistently of a mysterious "pulling in her head." In a flat voice she unfolds a life story so filled with disaster, loss and sudden death that it seems more the stuff of theater than medicine. From time to time, as she answers the questions of the young resident in psychiatry, she cries briefly; and yet for the most part she speaks in a curiously emotionless tone, as though telling someone else's story. The senior psychiatrist on the case, Dr. Thomas Szasz, sits quietly to one side, jotting on a yellow note pad. There are some twelve students in the consultation room, all juniors in the medical school: their expressions range from slight embarrassment to stern scientific interest.

"Well, what is your diagnosis?" Szasz asks, turning to them after the patient has been escorted from the room. He is a compact, curly-haired man in his early fifties, with a sharply intelligent face; his eyes are bright with mockery. Uncertain, the students look at him without answering.

"Come now," he prods ironically. "You are the *doctors* and she is the *patient*, so that means there must be an *illness*. Otherwise we wouldn't all be here, would we?"

"I think," ventures a young man with a sprouting blond beard, "that she's in a chronic depression."

"Oh, a depression," says the older man, nodding. "And you?" he asks, turning to the next student, whose appearance is almost anachronistically clean-cut. "What do you think?"

"I think that potentially it's a case of involutional melancholia. But for right now, I guess I'd concur in a diagnosis of chronic, severe depression."

Szasz looks at him with interest: "And then how would you go about treating this 'condition'?"

There is a pause. "Er . . . isn't there a drug called Elavil that's good for depression?"

149

The psychiatrist blinks several times, parodying extreme amazement: "So you would treat this 'sickness' she's got with *drugs*?" There are several uncomfortable, uncomprehending laughs from around the room. "But what, exactly, are you treating? Is feeling miserable—and needing someone to talk things over with—a form of medical *illness*?" Szasz gets to his feet, walks over to a blackboard and picks up a piece of chalk.

"I don't understand—we're just trying to arrive at a diagnosis," protests the student, his voice confused.

"Of what?" demands Szasz. "Has she got an illness called *depression*, or has she got a lot of problems and troubles which make her unhappy?" He turns and writes in large block letters: DEPRESSION. And underneath that: UNHAPPY HUMAN BEING. "Tell me," he says, facing the class, "does the psychiatric term say more than the simple descriptive phrase? Does it do anything other than turn a 'person' with problems into a 'patient' with a sickness?" He puts down the chalk so hard that a cloud of dust rises. There is a low muttering among the students as he returns to his seat.

"But if this woman comes in complaining of a 'pulling in her head,' and we can't give a name to what's wrong with her, how can we go about treating her?" asks someone indignantly.

Szasz turns to him with one of his elaborately astonished expressions. "What do you call 'treatment'? Suppose someone is sad because he's poor and I give him money, and then he feels happy. Is that 'treatment'?"

The student hesitates. "Well, yes, in a way."

Szasz laughs. "So then whatever makes a person feel better is 'medical therapy'; the term is infinitely elastic. But then, what *isn't* medicine?"

The group looks at him as if he were a minister who had suddenly started blaspheming in church. "Are you saying that psychiatry isn't?" asks someone in a voice tart with offense. "And if so, then why should we be wasting four weeks of our time on this service?"

Szasz cocks his head to one side comically: "You're asking *me*?" he demands. There is a moment's stunned silence; then everyone breaks into roars of laughter. In the wake of it come the questions—angry, confused, belligerent, intrigued. And the problem of diagnosing the patient becomes superceded for a time by Szasz's far more passionate and pressing concern—diagnosing what is wrong with the current practice of psychiatry.

Thomas Szasz is a psychiatrist and psychoanalyst in private practice, a professor of psychiatry at the Upstate Medical Center of the State University of New York in Syracuse and probably the most controversial figure in his profession today. For more than a decade he has mounted a virtually single-handed and doggedly persistent attack on the view of mental illness as a "disease" to be "diagnosed" by medically trained psychiatrists, "treated" and, one hopes, "cured." While mental-health organizations have been winning public acceptance of such propositions as "Mental illness is like any other illness," Szasz has infuriated many of his psychiatric colleagues by asserting that it simply does not exist. The concept of mental illness, he insists, is a metaphor run amuck. It is a mythical construct which, in common with most myths, serves covert social purposes. For one thing, it provides "reasons" and "explanations" why an individual may behave in ways that are different, disturbing, incomprehensible (i.e., because he has a "mental disease"); for another, it furnishes an acceptable, even humanitarian-appearing mode of controlling such behavior (the distressing person comes to be defined as "ill" and this justifies locking him up in a mental hospital until he is "well").

And yet, Szasz maintains, there is no such thing as a "sick mind" which can be cured by medicine, any more than a "sick economy" or a "sick society" can be. While the behavior and problems defined as "mental illness" certainly exist—people do become confused, guilty, excessively anxious, unhappy, unwilling or unable to play the game of social living—these represent problems in adjusting and communicating or what he terms "problems in living." They are not disease entities, nor indeed symptoms of any disease.

At present, vast numbers of people in this country are incarcerated in psychiatric hospitals for the care and treatment of their mental disorders: there are about half a million people in mental institutions, 90 percent of them on an involuntary basis. Nevertheless, according to Dr. Szasz, a diagnosis or finding of "mental disease" is an imposed social definition placed upon individuals who are either threatening to the community (the criminal, the deviant), or are disturbing or frightening people around them (the person who claims to "hear God's voice" or to be the Virgin Mary), or who are merely burdensome (old people comprise approximately 40 percent of the population of American public mental-health hospitals). Calling these people "mentally ill" is, says Szasz, a strategic tagging process facilitating their shipment out of the social order; it is a moral and political, not a medical, act.

Szasz is the author of more than 150 articles and seven books, including *The Myth of Mental Illness*, published in 1961 and now in its twelfth hardcover and seventh paperback printing. He is also a witty and moving speaker, whose unusual views—and verbal gymnastics—attract large audiences wherever he lectures. Szasz has been called everything from a crank and a paranoid to a prophet and passionate humanitarian. In reviewing *Law, Liberty and Psychiatry*, Szasz's third book, the late Manfred Guttmacher, an eminent forensic psychiatrist, complained; "A bird that fouls its nest courts criticism. Dr. Szasz doubtless enjoys the contention which he is creating."

Of the most recent Szasz book, *The Manufacture of Madness*, David J. Vail has said, "There is something in it to offend practically everyone." Nevertheless, Vail, who is director of mental-health programs for the State of Minnesota, concedes in the same article: "Szasz is like dry martinis. Szaszophiles, like dry-martini *aficionados*, may have their preference as to the potency. But they are hooked, and after that they find it virtually impossible to go back to the sweet stuff. . . ."

Szasz has hammered away at virtually every basic assumption of accepted psychiatric thought—and most vehemently at the practice of involuntary therapy. "One of my main concerns," he explains, "is trying to make clear the important distinction between voluntary and involuntary psychiatric interventions. I'm wholly in favor of the former, which I'd compare to the religious worship of one's own choosing. I'm unalterably opposed to the latter, which I'd consider similar to forced conversions or inquisitorial practices. You know, at this moment thousands of American citizens are being forced to submit to psychiatric 'therapies' against their will: to loss of liberty, to lifelong stigmatization, to extremely toxic drugs like Thorazine, to the brain-damaging assaults of electroshock, and until recently, even to such incredible barbarities as lobotomy. I submit that this is nothing less than a crime against humanity."

In a quiet, conservative city like Syracuse, the disputatious Szasz, who has appeared on popular televison programs such as the Dick Cavett Show, cuts an intriguing figure; he is viewed with some pride, some ambivalence, a bit of nervousness by his colleagues. "You know," remarks Dr. Donald Oken, chairman of psychiatry at the Upstate Medical Center, "when people hear that I'm head of the department *Tom Szasz* is in, they can't wait to hear what wild fantastic stories I've got to tell." Oken, who is in his early forties, laughs. "You'd have to know Tom personally to realize how ridiculous that idea is. He sounds caustic and polemical in his writing, but he's nothing like that. He's a warm, personable guy—there's absolutely nothing flamboyant about him. He wears a dark gray flannel suit to work every day, all day, every winter. He's a conservative person basically. He's also rather shy."

Oken takes out a cigarette, taps it against the back of his hand. "Tom is a great ego-ideal for many of the students here; they've taken it for granted, from his writings on individual liberties, that he's an uncompromising radical and wholly anti-Establishment. That's simply not true; he's a passionate believer in rights and freedoms, but also in responsibility, traditional authority, rules, standards. We had a moment of truth recently when the kids initiated a movement to abolish grading and found Szasz squarely against them. *He* was as shocked as they were; he couldn't understand why they'd expected his backing. 'Who do they think I am, Robespierre?' he asked me.

"But of course the material he's dealing with is controversial," Oken adds. "They mistake him for a zealot who wants to reform everything, not just psychiatry."

Says another colleague, "Tom is far more reasonable in person than in print. I think he does himself a disservice by writing in the antagonistic, inflammatory way that he does. When he starts calling psychiatrists 'jailers' and involuntary therapies 'tortures'—well, people just stop listening. And that's a shame, because he's making some important points."

Seated in his office, a long narrow room lined at one side with windows. Szasz is friendly, voluble, erudite. He is dressed in the expected gray suit and a striped tie; his black hair, very faintly tinged with gray, is cut short. "It's absolutely essential," he says earnestly, "that we look not at what psychiatrists *say* they do; but at what they actually do. They are not concerned with mental illnesses and their treatments. In practice, they deal with personal, social and ethical problems in living.

"As far as I'm concerned the concept of illness should be restricted to disorders of the body—things like diabetes, organic brain damage, cancer. Because, as the most simple-minded of observations ought to make clear, what is called 'mentally ill' is in fact behavior which is disapproved of by the speaker." Szasz speaks rapidly, his low-pitched voice intense.

"In our society the words 'good' and 'bad' are swiftly becoming obscured by notions about mental health and mental illness. And what is 'mental health' anyway? Ask six different psychiatrists what 'normal' means; you'll get six totally different answers. And if you asked me, I'd say normality is either a four-sided triangle or a square circle.

"So how do psychiatrists decide who is, and who isn't, 'healthy'? Well, Disraeli was once asked to define an agreeable gentleman, and he said: 'A gentleman who agrees with me.' In the same way, a normal person is one whose beliefs and conduct coincide with those of the examining psychiatrist. If the psychiatrist happens to think that homosexuality or suicidal inclinations are 'mental illness,' then by definition that person must be mentally ill. And yet what underlies this 'scientific diagnosis' is that the doctor *disapproves* of homosexuality; that he thinks trying to commit suicide is *bad*." Szasz shrugs, pauses. He turns and takes a sip from a steaming cup of tea which sits on a round table next to his chair.

"Take the Calley trial for instance," he resumes. "Why raise the insanity issue in a case like that? Many people seemed to assume that he must have a 'mental disease' to have perpetrated such a massacre; but such things have been going on for centuries; they're as old as history. Calley performed a perfectly simple act—murder. It was bad, not mentally ill."

The psychiatrist smiles slightly. "We seem to have mystified aggression in the same way that the Victorians mystified sex. Man is a predator; everyone knows that. But after World War II, perhaps in face of the horror of the Nazis, everyone began massively denying that fundamentally we are beasts and that the only things which keep men from murder are moral inhibitions or other people—that is, the sanctions of law. Look, for thousands of years people understood perfectly well why it was that Cain killed Abel. But now, of course, you couldn't have Cain stand trial without an insanity plea. Everybody would insist that he must be crazy because of what he did: He killed his brother!"

"But what," I inquire, "about cases which appear utterly bizarre? For example, one cited by an English psychiatrist in which a young man killed his mother, cut off her head and cooked it in the oven. Wouldn't you call *that* mental illness?"

"Why call it that?"

"Because the deed is grotesque. One doesn't understand what the motivations can have been; it's incomprehensible."

He gives me a pained look. "You've certainly just defined what 'mental illness' is. What cannot be comprehended about someone else is 'mental illness.' Now I don't know any more than you do why the man committed such a horrible act—he himself is the only one who knows. The explanation that it was because of a 'sickness' seems to satisfy you, to calm your intellectual disquietude. But as far as I'm concerned, it's exactly the same as attributing the 'cause' of his deed to witchcraft.

"The very essence of my work—what I've tried to point out over and over again—is that we have replaced a theological outlook on life with a therapeutic one. Psychiatry in this country *is* a form of religion. Just as we all recognize that there is a religion called Catholicism with a church in Rome, and a religion called Anglicanism with its church based in England, so we should all realize that there's an American church at the National Institute of Mental Health, and the name of the religion is Mental Health. The cardinals are people like Dr. Karl Menninger, Judge David Bazelon—all the evangelists of the mental-health movement—and they're pontificating not about how many angels can stand on the head of a pin, but about how many human acts are caused by 'mental diseases' which require 'treatment.'

"I think men like Menninger and Bazelon, who want to raise the question of insanity every time some poor jerk steals five dollars have been unwilling to commit themselves in simple understandable terms about what's good and what's evil. They claim that all crime is sickness and don't want to punish legally; they only want to punish psychiatrically.

"When someone is acquitted by reason of insanity," Szasz adds ironically, "he only gets a nonpunishing punishment; they call it 'treatment.' But as most criminals are aware, such an acquittal can result in their being locked up in a madhouse forever. In my opinion, 'treatment,' in a free society, can only be that intervention to which a person submits voluntarily. If he's incarcerated in a hospital that's punishment, no matter what his benefactors may care to call it."

"Then do you believe," I ask, "as some experts on law and psychiatry have recently suggested, that the insanity defense should be abolished?"

Szasz smiles disingenuously. "If there is no insanity, how can there be an insanity defense? Of course I think it should be abolished. I think societies should have a limited set of rules about what behavior is permissible, that these should apply to absolutely everybody, and that they should be enforced with savage consistency. *No* people who are merely 'suspected' of being dangerous or different or potentially antisocial should be committed to mental institutions. *All* people who break the law should be punished. But isn't what I'm saying simply— excuse the expression—what 'law and order' is supposed to be about? Punishing lawbreakers? Right now we've got two sets of law and order—legal order and psychiatric order."

The psychiatrist laughs. "I think the idea of 'helping' people by imprisoning them and doing terrible things to them is a religious concept, as the idea of 'saving' witches by torture and burning once was. As far as 'dangerousness to self' is concerned, I believe, as did John Stuart Mill, that a man's body and soul are his own, not the state's. And furthermore, that each individual has the 'right,' if you will, to do with his body as he pleases—so long as he doesn't harm someone else, or infringe on someone else's right.

"As far as 'dangerousness to others' goes, most psychiatrists working with hospitalized patients would admit this is pure fantasy—like those tales about Jews roasting Christian children and eating them for Passover. Both claims only justify seeking out and persecuting a class of scapegoats. There have in fact been statistical studies made which show that mental patients are much more law-abiding than the normal population. They're de-energized, cut off for the most part, less engaged in the real world. But, of course"—Szasz takes a sip of tea— "dangerousness is often not the issue."

He puts down the cup with a clatter. "Actually, what gets diagnosed as 'mental illness' is usually just behavior that other people don't want to tolerate. Say, for instance, a man goes walking around saying people are laughing at him and talking about him. Well, either those close to him will stand for it, or they'll try to cast him out of the social framework. Let's imagine that he's old and poor—most of those diagnosed 'mentally ill' are—and that his children don't want him. How do they get rid of him? By having him examined, and found to be suffering from 'senile psychosis'—instead of from children who don't want him. Then he'll be thrown into a New York State mental hospital where he'll be locked up and drugged, and have a far shorter life expectancy.

"This is the way that the mentally healthy help the 'sick' person; he receives 'therapy.' And, of course, it disposes of the problem in a rather convenient way."

Szasz, a Hungarian by birth, came to this country when he was eighteen. He and his family left their home in Budapest in 1938, four years before the Nazi invasion. Szasz had grown up in easy circumstances, in an upper-middle-class, nominally Jewish household. His father, who held a degree in law, was the overseer for a number of the vast, almost feudal, estates which persisted in Hungary until the Russian occupation. "The only problem I had as a child," recalls Szasz now, "was that my older brother George was a bit of a prodigy—he was a *wunderkind*. Life was a desperate race to keep up with him somehow."

He smiles. "The atmosphere of our household was intellectually very intense, and we were constantly making bets—it was a family rule that you had to put up money—whenever a statement or claim was questioned. Once, when we were in our teens, George dared me to bet that he could memorize Pi to thirty digits in fifteen minutes. He won. I couldn't do anything spectacular like that." He laughs. "I had to work harder. I was a plodder."

In 1939, Szasz entered the University of Cincinnati, where his uncle, Otto Szasz, was a professor of mathematics. In two years, he had earned an A.B. with honors in physics; he then continued on to an M.D., graduating first in his class. After an internship at Harvard, he trained as a psychiatrist at the University of Chicago clinics and, following that, as a psychoanalyst at the Chicago Institute for Psychoanalysis. He graduated at the age of thirty in 1950, and the following year met and married a young social worker, Rosine Loshkajian. In 1956, the couple moved to Syracuse, bringing their two small children; Szasz has been teaching there ever since.

Last winter, after nineteen years of marriage, the Szaszes were quietly divorced. "No one knows exactly what happened," remarks a friend. "Both Tom and Rosine are extremely private people. They didn't offer any explanations; and so everyone has simply accepted the situation for what it is." Their daughters, Margot, eighteen, and Suzy, sixteen, have chosen to remain with their father.

The publication, ten years ago, of *The Myth of Mental Illness* provoked a furious reaction in psychiatric circles and a major cataclysm at the Upstate Medical Center. In the shock waves which followed, the chairman of the psychiatry department resigned and many of Szasz's younger followers were, as he puts it, "purged" from the faculty. Far from being chastised, however, Szasz has mounted an increasingly virulent campaign against many accepted psychiatric practices; he has even questioned the motives and ethics of psychiatrists as a professional group. In his 1963 book, *Law, Liberty and Psychiatry*, he writes, "Offensive as the analogy may be, I suggest that, quite often, husbands and wives who commit their mates act like the bosses of crime syndicates. They hire henchmen—psychiatrists—to dispose of their adversaries." And in a later book, *Ideology and Insanity*, he characterized the whole of legal psychiatry and involuntary mental care as a "pseudo-medical form of social control."

Addressing the convention of the American Trial Lawyers Association in Miami Beach a year ago, Szasz declared, "More than the practice of any other medical specialty, many psychiatric practices make use of, and indeed rest on, force and fraud." And he went on to suggest that lawyers who succeeded in "freeing" involuntary mental patients ought to bring suit for false imprisonment, seeking heavy damages against the doctors involved.

Curiously enough, such provocative statements no longer arouse widespread reactions (the Miami speech evoked only a few protesting letters); they fall into a well of official silence. No professional colleague has mounted a serious counterattack against Szasz's accusations. Either he is simply ignored or—and this is coming to be far more common—he is conceded privately to be raising some important points.

Szasz, nevertheless, is still often regarded as psychiatry's thorn—a fanatic, troublemaker and extremist. Fellow professionals may agree that he has exposed important problem areas in the field, but they cite with distaste his popularity with groups like the John Birch Society and with odd sects such as Scientology. The Birchers, opposing psychiatry as some sort of Communist conspiracy, are delighted with this psychiatrist who attacks fellow psychiatrists. Szasz's articles have been printed in *The National Review* and are sent out with regular Birch-society mailings. The Scientologists, a quasi-religious society dedicated to salvation through "clearing the mind," have transformed Szasz into one of their spiritual patrons. Last year, when they were in danger of being outlawed by the South African government because of their vigorous campaigns against involuntary commitment of the mentally ill, the

Scientology group hired him to testify as their psychiatric expert. (The case is still undecided.)

On the other hand, journals of the far left, such as *The Radical Therapist*, are equally favorable to Szasz: many of the writers for that magazine stand solidly behind his position on involuntary hospitalization, and one recently proposed the establishment of an Insane Liberation Front. One well-known psychiatrist observes, "Szasz's thought has become the meeting place of radical opinion, both from the right and the left."

Says Szasz, "My involvement with these groups is practically nil. I think that most of what they say is nonsense. But in part we are all fighting the same battle, the battle against the legal and moral outrage of involuntary psychiatry. You know, there is an old Arab proverb: 'The enemy of my enemy is my friend.' We are all abolitionists!"

If "mental illness is a myth," says Dr. Alan D. Miller, Commissioner of the New York State Department of Mental Hygiene, "then it's a myth that patients all over the world act as if they believe in. If you visit a psychiatric ward anywhere, you'll see similarities in words, gestures, dress. Of course Szasz has a very legitimate point when he suggests that 'mental illness' is by no means a unified thing; the phrase is a catch-all and is misleading.

"There are, nevertheless, various categories of mental disturbance and they are quite tangible and real. One of the ways we deduce their presence is that someone starts behaving very differently. Admittedly, a psychiatrist's data may be more impressionistic than that of the internist who can point to a diseased organ. But the fact that you can't X-ray it or dissect it doesn't exclude the existence of an illness.

"Most people who have schizophrenia complain about it. Something funny is happening to them, and it's frightening. They start behaving in ways that make it impossible for them to cope, terrorizing not only those around them, but themselves. I think if we emptied the wards of all of the hospitals in Manhattan tomorrow it would be —cruel. Actually, most of the complaints we receive are not about our having committed someone unjustly; ninety-nine out of one hundred are because we've refused to admit a person whom we haven't thought needed hospitalization."

Yet despite wide areas of disagreement, Dr. Miller believes Szasz has played an important role as a reformer. "By taking an extreme position," Miller says, "and even questioning the ethics of people who considered themselves decent, hard-working doctors, he's managed to shock us all into some serious self-examination. That's upsetting; it's painful. But the effect has been to move the entire spectrum of the way people think about involuntary hospitalization. In New York State, for example, we're making a conscious move toward more open hospitals, with patients permitted to come and go freely. We're concentrating on short-term hospitalization and trying not to produce new chronic patients. In fact, the population of our public psychiatric hospitals has gone down 40 to 50 percent in the last decade.

"Also, very largely in response to the kinds of issues Dr. Szasz, among others, has been raising, the state has set up a mental-health information service. This agency gets in touch with every new patient, voluntary and involuntary, to make sure that he and his family know his legal rights; it continues in touch throughout his stay and serves on his behalf in the courts."

Since psychiatrists are empowered by our mental-hygiene laws to certify people, to detain them and to judge whether or not they are competent to stand trial, they are empowered, as one psychiatrist recently observed, "to condemn or absolve in our own ways."

Bruce Ennis, a young staff attorney with the New York Civil Liberties Union says, "Szasz was early in recognizing this as a clear civil-rights issue. He's a social philosopher, and two generations ahead of his time.

"The decision to commit someone usually revolves around a finding of 'dangerousness to self or others.' I think it's intellectually dishonest to lock up people who, for example, are suicidal but sane. Our present laws imply that anyone who attempts suicide must be mentally ill. But of course many suicidal people are either just physically sick, or have lost someone they don't want to go on living without, or simply have crummy jobs, horrible lives. They can't by any stretch of the imagination be called crazy.

"As far as 'dangerousness to others' goes," continues Ennis, whose present practice is limited to test-case litigation on behalf of involuntarily committed mental patients, "why is it that we're willing to confine people if they're dangerous and insane and not if they're dangerous but sane? We know that eighty-five percent of all ex-convicts will commit more crimes in the future, and that ghetto residents and teen-age males are far more likely to commit crime than the average member of the population. We also know, from recent studies, that mental patients are statistically *less* dangerous than the average guy. So if what we're really worried about is danger, why don't we, first, lock up all former convicts, and then lock up all ghetto residents, and then why don't we lock up all teen-age males?" He laughs briefly. "Then if we're still worried, we can try mental patients.

"The question Szasz has been asking," Ennis adds, "is: If a person hasn't broken a law, what right has society to lock him up? What Szasz has done is to make it respectable for lawyers to challenge the myriad psychiatric assumptions that are the foundations of our current mental-hygiene laws."

Last May, in what might seem like a fresh bid for unpopularity, Szasz put on display at the annual meeting of the American Psychiatric Association a paper entitled "The Ethics of Addiction." Its argument was that "dangerous" drugs, heroin, for example, should be available to adults in the same mildly regulated manner that alcohol is now, and that other drugs, such as marijuana, ought simply to be sold over the counter like aspirin and cigarettes. The decision as to whether to use or take drugs, asserted Szasz, should be a personal choice and an individual responsibility; the state should not respond in any way, either by calling the drug user "sick" and forcing treatment upon him, or by calling him "criminal" and imprisoning him.

"Clearly," he wrote, "the argument that marijuana—or heroin, or methadone, or morphine—is prohibited because it is addictive or dangerous cannot be supported by facts. For one thing, there are many drugs—from insulin to penicillin—that are neither addictive nor dangerous but are nevertheless prohibited; they can be obtained only through a physician's prescription. For another, there are many things—from dynamite to guns—that are much more dangerous than narcotics (especially to others!) but are not prohibited. As everyone knows, it is still possible, in the United States, to walk into a store and walk out with a shotgun. We enjoy this right not because we do not think guns are dangerous, but because we believe even more strongly that civil liberties are precious."

The reality of the situation, he suggested, is that our society is coming to value medical paternalism more highly than individual freedoms. "Our so-called drug-abuse problem is an integral part of our present social ethic which accepts 'protections' and repressions justified by appeals to health similar to those that medieval societies accepted when they were justified by appeals to faith. . . .

"Sooner or later," he concluded, "we shall have to confront the basic moral and political issues underlying the problem of addiction. . . . In a conflict between the individual and the state, where should the former's autonomy and the latter's right to intervene begin? . . . As American citizens, do we, and should we, have the right to take narcotics and other drugs? Further, if we take drugs and conduct ourselves as law-abiding citizens, do we, or should we, have the right to remain unmolested by the Government? Lastly, if we take drugs and break the law, do we, and should we, have the right to be treated as persons accused of crime, rather than as patients accused of mental illness?"

Szasz's paper will soon be reprinted in *Psychiatric News*, the journal of the American Psychiatric Association. Questioning him about the stand he has taken I ask, "Do you really think that the Government should abandon all attempts to protect its citizens, and that anyone should be able to take any drug—even to commit suicide—just as he pleases?"

"No," answers Szasz, "not as he pleases, but only without harming anyone else. A distinction certainly ought to be made between shooting oneself or blowing oneself up in a crowded airplane. If the latter attempt failed, I would insist that such a person be tried for attempted murder.

"I do think, however, that we should worry less about preventing suicides, and more about preventing homicides. We should worry less about people abusing their bodies by ingesting harmful drugs (the toxic effects of these drugs will be punishment enough) and more about people abusing other people through reckless driving, theft, assault, stigmatization and all of the countless other ways human beings have devised for injuring one another."

"But don't you think," I protest, "that if drugs became freely available to adults in the manner which you suggest, that addiction among children would rise?"

Szasz shakes his head. "I don't know what would happen immediately, but I'm convinced there would be a reasonable adjustment to it, as there has been to alcohol. I doubt, personally, that the drugs would be significantly more available to minors; they would only be more visible, and therefore more easily subject to parental control. In other words, the responsibility would be where it belongs—on the parents and their children.

"What do you think would happen if a child brought a bottle of gin into school and got drunk? Do you think the liquor store would be blamed as the pusher? Or would the parents and the child himself be blamed? Practically every home in America has liquor in it, yet you don't hear about that being brought to school. Whereas marijuana, dexedrine and heroin—things they are certainly *not* finding at home— frequently find their way into the school."

"But do you think the Government should prohibit nothing?" I persist. "What about such substances as cyclamates, which have been linked to cancer; shouldn't the state remove them from the market by fiat?"

"Absolutely not," Szasz replies. "No more than cigarettes, which have been linked to lung cancer, or ice cream and butter, which have been linked to coronary artery disease, or alcohol, which has been linked to all kinds of ills, including death on the highway."

"Do you then believe," I ask, "that the Government should exercise *no* protective public-health measures, like vaccination and fluoridation of the water?"

Szasz smiles, like a student who has just been asked the very question he is prepared to answer. "The Government should control those things which cannot be controlled by the individual, such as sewage, the level of radioactive waste, the labeling of poisons. In this sense, I suppose I would be against fluoridation of the water, because it imposes on an entire population something which is presumed to be beneficial for only a small proportion of it—that is, growing children. Certainly seventy-year-old women don't need it, and God knows what it does to them.

"I've no objection to the Government's advertising fluorides. And let them *offer* vaccines, as they did with polio. Beyond that, why don't we leave it up to the person himself, what he needs or wants in his own body?

"In other words," he adds, "let's distinguish between genuine protection by a decent government of enlightened citizenry— enlightened through warning—and the tyrannizing of a cowed, infantilized society by the paternalistic despotism of a corrupt government." He leans back in his chair confidently.

1971

Psychiatrist, Philosopher, Prophet, Social Critic, Cult-leader...
In Search of R.D. Laing

I had seen the glowering portraits of R.D. Laing on the covers of several of his books; I had seen other brooding, Byronic-looking photographs of him as well. I had heard him described as a frightening, almost demonic person, a "rabble rouser," a "brilliant paranoid schizophrenic" who was attempting to celebrate madness because he himself went mad periodically. *Life* magazine, in a spate of bad rhetoric, had characterized him thus: "His face is dour and pale, his brow furrowed, his eyes like bruises. He speaks in the thick and charmless tones of the Glasgow slums. . . ." Small wonder that, on meeting Laing, I found myself staring at him in surprise. R.D. Laing is a trim man in his mid-forties with a friendly, natural, somewhat exuberant air. He has clear brown-green eyes, smiles easily, wears his graying hair long, in curls that frame his head and give him the look of an aging della Robbia angel. After we had spoken with one another for a few moments, I heard myself blurting, "You're awfully different from the person I'd expected!"

"Oh?" answered Laing. And then he fell silent. I had an uncomfortable feeling that I had said something wrong, had offended him in some way. The expression on his face was unreadable.

I remembered, at that moment, the story an eminent psychiatrist friend of mine had told me. This man had gone to introduce himself to Laing when he'd been in London. After a brief exchange of greetings, Laing had suddenly stopped speaking. A battle of silence had ensued which, my friend assured me, had lasted almost a full five minutes. The same thing was now, as I could see, about to happen. Although I am usually no winner at such contests I determined that I was going to hold my own. And so R.D. Laing and I sat mutely staring at one another for what seemed like an extraordinary length of time. At last, however, he broke the deadlock with an impish grin, saying, "What sort of article are you proposing to write about me?"

164

"I'm not sure yet," I answered, smiling too. "Let's start with some interviews and then we'll see."

This vague reply appeared to satisfy Laing well enough; after that, we talked quite easily.

R.D. (Ronald David) Laing was in New Haven for a closely scheduled, high-paying week of public lectures, seminars, consultations at nearby hospitals. On the first two mornings of his visit, I talked with him at length, questioning him about various aspects of his work. I found him sensitive, intelligent, impressively erudite—not only very widely read but also original in the ways he thought about the things he had read. On the third day of his stay, I went to hear him speak before a large audience at Yale's Strathcona Hall. And there Laing put on a performance which, after my brief acquaintance with him, I would never have predicted.

Seated on a large, thronelike chair on the stage, facing a roomful of people who seemed to be well disposed toward him, he was inexplicably uncomfortable—hesitant and almost confused. He began a sentence and then paused in the middle, looking baffled, as if uncertain where such a thought might possibly lead him. His theme was the pursuit of inner experience through meditation (a kind of "trip" for which, as he observed in an aside to his mainly student audience, "you can't get busted.") A good deal of time was spent in tedious and seemingly endless discussion of one meditative procedure—concentrating intensely on the tip of one's nose while thinking carefully about the impact of the air as it strikes against the nasal membranes during breathing. But Laing himself appeared to be essentially disinterested in what he was saying; it was as if he were either physically exhausted or so bored that it was hardly worth continuing.

I could see the puzzlement on the faces of the people around me. Was this, then, the fiery counterculture psychiatrist who had declared that "normality" is a state arrived at through the "abdication of our ecstasy"? Was this the social critic who had written that the process of adjustment to a conformist and repressive society involves the "betrayal of our true potentialities?" He seemed tired.

The room became filled with small sounds, with the bored shiftings of bodies, with barely suppressed yawns, with sighs. After about a half hour or so, Laing simply ran out of energy and stopped. He stared out at the audience, then remarked limply, "Now what is one supposed, really, to make of all this meditation stuff? I don't know. . . . I haven't come up with any answers. In fact I've been listening for some answers all the time I've been giving this lecture. But I haven't heard any yet."

Not surprisingly, this observation was greeted with a few incredulous hoots of laughter. Laing added quickly, "It's a relief, anyhow, to discover that it's possible to get on with it, to do things, even if you don't have all the answers." Hearing some noises behind me, I turned. A scattering of people had gotten up from their seats and were leaving the auditorium.

Later that week, however, I saw Laing in a strikingly different guise. The occasion was a seminar with a group of young doctors, all residents in psychiatry at Yale Medical School. This time the group was small, and the format of the meeting unstructured: the students were free to ask Laing about any of the wide range of topics which he has explored in his hugely popular books.

I would have predicted, therefore, that he would be questioned closely about his theories concerning the "social" origins of schizophrenia. (Laing holds the view, a minority view in the field of psychiatry, that schizophrenia is a disorder of thought and communication which has its origin in a disordered and disturbed family environment.) I would have expected the students to quiz Laing about his more radical and "political" critiques of Psychiatry as a profession, of the Family as a social institution, of Western society as a whole, all of which he has called so lunatic that: "The condition of being asleep, of being unconscious, of being out of one's mind, is the condition of the normal man." But these young clinicians were far more interested in relating to Laing as Philosopher and Guru.

In the discussion which arose, he was clearly at his most forceful and lucid—every inch the scholar, the thinker, the wise man. The talk touched on the nature of reality and illusion, on various philosophical approaches to the understanding of what is "real" and what is "true." One had the definite impression that the students wanted to deify Laing; they wanted to make of him their holy prophet, have him point out the true path, provide them with "answers." But Laing, disarmingly rolling his Scots "r's," mockingly questioned the existence of any Truth, in the absolutist sense of the word; he even poked fun at the role he himself was playing, as social critic, as cult-leader. He had no "answers." All truths, he remarked, are contingent. While each of us—both as individuals and individuals living within a culture—take on certain belief-systems as ways of orientating ourselves in the world, none of these systems are more valid, more true, more "real" than the others. A monotheistic belief in one God, reigning above us, is not demonstrably truer than a pantheistic belief that God is everywhere, in all living creatures and in Nature. "Are you saying," burst out someone, "that what we call 'reality' is nothing more than a belief that a certain group shares? That it's like the emperor's new clothes; there isn't actually anything *there*?"

"What I am saying"—Laing smiled in reply—"is that there may not even be an emperor."

After the seminar I chatted with one of the psychiatric residents and asked him what he had thought of Laing's talk. "I'd trade in the whole last year of my training," he answered fervently, "just for this past hour-and-a-half."

Nevertheless, that same evening, I saw Laing repeat his "meditation" fiasco. Speaking before the New Haven Council for Human Relations, he became so bogged down, so disconnected, so sodden that a member of the audience rose and begged him to please just forget his lecture and use the time for answering questions instead. To which a bored, fatigued Laing acceded with obvious relief.

Laing's position in regard to his fellow psychiatrists is a curious one: He is, in the eyes of many, a sort of shining knight who galloped off on his white steed to do great deeds for psychiatry; and then at some point veered round to attack the very ramparts of the castle itself. Despite a good deal of bitter criticism of him, however, I found that most psychotherapists with whom I spoke tried to be scrupulously fair in distinguishing between his later "polemics"—his anti-psychiatry, anti-mental-hospital stance as well as his notion that much of what is psychiatrically classified as crazy is merely a sane response to an insane world—and his earlier work, particularly his scholarly study of schizophrenia, *The Divided Self*.

This first book, published in 1959 (when its author was thirty-two), is undoubtedly Laing's most significant and interesting contribution. Deeply influenced by existential philosophy and psychiatry (works of Sartre, Tillich, Binswanger, Boss and others), Laing set himself the task of explaining how madness may be understood as the lawful and logical outcome of an individual's way of experiencing his world. The book points out the ways in which, if one makes the effort to articulate the psychotic's own view of his reality—that is, his situation as he sees and lives in it—one can translate his apparently random, "crazy" behaviors and statements. Such behaviors and statements are not gibberish, not "symptoms" of a mysterious illness, but meaningful parts of a system that a person has been forced to construct in order to go on living.

Laing's central thesis in *The Divided Self* has to do with the notion that there are individuals who are insecurely based in their bodies, who feel unenclosed, fragile, vulnerable, uncertain about what is "in" them and separate from other beings and the world, and what is outside them. Such persons lack the most primary security—the sense that there is an experiencing "I" that is whole and real and that exists within and is bounded by the body; they lack this inmost sense of privacy as well. Such an individual may, observes Laing, become totally preoccupied with preserving his precarious sense of his own existence. He may, as a kind of defensive mental operation, withdraw his "true self" from that body which he experiences as an exposed, unsafe, unprivate place; and leave it, like an abandoned fortress, under the sway of a pretender, a "false self," a façade, a creature who is "not really him." The "true self" is then hidden away from outer reality, from the intentions and expectations of others, while the "false self-body" system maintains an outer mask of normality, a "false face" which negotiates with and experiences the world. Such a cleavage of the self represents a split between body and mind.

What is called *psychosis* is, Laing writes, sometimes no more than the dropping of the mask which has been turned to the world. It is the cry of the individual's "true self" *to be*, to communicate the real truth of that person's existence. "Undoubtedly," observes Laing, "what most people take to be 'really true' has to do with grammar and the natural world. A man says he is dead but he *is* alive. But his 'truth' is that he is dead. He expresse(s) it perhaps in the only way common (i.e., the communal) sense allows him . . . and is seriously bent on communicating his truth. The price, however, to be paid for transvaluating the common truth is to "be" mad, for the only *real* death we recognize is biological death. . . ."

What is most striking to the reader of *The Divided Self* and of Laing's later works, is the difference in the postures he appears to take vis-á-vis the schizophrenic experience. For the patients discussed in this first book are no hyper-sane prophets or seers, no magical shamans. Peter, who believes his body to be giving off the musty smell of rot; Julie, the haunted "ghost of the weed garden"; James, who comes to Laing complaining that he is an "unreal man"—they may be, in their psychoses, living out the existential truth of their lives; we are left in little doubt, however, about the fact that they are in a thoroughly bad way. They are individuals who are lacking in a sense of personal unity, who have failed to establish the ego-boundaries which are usually differentiated during normal childhood development; they are profoundly uncertain, in effect, about where the realm of the "self" ends and the province of the outer world begins. The book is filled with images of their personal desolation: the sense of emptiness, vacuum, terrifying void—a far cry, seemingly, from that madman "irradiated by light from other worlds," off on a psychedelic exploration of "inner time and space," whom Laing came to celebrate in his 1967 book *The Politics of Experience.*

I was, as many of Laing's readers have been, curious about this apparent shift in his thinking. "*What was it,*" I asked him, "*that led you to change your views about schizophrenia?*"

LAING: There hasn't been any shift or change in my views.

SCARF: *But in* The Divided Self *you talk about the experience of the schizophrenic in terms of deadness, ashes, ruin. You speak of that individual as encapsulated in a kind of closed system, where the breath of outer reality is never permitted to penetrate, so that in effect the inner world comes to be experienced as a vacuum, as dried-up, burnt-out, a "weed garden"—a very different approach from* The Politics of Experience, *in which you talk about madness as a possibly enriching experience, as "potential liberation and renewal," as a kind of "breakthrough" to a super-sensory reality.*

LAING: What I'm doing is, I'm saying two different things in the two books; I mean I'm taking a focus on one aspect of the situation in each of the books, but I don't feel a shift. It's just a matter of concentrating on first one feature of the matter and then on the other.

SCARF: *And yet some of the things you say in the two books would appear to be mutually contradictory. In the first instance the schizophrenic is someone who needs help, understanding, who is not in a desirable condition: he lives in a terrifying fantasy world where indeed "anything is possible." And in the second book, he's someone off on a mystical voyage, someone able to pierce beyond our shared "normal" reality to something which is deeper, "truer." You don't entertain these two views of schizophrenia simultaneously, do you?*

LAING: Yes.

SCARF: *Well, in one book you're speaking about the deadness of the schizophrenic individual himself. And in the other you seem to be talking about the deadness, the alienation of an entire society. In this latter instance there's the suggestion that the only difference between the madman and the rest of society is that he* knows *he's dead.*

LAING: . . . that the weed garden is everywhere.

SCARF: *Yes. In effect the message is that we "normal people" are living in the weed garden, and that if there's any truth to be found anywhere— untainted by our shared social delusions—it is in madness.*

LAING: No, no, not at all. A lot of people have taken me to say that, but I say to them: "Show me anyplace where I've said that!" These books are not, as far as I'm concerned, supposed to be expressions of what people commonly call madness. They are presented in an idiom which I expect, in our day and age, most people regard as being sane.

SCARF: *I don't understand.*

LAING: Well, I'm not trying to say things in the idiom of madness myself. I mean the suggestion that the sane world is just a crowd of lies and that the only truth that exists is what is regarded as "mad"—I haven't said that and I haven't practiced it.

SCARF: *But you are . . . how shall I say this? . . . identified with a "romantic" kind of movement in psychiatry.*

LAING: So people seem to think. But actually I don't believe there is a romantic movement in psychiatry at all. The people I work with—the people who come over to London to apprentice themselves to me, and the people I meet who are doing work in this country—I think their actions and experiences are anything but romantic.

I mean there's nothing particularly romantic about someone who's desperately freaked-out and is terrified, raving and exhausting himself or herself; who can't find any place of solace or comfort or rest; who might be in a state of continual panic about every breath, every heartbeat.

SCARF: *And yet what you've intimated in* The Politics of Experience *is that they may know something, see something, learn something that we can't do, perhaps because we're not in a perpetual state of panic, terror . . . Whereas in* The Divided Self *the madman is someone burnt-out, in the weed garden, closed off to possibility . . .*

LAING: But there I didn't say they'd closed themselves off to possibilities—not at all! I said they had opened themselves out to possibility and closed themselves off to fact.

So there's a dreadful possibility, the awful silence of infinite space and . . . that sort of thing. That's extremely scary, and many people prefer to cocoon themselves off into something that precludes them from ever confronting that. I don't mean to say, by the way, that if that possibility opens out to someone it is an index of his being psychotic; or that, on the other hand, people who are psychotic are *ipso facto* open to this kind of possibility, this kind of experience.

But let's say this: We all have a tendency to try to subsection off the darkness, to give ourselves a sort of pathetic impression that we are orientated in the total scheme of things. And so the person who may become involved in these unusual kinds of experience will be regarded as someone outside, "psychotic." He is considered to be someone without anything to say that an intelligent person—such as a psychiatrist— might find useful for himself. I mean *for himself*: Not as a research project, or to report to colleagues about the psychotherapy of a schizophrenic, but actually of relevance to himself as a person.

SCARF: *I believe you're saying here—as you said in the* The Politics of Experience—*that the dissociated schizophrenic might be looked upon as "validly mystical" rather than "invalidly mad."*

LAING: To be perfectly straightforward, I don't find any of these "definitions" of sanity and insanity—the ones that are out in the market place—very convincing. And I believe quite literally that the definitions of madness are different under different socioeconomic conditions— just as, for example, a black man under all conditions has a black skin; but only under certain socioeconomic conditions is he defined as a slave.

Similarly, only under certain socioeconemic conditions is a person labeled "mentally ill" or "mad."

I mean there are some areas, and some places where a person could go around in quite a bit of a dither, and no one would trouble him at all. But suppose I, for instance, am walking along on my way here, and I'm coming along a very nice, well-tended suburban street. And I see a man standing in the middle of the road; and, from his manner, he seems to give the impression that he hears some voices speaking to him from directly over his head, and he acts as if he is in the company of some person or persons whom I can't see. I wouldn't feel impelled to sweep him off the street, to give him "treatment," to help him if he didn't ask for help.

But many people would. Because that is strange behavior in our society and not socially sanctioned. On the other hand, if he were in a church, down on his knees, babbling away in communication with the Unknown, that would be okay.

SCARF: *But if he were out in the street, hearing and talking to voices, he might be completely confused.*

LAING: So he might be, as we all may be; and we may be without being regarded as mad, or without our orientation in this world being in a state of total disorder or disarray. Let's say this, as a rule of thumb and for all practical purposes: In order to pass in this commonly shared space, we should expect to be answerable to our name, to give our address, telephone number, our social security number . . .

SCARF: *Wait, I don't know my social security number—*

LAING: Yes, well, I can't ever remember the number of my driver's license, but I do know where to get my hands on it right away. It's very seldom that I allow myself out in the street in a state of mind in which I haven't got that minimal grip on socially shared reality; I would regard it as very dangerous to venture out under these conditions.

SCARF: *Are there times when you feel you don't have that grip? Because I can't think of any time in my own life when I wouldn't have been capable of reciting my own name, address, and so on.*

LAING: Oh, I have it pretty well. But I can allow myself to go into states of mind where that is . . . where I might not be able to put my mental hand onto my particular files. In some states of meditation, for example, one might become completely abstracted. But I do make sure, as far as I am able to do so, that I'm *known* to be meditating. And so then that's all right.

Laing has taken some pot shots at the Family as a social institution, calling it a "mutual-protection racket" whose real function is to "repress Eros," to create "one-dimensional" man, etc. Not surprisingly, he stands firmly on the "nurture" side of the "nature-nurture" controversy as it relates to the question of what "causes" schizophrenia. He considers this most widespread of mental illnesses to be "no illness at all," nothing organically based, nothing "in" a person in the physical, constitutional sense; but, very simply, "a special strategy that a person invents in order to live in an unlivable situation." In a tradition which includes Harry Stack Sullivan, Frieda Fromm-Reichmann, Theodor Lidz and others who have emphasized the crucial role of the family in the psychogenesis of mental disorder, Laing believes the strange behaviors of the person who comes to be labeled "schizophrenic" to be realistic reflections of and reactions to disturbed patterns of communication existing within the home. "In his life situation," said Laing in *The Politics of Experience*, "the person has come to feel that he is in an untenable position. He cannot make a move, or no move, without being beset by contradictory and paradoxical pressures and demands, pushes and pulls, both internally from himself and externally from those around him. He is, as it were, in a position of checkmate. . . ." From this theoretical vantage point, schizophrenia may thus be seen as a particular mode of adaptation (albeit maladaptive): It represents an individual's flight "inward" from a too-painful social reality. It is a kind of last exit in a no-exit situation; the escape hatch for the individual who, in attempting to adjust to his family environment, has found that no such adjustment is to be permitted or possible.

Such a viewpoint minimizes the role of "nature" in the etiology of schizophrenia; it seems to ignore or dismiss the possible influences of heredity. I asked Laing about this.

SCARF: *Just recently there have been a number of studies of children of mental patients that do seem to point up the significance of a genetic factor in the causation of mental disorders. One research group, for instance, took a random sample of Danish children (some of whom had*

*been born to schizophrenic mothers) who had all been adopted shortly
after birth. They found that where the natural mothers had been
schizophrenic, there was a much higher incidence of development of
schizophrenia in the children. Now all of these kids had more or less
shared the same fate as far as "nurture" is concerned; they were all
adopted. So doesn't that suggest very strongly the existence of some
genetically transmitted vulnerability?*

LAING: I haven't actually read that study, and so I can't really comment
on it; not without going over the research. But if that is being put up as
evidence of some "genetic predisposition" to mental illness then that is,
in my mind, a lemon.

SCARF: *Why a lemon?*

LAING: Because I haven't ascertained what sort of transmission of
nonverbal information could have happened between the foster parents
and the agencies through which the supposedly vulnerable children were
being adopted.

SCARF: *A number of psychiatrists, however, looking to these genetic
studies, have come to believe that schizophrenia may very well be a
stress disease in which the target organ is the brain. That is, just as one
individual develops peptic ulcer when exposed to too much strain—
because his vulnerable organ is his intestine—and another develops
hypertension because in that case his vascular system is his bodily "weak
link," so schizophrenia may represent a disturbance of brain function
resulting from too much environmental stress. In this case since the
brain is the organ of thinking, the "symptoms" would be impairment of
thought processes rather than high blood pressure or something like
that. Does this model make sense to you?*

LAING: Let me say this: In this country it's not uncommon to see—say,
in a taxi—a sign put up by the driver which says: "No Smoking, Driver
Allergic." Now allergy doesn't mean, in most people's minds, some
genetically, constitutionally disposed weakness whereby one is unable
to respond adaptively to an ordinary, good-enough environment. But
allergy can be taken to be the persistence in some people of a vital,
healthy response to an anti-biological environment which surrounds
one with noxious stimuli.

So some people continue to sneeze when their nasal membranes
encounter an irritant. Many others have stopped sneezing: Their skin,

their eyes, and so on, don't react allergically either to a stimulus that irritates that part of the body. Now the responses, the behaviors and experiences which tend to get called schizophrenic can be looked upon in different ways. One could say perhaps that some people are in a disorientated environment; and perhaps that environment presents multiple signals and messages that are contradictory and paradoxical and cannot be put together at the same time and coexist together.

All right, if that's the nature of the input, then there may be a genetic predisposition—a genetically programed capacity—which some individuals have for tolerating lies and deception and hypocrisy. Whereas other people who are in the same situation might find themselves "allergic" to a low quotient of truth in communication. (So if you want to think of it in terms of, say, a vitamin deficiency, then some people are mysteriously able to tolerate a greater amount of vitamin deficiency without developing any syndrome of it, such as scurvy. But I wouldn't regard someone who develops scurvy as suffering from anything the matter with him in himself.)

It doesn't matter; it doesn't matter a damn anyway, from a therapeutic point of view. Because the obvious thing to do, whether or not, say, diabetes has a genetic, constitutional component, etc., is to give that person who has it insulin. . . .

The whole point here is this: If you want to treat a person for T.B. you don't put him into an environment loaded with tuberculous bacilli. And if you want to treat people for a certain fragility in being able to tolerate confusion, mystification, lies, then you don't put them into mental hospitals—which present in themselves a disorientating, deadening, anti-biological and highly paradoxical kind of environment. Putting such people into mental hospitals is like putting someone with a heart condition into maximally stressful situations, so that that individual will decompensate.

We'll all decompensate if put under sufficient stress. And if some people find the type of stress which we all find difficult to tolerate— which is suffocating, dulling, draining of our energy and vitality—too much for them, more than they can take; and if they really curl up and put their face to the wall, or start to scream, or tear their hair out, or cut off communication . . . why I don't blame them for that. I don't feel there's necessarily anything wrong with their innate genetic constitution if they find things to be more than they can bear. I'm mainly surprised that more people don't find it so; at how many people manage to stick it out somehow.

SCARF: *I'd like now to change the subject slightly. There are, as you know, a great many different theories concerning the etiology of schizophrenia. One intriguing notion, suggested by Sarnoff Mednick, one of the researchers involved in the studies of the "vulnerable" children of mental patients, goes like this: Certain individuals may be born with abnormally functioning central nervous systems, so that they're in a state of continual bodily arousal—the kind of arousal normally present only in situations of great stress or danger. They're predisposed toward experiencing a great deal of anxiety. And it may be that a child who is continually in this state gets an erratic thought in his mind, and this thought stops the flow of his anxiety-laden thought processes and has a more-or-less tranquilizing effect upon him. He may then begin "using" erratic thoughts, may "condition" himself to their use, because these thoughts calm the overactivity, soothe his tension.*

LAING: That's pretty well what everyone does.

SCARF: *No, not really. I mean . . . let's make up an example. Suppose that I, sitting here, got it into my head that you didn't like me. That thought might be anxiety-arousing, but I could compensate for it by thinking: "My husband likes me," or "My children like me," or "I have friends who like me." These thoughts would offer solace, but they wouldn't be erratic or unrealistic in the sense that I'm not saying: "The trees like me," or "The birds like me."*

LAING: But there are things that have been quoted to me—about the Russians having established that there actually is some rapport between human beings and plants, trees, flowers, and so on.

SCARF: *No, you're taking literally what I meant figuratively.*

LAING: I mean it literally. You see, if someone said to me that the trees liked him, I might feel it possible that he—having been pushed out of human society by a combination of his own thoughts and of other people's—had come to a position where no one he knew actually liked him. Now if anyone did say that the trees liked him, people would of course back away and say, "Oh, that's a symptom of paranoia." But it's perfectly true, in many cases, that there are persons of whom one could say—and it's a terrifying thought—that no one likes them in particular.

And in that event it doesn't have to be the trees that like him; its often a dog or cat or some animal. But I mean it's regarded as a typical schizophrenic behavior when someone withdraws from human company, "seeks companionship with pets and animals and even plants and flowers," and all that. But people who treat that sort of thing in a superior kind of way, who pooh pooh it, who have a defensive reaction against it and treat it as illusory, may just not know about what those people who have gotten into the world of plants and flowers have really found there for themselves. I mean in reality, not as a delusion.

My interviews with Laing, which took place over the course of a couple of successive mornings, were tape-recorded in my own home. Laing and I sat in a brilliantly sunny (it happened to be extraordinary fall weather) little room which opens out from one end of our living room. Since on both occasions we got started rather early in the morning, I kept a pot of coffee plugged in all of the time. I also brought in a tray with a plate of toast and a basket of fruit on it; we kept this nearby. Our conversations ran for a little over three hours each time. When they were over, I drove Laing to his next appointment.

At the end of our second, and final, long talk a curious thing happened on the way to the back door. We were, as a matter of fact, just going past the kitchen—on our way towards the car—when Laing hesitated and asked somewhat shyly whether I had any extra fruit that he might take back to his room. He was, he explained, staying in the guest suite of one of the Yale colleges, and he sometimes got awfully hungry during the night. "There's nothing around to eat at all," he said. "It'd be awfully nice to have some fruit there."

I told him—naturally—that I'd be happy to give him some apples and oranges, or whatever he'd like to take back with him: I felt a little embarrassed myself, however, afraid that I'd try to load him down with too much. So I invited him to come to the refrigerator himself, and then I pulled out the groaningly heavy (luckily!) fruit drawer, inviting him to choose whatever he pleased. To my astonishment, instead of selecting a few pieces of the fruit, he reached in and scooped out a great armful—so much that he simply couldn't hold it all; it began slipping out of his hands and went bouncing and rolling all over the kitchen floor! Trying hard to prevent myself from laughing, I merely smiled and inquired ironically: "Would you like to have a paper bag to put all those apples and oranges *into* . . .?"

I expected him to smile too, I suppose. That scene, with the fruit rolling all about, was so completely preposterous. But to my surprise, he took the offer quite seriously: "Why yes," he replied promptly, "that would be nice."

And so I went to the broom closet and took a big brown paper bag from a storage shelf, and gave it to R.D. Laing. He, without further ado, filled the sack with most of the contents of our family fruit drawer. Then, thanking me kindly, he held the kitchen door open while I went through; the two of us walked down to the car. (Later, I recounted this story to a local psychoanalyst—and friend—and asked him what it meant. "It probably meant," replied the analyst, "that Laing was feeling depleted." Which may be, for all I know, the truth of the matter.)

Part 3

In the "Therapeutic Community" the Patients Are Doctors

I t is a mild spring morning, and the patients' day room is warm with sunshine. Several of the tall windows are open, and their light plaid curtains stir in the breeze. From outside there comes the muffled noise of traffic, and the distant clatter of a pneumatic drill. Here, in chairs arranged in a large oval, the entire patient population and the staff—including psychiatrists, residents, nurses, social workers, psychologists—of "Tompkins 1" are gathered.

Tompkins 1, called T-1, is a small (30-bed) unit for the short-term treatment of acute psychiatric disturbance. It is located on the ground floor of the Yale-New Haven Hospital, a general hospital serving the city of New Haven, and affiliated with the Yale Medical School. Today's meeting, one of three weekly gatherings of the ward's patient-staff community, is being led by T-1's director, Dr. Gary Tucker.

Tucker, thirty-four, rangy and brown-haired, slouches down relaxedly in his chair, one knee crossed over the other. He has just reopened the case of Susan, a seventeen-year-old girl who had been admitted to T-1 just prior to the weekend. Susan, diagnosed as pre-schizophrenic with thought disorder and possible hallucinations, attempted to walk off the unlocked ward on Saturday. Although a community meeting was called immediately after this incident to give the other patients a chance to express their own panic and concern, a sense of uneasiness has persisted. Now Susan sits rigidly in her chair, staring straight ahead.

Dr. Tucker: "I wonder what people in the community are thinking about Susan."

Adolescent male patient: "I had her on patient special. She's very hard to special." ("Specialing," means accompanying a patient constantly during a designated time period.)

Older male patient: "I think Susan's having a hard time trying to come to grips with the facts. Her illness."

Young female patient: "I think she seems slightly better this morning. Her eyes are open more of the time."

Same older male patient: "She seems to have a phenomenal need for sleep."

181

Middle-aged female patient: "I specialed her this morning. I asked her was she sleeping, and she said no. So I asked her: 'Are you thinking?' and she said yes. So I asked what about. But she just shut her eyes again, and acted like she'd gone to sleep."

Dr. Tucker: "Susan sounds a bit crazy and bizarre. Maybe that's her way to keep people off."

Same middle-aged female patient: "Maybe that's the way she protects herself from personal questions."

A male patient in his early thirties sits forward on his seat, looks around at the rest of the group tensely. "Look, I'm not sure what you mean by the word 'crazy.' I'm not sure what that word means."

Staff psychologist: "You don't know what crazy is? Well, just look at Susan for about five minutes. That's 'crazy.'"

There is a pause, then everyone bursts out laughing.

Same patient (angrily): "Do you think that's right, to call someone crazy?"

Young male patient: "Susan gets especially bizarre when she really wants someone to give her agitation medication."

Susan (looking at him): "What do you mean, bizarre?"

Male patient: "Well, the way you walk. The way you sit. You're so stiff. And even when you talk, it sounds flat, like a paid political announcement."

Dr. Tucker: "Apparently Susan isn't aware all the time when she's acting bizarre. She should have some feedback from the community."

Young female patient: "She came up and asked me yesterday if I thought she could be a nurse's aide."

Dr. Tucker: "Susan needs some reassurance. She needs to find out from the rest of us what is bizarre and what isn't." He reaches for a pipe in his jacket pocket, begins packing the bowl, glancing at the same time over the mimeographed list which sits on his lap. The room is filled with rustling noises: everyone is scanning his own copy of this paper. At its head, eight names are listed. Then, directly below:

PATIENT ADVISORY BOARD
May 13, 1969

1. Frank M. requests a Work Pass, May 15, from 9 A.M. until 3 P.M. Vote: 8 yes 0 no

2. Ann J. requests that she be placed on Independent Status. Vote: 7 yes 1 no

3. John R. requests that he be placed on ten-minute checks.
Vote: 0 yes 8 no.

(There are over twenty items all together.)

One of the young residents in psychiatry raises his hand: "On item 3, I notice that John wanted to be moved up from patient special to ten-minute checks. And that the Patient Advisory Board denied it unanimously."

Patient: "We don't trust John yet. When he came in here he kept saying he was a saint, and he was going to be martyred. Yesterday he started jumping around, telling the nurses he was turning into a grasshopper."

Everyone turns to look at John, a tall, cadaverous adolescent with blond, almost shoulder-length hair. He sits, a hand on each knee, staring downward. "I know I'm not a grasshopper. I know I'm not a saint. . . ."

Tucker (with a smile): "Good, we've had three already this year."

Young female patient: "John says he's physically ill. He says the medication he gets is making him sicker."

Tucker (looking around): "Who knows why John is here?"

Young female patient (with a laugh): "He's crazy!"

Susan (speaking up suddenly): "You mean you just look at him five minutes and you know it?"

Every face turns toward her in surprise; she smiles a droll smile; in a moment, everybody is rocking on his seat with laughter. Then Dr. Tucker turns back to the boy. "Perhaps, John, you could tell the community why you are here."

John (his voice low): "I was out of touch with reality. I took a mind drug. I was having trouble with my parents."

Tucker: "Well, I think we're all still quite concerned about you; and that the community is probably right in wanting to hold you back on patient special for awhile." He pauses, looks down at the list on his lap, then up again with a smile. "Anyhow, if you do turn into a grasshopper, we want to make sure someone is with you. . . . The rest of us wouldn't like missing it." John glances up at him, concedes the joke with a shrug and a self-mocking grin. Then this group therapy-*cum*-town meeting continues.

A pretty social worker raises her hand to ask how the community feels about items 6 and 7, two extended passes away from the hospital granted to Ezra, a male patient in his late forties. A theoretical physicist, he was hospitalized six weeks ago during a severe depression. "Yes, I wonder if there was much discussion about those passes," asks Tucker, looking around. "And I'm wondering also what people think about Ezra's imminent discharge. Do you think he's being pushed out too soon, and that he's not really ready yet? We all know the problems he has with his wife. Is the community comfortable about his going, or do some of you think we're throwing him right back into the lion's den?"

Hand after hand goes up, as fellow patients and staff members contribute bits of information about Ezra—conversations they have had with him; what his recent moods and attitudes have been; how he has behaved during visits with his family; comments he has made during individual or group therapeutic sessions; how willing he has been to approach others in the community, and how often he has been isolating himself. There is nothing about Ezra's problems, his illness, his life situation, which is not known to the full patient-staff body, and which cannot be discussed openly in his presence. On Tompkins 1, there are no secrets.

"Open communication and complete frankness are the 'party line' of this ward," explains Dr. Tucker. "In this sense you might say that each patient's business is everyone's business, which is just a harsher way of saying 'everyone's concern.' The whole therapeutic-community idea is predicated on the notion that everyone is involved; that it's not just a group of doctors treating a group of patients, but also patients who are treating one another. It is the social organization itself, and the intense interaction that it promotes, which is supposed to do the healing—the community is 'the doctor.'"

The concept of the therapeutic or curative community was pioneered and developed, for the main part, in English psychiatric hospitals, shortly after World War II. It may be described as an arrangement in which all of a patient's time in the hospital—not just the time he spends in therapy—is thought of as treatment. The milieu in which he finds himself, *i.e.,* the hospital, is seen as exerting a powerful influence upon his emotional life and behavior. Every contact, every casual conversation with a fellow patient, a nurse, even a kitchen helper, is regarded as potentially therapeutic. "Milieu therapy," as this approach is called, is an attempt to take into account what psychiatrists have called "the other twenty-three hours in the day"—to treat mental illness through a careful structuring of the social environment.

"What we see in the majority of our patients," says Tucker, "is that a period of great withdrawal has usually taken place just before hospitalization. They've become isolated from their families, their social setting; the very fact of needing hospitalization illustrates quite clearly that the person can't function any longer in his ordinary environment. His communications with those around him, if they exist, are distorted. And the dramatic symptoms we see on admission—delusions, hallucinations, excitement—are often being used by the patient to distance himself from terribly real, terribly painful problems."

One of the major efforts of the ward, therefore, is toward boldly forthright communication. A new arrival at T-1 may be startled at first by other patients coming up, asking, "Why were you brought here?" and then launching into explanations of their own illnesses, their situations, and their current problems.

But the new patient quickly learns that such behavior is not only accepted, but expected on the ward. Withholding information, maintaining privacy: these are viewed as antitherapeutic, both for the patient and the community as a whole. Secrets, be they between patients, or between a staff member and a patient, are not tolerated; this even includes information which a patient may offer his therapist during individual treatment.

"Of course, we on the outside tell half-truths sometimes, don't go into details," explains Tucker. "We can tolerate ripples under the surface. But by the time a breakdown has occurred, the person is in need of a climate where communication is straightforward, simple and understandable. He needs to be able to say out loud the things that preoccupy him privately, to talk to others honestly and know that the responses he is getting are honest. For whatever bizarre actions or thought may have preceded his hospitalization, they've doubtless been confusing to those people who are close to him. And they, we often find, have begun responding in ways that are equally bizarre and irrational."

New patients on Tompkins 1, after initial evaluation, are generally placed on some form of medication—either a tranquilizer, such as Prolixin, or an antidepressant, or one of several experimental drugs now being tested on the ward. Drug therapy is widely used: approximately 80 percent of the patients are treated with some type of psychopharmacological agent. "We usually start out with fairly low dosages and then increase according to need," explains Tucker. "Our guide is sleep; how much the patient needs in order to sleep." Occasionally, however, a new patient is placed on high dosages immediately. "It depends," Tucker admits, "on how scared we are."

A patient admitted to a mental hospital in the acute phase of disturbance, displaying such symptoms as hallucinations, excitement, delusions, is in such turmoil as to make him doubt the very existence of reality as he has previously conceived it. The experience of seeing or hearing things others do not see or hear, or of losing control, of being unable to think and communicate with others in an understandable way, has shattered his image of himself as someone capable of functioning within a normal society. The purpose of drug therapy is to reduce his discomfort during this intense stage of illness. "What people don't realize is how appallingly uncomfortable psychotic patients are," maintains Tucker. "There seems to be a popular idea that, once someone has gone around the bend, the rest is just picking up daisies. He's happy, you know, no responsibility, no cares. Actually that's not true; most psychotic patients are intensely unhappy and unhealthy."

During the first few weeks after arrival, as the patient's turmoil is lessening, the powerful social pressures of the ward begin to draw him in. Opposition to his symptoms or "craziness" is manifest, from the beginning. Although it is understood, he is told, that he may have crazy thoughts or ideas, he is not expected to act upon them. They are under his control: there are "appropriate" and "inappropriate" ways to handle them.

"'Appropriate' is a big word around here," says Julie Adams, a handsome blonde in her mid-thirties, who is the ward's recreational therapist. "There is a lot of push toward suppressing and controlling symptoms, toward knowing when and to whom one may talk about them; in other words, when is it socially appropriate? . . . For instance, suppose you have a paranoid patient sitting in a room and suddenly he gets the idea that everyone is laughing at him, making fun of him. The thing he must learn is that he needn't go up and start a fight about it; that it can be handled in a more acceptable way if he gets someone who will understand, a staff member or even another patient, and talks these thoughts out . . . and this is something the patients do seem able to learn. People—even very sick people—respond amazingly to others' expectations of them."

Mrs. Adams, who has worked on Tompkins 1 for the past four years, had "no special training for the job. I'm not a regular occupational therapist. We don't stuff bunnies or make ashtrays; in fact, the patients are not encouraged to isolate themselves with 'things.' The main emphasis here is on the interactions—and they're quite intense—between members of the community, on taking responsibility, first for yourself, then for others. That is, getting on what we call 'the ladder,' and then moving up.

The T-1 ladder is a graduated series of social exercises which, because they are incorporated into the very structure of the system, force each individual patient into intense contact and extensive negotiation with the rest of the group. Such interaction—often painful for the ward newcomer—is, like the exercise of a wounded limb, oriented not only toward the work of repair but toward preserving those functions which remain unaffected. Each patient, at the time of admission, is assigned some position on the ladder. "It doesn't take very long for them to understand this," remarks Julie Adams, "or to begin feeling the pressure to move upward."

At the lowest rung of the ladder are those patients who might possibly harm themselves, or who might lose control and injure someone else. They are on "staff special"; each such patient is accompanied by a nurse at all times. When discomfort and symptomology have lessened, however, the patient on "staff special" may prefer being accompanied by other patients, rather than by nurses. In order to gain this privilege, he must take his first step upward and achieve the next level, "patient special."

Movement upward is determined by the powerful Patient Advisory Board, a group of eight elected patients who, according to the ward's written constitution, "manifest an awareness of responsibility." This board meets five times a week with the entire patient group to consider applications for changes in status, pass requests, for going out of the hospital, and disciplinary action for rule infractions.

Patients' requests are formally submitted to the Advisory Board in writing. Each item is read aloud by the board chairman before the assembled group; the petitioner is then expected to explain his request. If, for example, the patient had been hospitalized following a suicide attempt and were now requesting a move from staff special to patient special, he would have to persuade the rest of the group that he could handle the added measure of freedom. After the patient himself has spoken, discussion is thrown open to all patients present.

Finally, a vote of the eight-man board is taken by open show of hands.

The move from staff special up to patient special is a first, very small step toward independence. The next level for which a patient may apply is one at which he is "checked" at ten-minute intervals throughout the day. Beyond that, once his ability to assume responsibility for self-control is established, the patient may request "independent status." This is the mid-point of the ladder: at this point, the person is considered to require no special help whatsoever.

Nevertheless, patients are encouraged to move onward from independent status as soon as possible. "It's a level at which they're neither putting in nor taking out anything from the community," explains Mrs. Adams.

Once above independent status, the patient begins to take on responsibility for other, sicker patients. He may do this by volunteering for such duties as patient special, or by becoming a "checker" for those on ten-minute check status. Or, he may become a ward monitor. This job, which rotates daily, is shared by two patients; it consists of overseeing patient activity in the community. Monitors are responsible for making sure that all specialers and checkers are performing their tasks, and that no inappropriate behavior is taking place. They also act as semiofficial assistants to the nurses, helping with morning blood pressures, etc. A monitor's day is arduous and involves handling a variety of complex situations; only a fairly well integrated patient can manage it.

Movement up the ladder has been geared thus far to assuming responsibility for the self, and after that, responsibility for others. At the top of this simple status hierarchy is the "buddy system" and the final responsibility—that of freedom. A patient admitted to the buddy system may, for the first time, be permitted to leave the ward. Initially, he will go out only in the company of similarly privileged "buddies"; and responsibility for one another will be shared and explicit. Once his ability to function outside the hospital has been demonstrated, however, the patient may apply for pleasure passes to visit home or friends, and/or work, school or outside-therapy passes.

Each of these pass requests, like movements upward along the status ladder, must be submitted for full discussion by the patient community and voted upon by the Advisory Board. In this way, responsibility for decisions involving each individual member is assumed by the group as a whole. "The patients here have real power," observes Mrs. Adams, who sits in on board meetings as liaison between patients and staff.

Although the staff retains the right to veto "unreasonable" Advisory Board decisions, this prerogative is exercised with surprising infrequency.

Traditionally, since the great reforms in the care of the insane instituted during the late eighteenth century, the model of a mental hospital has been that one embodied in the Greek word *asylum*—an inviolable refuge. Situated, customarily, outside of city or community, the institution offered the suffering patient protection from the stress of daily social activity, and distance from whatever family pathology might be contributing to his illness. Within such hospitals no demands were or are placed upon the ill person; and he is not expected to make decisions, exercise judgment or function in any responsible way.

That such treatment might possibly have harmful effects has recently come to be recognized. While it would seem just and moral to remove a sick person from stress and responsibility, the prolonged helplessness and dependence caused by this type of hospitalization may actually prevent his return to ordinary life. Those social skills which he formerly had, and which may have remained intact during the period of acute illness, have often fallen into disuse: he no longer feels competent to face the demands of the outside world. At the same time, ties to family and friends have been seriously disrupted. Separated by physical distance from his former community, the patients may suspect that his place in it no longer exists, and concomitantly, he may be uncertain that he can function well enough to fulfill it if it does. The person who becomes "cured" in the hospital setting and then collapses on the front steps is a familiar one to most psychiatrists.

A unit such as Tompkins 1, within a general hosptial, which is in turn in the midst of a busy community, is well situated for resisting the process of gradual estrangement which many psychiatric patients experience. As Dr. Thomas Detre, the ward's first director and its "founding father," pointed out in an article, published in 1963, "in order to counter effectively the isolation to which . . . [patients] . . . are liable, our open doors should be doors that swing both ways. Families, friends and employers must be encouraged to visit the patients, maintain the patients' community contacts. A breakdown in interpersonal relationships cannot be mended by separating the patient from the community to which he must return."

While it may be true, concedes Detre in the same article, that family members are often as disturbed as the patients themselves, ". . . we fail . . . if we do no more than blame them for patients' illnesses. If we consider relatives as participants in a disturbed transaction, they must become part of the over-all treatment program." The much-increased knowledge of family dynamics, he adds, can help both patient and family to decode each other's distortions, while new drugs and drug therapies "afford the patient sufficient comfort to tolerate this decoding process."

Detre, presently director of psychiatric services at Yale-New Haven Hospital, views the need for inpatient care not only as the culmination of an intrapsychic process, but in its broader and more sociological sense, as dramatic demonstration that a certain individual can no longer exist within a certain setting. "As most administrators are aware, the majority of mental patients land in a hospital because they are annoying or frightening those around them," says Detre. For this reason, the T-1 approach has been to focus not only upon the illness itself, but upon the social context in which it occurred—the patient's most intimate environment, his family.

There is in many mental hospitals a prevalent belief that patients' conditions deteriorate after visits with their families; frequently, it is recommended that relatives should be politely but firmly kept away during the first four weeks of hospitalization. T-1's position is the opposite: From the moment of admission, it is made clear to the patient's family that they are expected to play an important role in his treatment. In the early weeks of hospitalization, the patient's close relatives are seen by a ward social worker on a regular basis. These interviews, taking place once or twice weekly (or daily, if the family is very shaky), help family members to clarify their own feelings about the patient's hospitalization. They also serve to give the staff some insight into how the family functions; and what understanding they may have of the series of events which finally necessitated inpatient treatment.

At the same time, the patient is seeing his therapist in small-group therapy (in individual therapy also, if this seems indicated; most often it does not, for the ward view is that some patients use it to "isolate" themselves). And both patient and family get together regularly, not only during visiting hours, but at large patient-family gatherings, so-called "family meetings."

Family meetings take place twice weekly throughout the entire period of hospitalization. Led by a staff or resident psychiatrist, they are attended by patients, families, social workers, and generally a number of recently discharged patients, accompanied by their close relatives. Because the patient spectrum includes people in so many different phases of treatment, family meetings actually serve a variety of purposes. For the new family, the group is useful in providing orientation, in helping to draw them out and counter their feelings of isolation, and in offering reassurance that the acute phase of illness does subside. For families where the patient is further along in treatment, the group ideally serves as a sort of verbal reflector, pointing out to both family and patient the ways in which they interact, and what games they play. And finally, for the just-discharged patient making the difficult transition from hospital back to the community, the family meeting provides a safe place to return to, a place where the problems are known, and where one can talk out the early difficulties of readjustment. "Although the idea of these meetings often frightens relatives at first, they soon find them helpful," says Dr. Detre. "In fact, we've had cases where family members keep on coming back long after the patient himself has ceased attending."

Most patients, after two or three weeks on the ward, have almost or completely suppressed symptomology; it is difficult to surmise what they might have been hospitalized for. (Indeed, visitors on T-1 are often under the impression that the ward only admits mildly ill people.) Once his symptoms are under control, and the patient seems generally able to communicate in a less agitated manner, meetings called "four-ways"— the "ways" being patient, family, psychiatrist and social worker—begin to take place.

The purpose of these meetings is to sort out the issues and difficulties associated with the onset of illness, to try to work out some of these difficulties and, if possible, to modify the way patient and family interact in attempting to handle them. "Of course, in the eight or ten weeks that a patient is hospitalized, we can't effect a major change in his family structure," allows Dr. Detre. "Nevertheless, the attempt is to return him to a somewhat more flexible environment, where at least some understanding of the problems has been gained."

Dr. Detre was director of Tomkins 1 from the time of its establishment in 1960 until June of 1968. (As the hospital's psychiatrist-in-chief, he still has the unit under his administrative charge.) In his early forties, of medium height, Detre is a man of immense personal force. A sociological study of the ward, carried out in 1961, described him as a "charismatic leader."

". . . And I've been called a number of other things," remarks Detre, with a perennial amused half-smile. "During the infant days of this ward, there was a great deal of criticism of our methods and our setup," he explains. "To many people, the mere idea of treating acute psychotics on a short-term basis, and in an open unit, seemed slightly preposterous. Then, there was opposition to the use of drugs—the drugs themselves were fairly new; the major tranquilizers had only come into use in 1954. Many psychiatrists, both in New Haven and at Yale, disliked them; they felt the drugs were a way of dealing with symptoms, and yet ignoring the long-term problems that existed."

Early objections to T-1 centered not only on drug usage, but on the demanding, pushy, behavior-oriented techniques of milieu therapy. Professionals in the area, more sympathetic to the goals of long-term intensive psychotherapy, disliked the intense social pressure brought upon patients in order to manipulate behavior and force them to suppress symptomology. Compelling someone to behave as if he were well, they argued, did not make him well in fact; and there was some feeling that the new ward was, in effect, putting Band-Aids on deep wounds.

"Actually," points out Dr. Detre, fishing for a cigarette, "my own bias is that the hospital is not the place for dealing, at a fantastic cost, with the patient's long-term problems; I mean with the life history of his pathology. The only purpose of hospitalization, as I see it, is to end hospitalization, to restore the *status quo ante,* so to speak, the patient's level of functioning before the acute flare-up, so that it becomes possible for him at least to survive, to manage outside the hospital. And then to explore the long-term difficulties on an outpatient basis." For this reason, follow-up care is considered an integral part of the treatment scheme. Such care is arranged for every patient discharged from the patient service.

Today, almost ten years after its establishment, Tompkins 1 wears a slightly more respectable, less radically experimental air. Drugs are, in general, no longer considered quite as objectionable: modified drug usage is practiced in many mental hospitals, as are a number of varying adaptations of the therapeutic-community approach. "Of course, we were by no means the first hospital to implement the methods of the therapeutic milieu," Dr. Detre says. "But ours was the earliest attempt to apply these methods to short-term treatment of acutely ill psychotic patients."

Unique in this country initially, T-1 is no longer the only unit of its kind in operation: hospitals such as Langley Porter in San Francisco, the Washington Psychiatric Institute, Fort Logan in Denver, Colorado, have organized programs that are quite similar in orientation. Of the new hospital services opened during the past five years, a major proportion, according to Dr. Detre, "have been constructed along a model quite comparable to ours. I think this is part of a general shift which is taking place, a shift toward viewing the patient not only as an individual, but also as a part of a social system, a member of the society in which he lives."

Studies of Tompkins 1, and of its treatment methods, have been carried out with great frequency. Because the unit is a teaching and research ward affiliated with Yale Medical School, every aspect of its program is still subjected to constant scrutiny and re-evaluation. Aside from informal studies, there have been over fifty published investigations of the ward; these have included research on such questions as the relationship between sleep disorders and symptoms; how disputes among staff members affect the patient community, and even a paper on the tablemate choices of psychiatric patients as a guide for measuring social contacts.

During the past four years, Kenneth Keniston, associate professor of psychology at Yale and author of *The Young Radicals*, and two young psychiatrists, Richard Almond and Sandra Boltax, have been engaged in a long investigation of the ward's social culture. Specifically, their questions have centered about the interesting notion that therapy on T-1 might be a process comparable to thought-reform or "brainwashing." Noting the application of intense social pressures to bring about changes in attitude and belief (so that "openness" becomes a more important value than that of maintaining confidentiality or privacy; "taking responsibility for others" becomes more highly prized than not interfering, etc.), Keniston and his associates devised a series of questionnaire studies that would attempt a measure of patients' values and beliefs at the time of admission, one week later, one month, at discharge, and then fifteen months later.

At the end of one week on the ward, the researchers found, patients' values had already begun altering in the direction of the dominant ward culture. Agreement with such written statements as "each patient's

major problems should be known to the staff and other patients" had
grown considerably, while statements such as "patients shouldn't have
to tell each other how they came to be on the ward" were increasingly
rejected. This first week's swing toward the community value system
was, for many patients, accompanied by the enormous discovery that
with drugs, and the support of the milieu, it was possible to bring a good
deal of bizarre behavior under control.

"We found that this trend, increasing acceptance of the ward's
values—which revolve mainly around the themes of openness, taking
responsibility, sharing problems and belief in the community—
continued throughout the period of hospitalization," reports Keniston,
whose questionnaire methods were supplemented by patient interviews
and observations of the unit. "And this acculturation seemed to reach its
peak, quite consistently, right around the time of discharge."

Fifteen months later, however, in a follow-up study of the same
group, it was found that patients' attitudes had undergone changes in
the reverse direction; they were now actually fairly similar to what they
had been before admission. Thus, although some selective
"brainwashing" or value change did seem to be taking place measurably
during the course of therapy, it was, in Keniston's words, "relatively
specific to the ward and the life within the therapeutic community."

Of the fifty-nine patients contacted during the Keniston-Almond-
Boltax follow-up study, none were in the hospital. (Neither were four
other patients included in the original study, who had moved out of the
area in the year-and-a-half interim.) "As a group," says Keniston, "we
found them doing awfully well; they do feel improved. Out of the fifty-
nine people interviewed, forty-nine were working full-time, seven
weren't working, three were working part-time.

"Of course, T-1 tends to be a middle-class ward, which means in plain
words that patients are likely to have a better stake in the outside
community—better living conditions to return to, careers, schools. But
still, when I look at some of these diagnoses, and at how short the period
of hospitalization was, and then think what a really major accomplishment it was twenty years ago, just getting someone discharged from a
mental hospital at all . . . Well"—he smiles, gives a little shrug—"I'm
impressed."

                                                                1969

Behavior Modification

And now," Dr. Davison was saying, his voice low and somewhat hypnotic. "I'd like you to tense your left hand. Study that tension; study the way it feels . . . And now— relax it. Let your whole hand go limp." I was stretched out, eyes closed, on the marble floor of his office; I let my hand drop to my side. "Feel the difference between the way it felt when you were tensing it," his voice continued in its singsong rhythm, "and the way it feels now. And now, relax those muscles even further. Further and further . . . relaxing all the while . . . relaxed."

I had not thought that these deep-muscle relaxation exercises could possibly have any effect upon me. I was too taut. It had just begun raining very hard, and I was concerned about my return flight across Long Island Sound later on this evening; it was liable to be canceled. If that happened, what was to have been a ten-minute air journey across the water would develop into a six-hour train trip: First, I would have to travel west from Long Island into New York City, and then turn around and go east from Manhattan toward my home in New Haven, Connecticut. I couldn't possibly get into Penn Station until close to midnight. Would I be able to make some reasonable connection to New Haven? When did the trains stop running regularly? I had out-of-town guests arriving for lunch the following day; and if I got in at three or four in the morning, there wouldn't be much chance of sleeping late. I would have to get up and shop for the groceries . . . "And now," Dr. Davison said, "place both hands by your sides, the bottoms of your palms on the floor, and then raise your fingers toward the ceiling and tip them back in the direction of your head. Now, bending those hands backwards at the wrists . . . feel the tension in your forearms. Study those muscles; study the way they feel. And now: Relax." I let my hands flop down by my sides once again.

A floating sensation was beginning to steal over me. I felt a funny tingling in my fingertips. (Later, Davison was to mention to me that many of his patients experienced those tingling feelings; and that the

195

floating sense of bodily "letting go" made some people panicky; they felt that they were losing control.) I became aware that I had started to breathe very deeply, the kind of long, drawn-out breathing that usually precedes sleep.

There was nothing that could be done about the airplane flight anyway. The thought, far from causing an upsurge of fresh anxiety, seemed to traverse the cloudless sky of my consciousness. I was feeling pleasant—at a comfortable distance from myself and my sense of daily pressures and obligations. The psychologist's voice was behind me, coaching me, as I went on alternately clenching and relaxing muscles— in my upper arms, my neck, my forehead, stomach, buttocks, upper legs, calves, toes. We ended this session of relaxation training with my pointing my toes toward the ceiling and then bending them very hard in the direction of my head (as I had pointed my fingers in the hand exercise) and feeling the muscle tension in the lower back of my legs. And then relaxing it . . .

At this point the behavior therapist instructed me to draw in a very deep breath, hold it, and then let go of all my muscles even further, as I expelled the air from my lungs. This deep breathing exercise was repeated several times. Then—again reminding me of a hypnotist— Davison suggested that I relax my muscles further and further, with each count, as he intoned the numbers from one to ten. "One. And relaxing even more. And two. Further and further . . ." I began to notice, as if from afar, that the sides of my mouth were curling upwards in a contented smile. The psychologist's voice, again sounding distant, suggested that I continue to breathe deeply for several moments and, on each exhalation, try to picture the word *calm*. "Try to associate the state which your body is in at this moment," he said, his own voice somewhat drowsy itself, "with the imagining of that word, *calm*." I did so, and a feeling of great peace, touched with slight exaltation, filled my body.

After this demonstration of deep-muscle relaxation technique (which is, says Davison, designed to teach people the difference between bodily states of tension and relaxation: "If you're going to relax yourself, you have to know when you're tense") I felt refreshed and curiously happy. It was as though my churning brain had been bombarded by messages from my muscles—"Hey, we're calm, we're feeling relaxed"—and that had affected me psychologically, inducing a mood of tranquility.

The mood persisted even when, on getting to the Islip airport, I learned that my flight had been delayed for several hours. Davison had mentioned to me, in passing, that while deep-muscle relaxation is generally used by behavior therapists in conjunction with other techniques, it is "like chicken soup. It's good for everyone, and it simply can't hurt you." And so at midnight, when my plane was finally canceled, I went to a nearby motel and played over the tape-recording I had made of those progressive relaxation exercises.

And then I went to sleep.

Behavior modification is a form of psychotherapy which stems directly from experimental research carried out in psychological learning laboratories. The various methods and techniques are based upon what are now well-established principles relating to the ways in which organisms acquire behavioral responses, and the ways in which "unlearning" of such responses occurs as well. The unifying theoretical notion which underlies all behavior-change-directed procedures is that habitually maladaptive responses—"symptoms," or self-destructive, pain-producing behaviors—are responses which at some point in the individual's life have been *learned.*

The neurotic behavior may have been acquired through a process of simple conditioning. This was the type of learning displayed by Pavlov's dogs when they began habitually salivating at the sound of the bell which preceded feeding, just as if the bell were the same thing as the sight and smell of the food itself. In this instance, the person's problems may have to do with the fact that she or he persistently responds to one stimulus as if it were something else—an example would be responding to a great many authority figures as if they were the same individual as one's punishing father.

The problem behavior may, on the other hand, have been acquired because it was initially rewarding or reinforcing. Perhaps it once served to reduce anxiety. The person might have responded by withdrawing, or eating, in situations that aroused fear; and if one or both of these behaviors reduced fear, they are very liable to recur. Many neurotic responses are acquired because they serve, in the short run, some useful purpose for the organism. If the withdrawal and eating become, over a period of time, pathological withdrawal and/or compulsive overeating, then what is called "neurosis" may be recognized as equivalent to "maladaptive conditioned responses." No matter how the learning may have taken place, however, the behavior therapist's efforts and entire treatment approach are based on the supposition that what has been learned can be unlearned.

Seen from this standpoint, the "cure" of neurosis lies not in helping the person to gain insight into the "why's" and "because's" of what he or she is doing, but in simply helping him to *change* his habitually disturbed modes of behaving and responding so that the way may be cleared for other, more satisfying, and ultimately far more rewarding kinds of learning. Getting better involves, in other words, modifying the things the patient *does*—how he reacts in the presence of what are, for him, particularly "sensitive" stimuli.

The best-known behavior modification procedure is, of course, aversive conditioning. Indeed, aversive therapy is often considered to be synonymous with behavior therapy. It is not. It is merely one kind of behavior-change directed treatment and is usually used in cases where the problem involves the unlearning of a bad or self-destructive habit or a deviant practice: overeating, smoking, homosexuality, transvestism, fetishism, are examples.

Aversive therapy depends upon the carrot-and-stick approach to human behavior—with the emphasis on the stick. It establishes a negatively conditioned emotional response to stimuli connected with the problem behavior, usually, by pairing these stimuli with noxious or painful or disgusting ones. For example, in the case of an alcoholic, the drinking of liquor may be presented in conjunction with the ingestion of a vile, nausea-inducing drug: The rationale is that the alcohol then becomes associated in the drinker's mind with retching and illness rather than with anxiety-relief or euphoria. Similarly, in the case of the compulsive child-molester, photographs of alluring children might be paired with mild electric shocks to the fingertips. The attempt is, once more, to replace aroused, erotic responses to children with responses that are closely assocated with anxiety, displeasure and fear.

Such counterconditioning of unwanted behaviors is sometimes accompanied by the rewarding and reinforcing of more desired responses. Male homosexuals may, for instance, be given shocks when they look at pictures of naked men; and granted relief from the shocks while viewing female figures. But whether or not "rewards" are used, the therapist endeavors to apply the principles of learning, conditioning and deconditioning in order to eliminate disturbed and deviant responses.

Aversion therapy has raised a storm of controversy in psychological and psychiatric circles, and among civil-libertarians as well. Critics decry the use of physical punishments, the emphasis upon treatment of symptoms rather than attention to "underlying causes"—and there is a general uneasiness, some feeling that behavior therapists may be manipulating their human patients as if they were so many laboratory animals. The debates have raised a number of fascinating questions, among them the very cogent problem of how "free" an individual may be when she or he is compelled by inner needs to behave in certain self-destructive and self-punishing ways. As one behavior therapist asked me, in a somewhat puzzled tone, is he to see himself as cold, mechanistic and cruel if he gives the child-molester the option—the purely voluntary option—of attempting to countercondition or "unlearn" those deviant responses to children which lead to constant trouble and repeated imprisonments?

According to psychologist Gerald C. Davison, a professor at the State University of New York, Stony Brook campus, and an expert on behavior modification, the disputes about aversion therapy have totally distorted the public image of what most behavior work is about. "Aversive conditioning—by which I mean some technique involving mild physical punishment—is not an important part of the ordinary behavior therapist's clinical practice. I myself have never used it with a patient. I have, however, sometimes used aversive imagery: For instance, in working with an obese client it can be quite effective if you train the person to imagine herself as nauseated, ill, throwing-up, and so on, each time she reaches for something sweet or fattening."

To the major charge leveled by more traditional, psychoanalytically oriented psychotherapists—that behavior modifiers cure symptoms rather than the underlying neurosis—the behavior therapists reply that the symptom often *is* the neurosis. If you change the ways in which the individual repeatedly responds, then you may expect to effect changes not only in the person himself, those with whom he is interacting, but in the very nature of the problem situation itself. For this reason, the therapist often commences treatment by trying to isolate the difficulty or difficulties in terms of the question: What is the behavior that needs changing? What are the critical distress-producing situations, or people, or objects—and in what ways is he or she responding to them? "If, for example," said Davison, who is in his mid-thirties, has dark curly hair and an intense manner, "someone comes in to me and says that he is very afraid in social situations, can't mingle with other people, and is feeling lonely and depressed, then I would want to concentrate on and pay particular attention to stimuli relating to other people—and the precise ways in which those stimuli elicit responses of fear, avoidance and escape."

The assumption made here is that the patient who comes in for help with this kind of problem has acquired his fear the way an animal in a laboratory acquires a fear-response—that is, through association with painful and punishing events. Just as in the psychological laboratory a rat can be quickly conditioned to fear a tone which is followed by shock, or the white walls and grid floor of a cage in which it has received shock, so it can be inferred that the human being with enormous anxieties relating to other people has *learned*—through early aversive experiences—that "other people" are stimuli which may have very punishing properties. In the case of the experimental animal, it is well known that the fear of the tone or the white walls of the cage will persist for great lengths of time after the shock has been permanently turned off. In the case of the psychiatric client, the anxieties aroused by other people and by social situations in general may have far outlasted the circumstances in which this maladaptive learning first took place. In this situation, a procedure called "systematic desensitization" often proves remarkably effective.

Systematic desensitization is a method that has been very widely used, and with quite striking successes, in the treatment of anxiety-related problems. Indeed, it has proven effective with such diverse complaints as phobias (i.e., irrational, persistent and morbid fears which center upon some harmless situation or object—such as fear of cats, of enclosed places, of being outside on the street, and the like), obsessions and compulsions, fears relating to sexual intimacy, reactive depression (depression which occurs in reaction to some disturbing or traumatic life-event); and psychosomatic disorders, such as ulcers, asthma and hypertension.

The technique involves, at the outset of treatment, defining as narrowly as possible those people, objects and situations which tend to trigger the patient's anxiety. This entails drawing up what is called a *stimulus hierarchy*—a fancy name for something which is simply a graded list of the individual's fears. If, for example, the person suffers from agoraphobia (intense and crippling anxieties relating to being outside on the street, in places crowded with other people, etc.), then the "fear-list" might begin with a relatively unfrightening item such as "going for a walk around the block." This might be followed by a trip to a nearby supermarket, then a short bus ride, then a journey to the other side of town, up to the potentially overwhelming excursion to a busy department store.

At the same time as the list of fears is being carefully worked out, the client is given intensive instruction in deep-muscle relaxation. After that, in much the same way that a mother gradually accustoms her child to play in the ocean surf—by gradually approaching the water, dipping in one of the baby's feet, then the other; wetting the child's hands, and so on—the therapist slowly assists the patient in learning to confront those stimuli which arouse neurotic anxieties and to consciously relax himself in their presence.

The principle that underlies this treatment-approach is that an organism cannot display two behavioral responses—relaxation and fear—to the same stimulus, at the same time. As psychologist Dr. Joseph Wolpe, a pioneer of the behavior modification movement in psychotherapy, has suggested, the learning of a new response to a certain stimulus will inhibit the elicitation of the old response.

Systematic desensitization (the method is sometimes called gradual habituation or toleration) may be carried out in vivo, or "real-life" situations. In the case of the agoraphobic patient, this might involve the therapist's literally accompanying him on a series of outings which are graduated according to lengthiness and stressfulness, while at the same time offering him psychological support and continued coaching in the use of deep-muscle relaxation techniques. Such step-by-step exposure, in the presence of the behavior therapist, enables the patient to face up to those things which tend to evoke irrational anxieties; and to learn to relax himself consciously in their presence. Desensitization is certainly, at times, carried out in this manner.

Often, however, in vivo treatment is infeasible—either because it makes such expensive demands upon the therapist's time or because the anxiety-arousing situations are too diffuse and relate to interpersonal interactions which cannot be "planned out" in advance. An individual with intense and unrealistic anxieties about the way he is performing on his job cannot, for instance, predict the precise moment when his supervisor or a colleague may offer a criticism about the way he is doing something. Therefore, a method called "desensitization in imagination" tends to be used far more frequently than is desensitization in real-life situations.

This treatment, as its name implies, involves the conjuring-up of mental pictures of the feared stimuli. For example, treatment of someone with a straightforward phobia about elevators, tunnels or other enclosed spaces (claustrophobia), would entail the patient's imagining himself in a series of more and more demanding situations— being caught in a jammed elevator, stalled in a subway tunnel, and so on. Then, as in the "real-life" paradigm, he becomes trained, in graduated stages, to calm and relax himself consciously in these very anxiety-evoking situations. Hopefully, the learning done during these "fantasy confrontations" will generalize over into the patient's acutal life experience, and, as a wealth of follow-up data has demonstrated, this generalization does seem to take place very readily.

I questioned Dr. Davison about what made people believe in these imaginational situations to the degree that they were able to equate them, emotionally speaking, with situations in their real lives. "Isn't the client always aware that he's only taking part in a kind of a game—that he's only role-playing, as it were—and not really stuck in an elevator at all?"

Davison smiled in reply. "What makes theater, actually?" he asked. "People can involve themselves deeply in make-believe situations even though they know they are make-believe. And they can become totally aroused by those make-believe situations, not only psychologically but physiologically as well. I mean, you could measure the person's heartbeat, or breathing-rate, or the rate at which adrenalin is being produced, and you would find that, by all objective standards, that individual is truly afraid. I've had, as a matter of fact, patients who become literally frozen with terror, right here in my consulting room, while acting out these purely imaginary situations. And of course I do try, during the session, to make the whole thing as real as possible."

Phobias, because they are fairly specific fears which have become localized around particular kinds of situations or objects, are foremost among the complaints which have proven amenable to treatment by this gradual deconditioning method. Indeed, a number of psychological studies have shown that systematic desensitization is more effective in the treatment of phobias than is any other form of psychotherapy. Dr. Davison told me about one client, for example, who came to him after spending a great number of years in psychoanalysis.

"What this woman had was a simple phobia about birds," he remarked. "But her analyst had interpreted this fear of birds as something related to the repression of her aggressive feelings toward men. The bird was supposed to be a symbolic representation of testicles; and her secret wish was that of squeezing a male's testicles until he screamed in pain." Dr. Davison shrugged. "In addition to this theory's being, in my opinion, the most absurd nonsense, it wasn't proving at all useful in therapy. Because after her bird phobia had been 'revealed' to her as a defensive protection against her acting-out of her hostile feelings toward men, she was still as afraid of birds as ever."

The case was, he observed, a classic one. "I took a standard desensitization tack with her; it went well and she turned out just fine. She lost her fears about birds completely." He laughed. "I know this sounds like a silly kind of phobia, but while I was seeing her, I myself got very sensitized to the presence of birds. There are a lot of them around here on Long Island, especially in the spring. And her fear was so intense that she would have to stop her car in the middle of the highway if a bird flew too close to the windshield; she would become panicky. Some days it was impossible for her to go outside at all, so terrorized was she by the large number of birds."

Other types of phobic difficulties that he has treated, said the psychologist, have ranged from one patient with intense fear of earthworms to a number of patients with inordinate and unmanageable neurotic anxieties about giving dinner parties. The latter type of problem is not uncommon. "Many of my clients have disturbances which relate, in one way or another, to their social functioning. In fact, the most prevalent kinds of anxieties that I (and most other therapists, I believe) tend to see in the consulting room are those which might be called *social evaluative anxieties* or *interpersonal performance anxiety* or just vivid fears relating to real or imagined criticisms. I see a great number of people who are so concerned about what others may think of them that they become crippled, in one way or another, by their anxieties. I see people who can become literally overwhelmed by the mere notion that they might make some tiny mistake or blunder. And people who are so frightened at the idea that someone—anyone—might dislike them, or disapprove of something they are doing, that they live in a state of perpetual anguish. Or they become socially withdrawn, or they do both."

For patients with these somewhat more diffuse, mildly phobic types of social anxieties, treatment may be carried out by means of another important behavioral-modification method, "assertive training." Assertive training is another technique that is based upon the theoretical idea that certain other responses are incompatible with fear-responses. In this instance, however, it is assertive responses rather than muscle-relaxation ones which are used in the counterconditioning of fear.

"If a patient comes to me," explained Dr. Davison, "with a presenting complaint which she terms *frigidity* it often develops that the problem is deeply intertwined with the person's difficulties in asserting herself, in expressing her own feelings and preferences, in telling her sexual partner what it is that she does or doesn't like about the things that are going on between them."

Davison described to me a recent case he had treated, that of a very inhibited young woman who had come in to see him convinced that there was something profoundly wrong with her sexual functioning. "She was, as it happens, an extremely attractive girl—she had no trouble in getting men to approach her. But she was also someone who felt that she had no right to express her own likes or dislikes in any way, shape or form; she was always demure and accommodating. Her trouble in being candid about the ways she wanted things—which was connected to her overwhelming fears of being criticized—extended all the way from decisions about which restaurant she and her boyfriend should eat at, to honesty about kinds of foreplay and the things that were taking place in bed. The consequences of her lack of assertion were the problem that she came in with: She just didn't have orgasms."

Assertive training often proceeds along lines which resemble sessions of dramatic coaching. The patient is literally taught new ways of behaving—new "roles"—during these staged interactions. The method which, for obvious reasons is sometimes called *role-playing* or *behavior rehearsal,* entails the acting-out of stressful situations and problematic interchanges in the client's life. The behavior therapist takes the role of the person or persons who ordinarily evoke anxiety and then attempts to point out to the patient the response options that he realistically has at his disposal. Or the therapist may assume the client's part directly, actively demonstrating to him the ways in which it *could* be played. (The latter method, called *modeling,* is very similar to what mothers do when they encourage their children to copy, and to learn, a new form of behavior through a process of simple imitation.) The patient can then, in the relatively protected atmosphere of the consulting room, practice showing assertive behaviors in situations that are progressively more demanding and anxiety-arousing.

"Again," said Davison, "as in treatment with systematic desensitization, there is made every effort made to create a vivid feeling of immediacy—of being *in* the situation, of having it happen right here and now. For instance, in the case we were just talking about before—the woman who couldn't have orgasms—there was a particular session during which I acted the role of the boyfriend. And I called her on the telephone and asked her whether she'd prefer to go out to a restaurant or to Jake's party that evening. That sounds rather innocuous, doesn't it? I happened to be aware, however—because the behavior therapy was being carried out in conjunction with traditional 'talking' therapy—that she didn't want to go to Jake's party at all. But for her, as the interaction quickly demonstrated, simply making the decision, saying what it was that she wanted, was an absolutely impossible thing to do.

"In that little imaginary exchange," he continued, "I—as her surrogate make-believe partner—did give her her choice. But she immediately said: 'You make up *your* mind.' And so I stopped the whole thing right there and asked her directly how she was going to like finding herself at that party, when previously she had expressed such negative feelings about it."

After that brief interruption, both therapist and patient engaged in a fresh enactment of the same interchange. "This time she was encouraged to try a new response, such as: 'Oh, I might prefer going out to dinner, if that's all right with you,'" Dr. Davison continued. "Once we obtain a new behavior, we can go to work on it, hone it up, sharpen it. I might, for example, encourage her along the lines of sounding less apologetic, of becoming more direct about her own wishes. As a rule, I try to work on successive changes in the style of the person's responding."

Sometimes, noted the psychologist, even in the imaginational situation as it is played out in the therapist's office, the patient becomes too frightened at the idea of making an assertive response; he or she simply cannot get the words out at all. Such responses have been powerfully inhibited in the past, often because the individual has pathological fears about displaying even the minimal amount of aggression required in order to make them. The whole dramatic scenario, as well as the suggestion that he might play an assertive role in it, may put the patient into an anxious panic, or paralyze him with fright. If this occurs, then assertive training is suspended while the patient receives instruction in deep-muscle relaxation. Then, when he reaches the point where he can relax his tensions sufficiently to emit an assertive response in the first place, the training sessions are resumed.

The focus of this treatment-approach is on rewarding the person for showing more forceful, less fearful kinds of behavior. If, for example, the woman who is frigid learns how to make her wishes and preferences clear to her sexual partner—and if both are rewarded by a new pleasure and mutuality in the experience—then it will be easier for her to learn more assertive responses, since they help in getting her needs met and in achieving her goals. For the neurotically timid, anxious, fearful person who has difficulties in communicating the smallest wish or demand, assertive training provides a situation in which it becomes possible— through dramatic rehearsals—to learn how it might sound if one made one's demands known and explicit. It also provides the opportunity for learning that one's world will not break apart if one dares to do so.

The Anatomy of Fear

rivial happenings and ordinary conversations: Early on a Saturday morning the telephone rings. It is my next-door neighbor, her voice panicky: a "suspicious-looking" service man is at the back door, saying he wants to check the meter. "I'm alone in the house," she whispers. We agree that I will call her back in a few minutes to make sure that everything is all right. I do, and she is. That same afternoon, while shopping, I get into a conversation with an elderly saleswoman. Her husband has recently retired and is having trouble figuring out what to do with his time. "There's a lovely big park not far from our home," she says, "but with everything going on these days—you know—he doesn't like taking any chances. So, what can he do? He just sticks to the streets and to the sidewalks." In the evening, at a party, a journalist friend visiting us in New Haven says: "I am more frightened, living on the West Side of New York, than I ever was during my years in Vietnam. There at least you knew where the danger was or where it might be coming from. You could make your own choices about whether to move closer or further away from it. But in Manhattan you have the feeling that anything can happen at any time, day or night, in any part of the city. And these muggers would just as soon kill you as rob you."

Why, I wonder, do we all spend so much more time ruminating about this kind of menace than about other sorts of dangers which we also realistically face? I have never, fortunately, been the victim of any crime, and yet such conversations—which make some kind of victimization seem not only possible but imminent—bring forth from me immediate and intense emotional responses. Why don't I react similarly to the threat of injury or death in an automobile accident?

Some of the answers to these questions may lie in the vast body of psychological literature which has emerged from the experimental study of fear. These studies have raised the suggestion that the degree of fear we feel about a potentially harmful event may be linked primarily, not to the degree of threat (in terms of the probability that it may actually happen to us), nor even to the amount of injury one imagines one might sustain if it did happen, but to the quality of the event or situation itself. Some *types* of external threat evoke far more fear than others. To put it another way, given the possibility that bodily damage might be equal in both cases, most people would find the idea of being injured in a violent encounter far more frightening than the idea of being hurt in a traffic accident.

The two potential sources of danger—violence and automobiles— deserve comparison. Generally speaking, in a given year there are three times as many traffic fatalities as murders; the figures for 1972 cite 18,520 deaths from violence as compared with 56,590 deaths in automobiles. In other words, the murder rate is 8.9 per 100,000 population per year; the automobile fatality rate is 27.2 per 100,000. We are, however, rarely preoccupied by the menace presented to us by the automobile—while fears of random crime touch most of us, affecting a variety of aspects of our thinking and behavior.

The above figures are, of course, calculated on a national base and will be altered when broken down into differential bases. Someone living in what police call a "hot crime" area of a major city is clearly going to have a higher probability of being killed during the commission of a felony offense than is someone who lives in a rural area of Vermont. (The Vermonter has a correspondingly higher chance of dying in a traffic accident.) But if one eliminates from that over-all murder total— 18,520 in 1972—those deaths resulting from spouse killing spouse, parent killing child, other family killings, romantic triangles, lovers' quarrels, etc., one is left with a very low figure: Some five thousand murders linked to the currently widespread fantasy of "being killed by a stranger during the commission of a random crime." This means that for the average citizen there is an infinitesimal 1-in-40,000-per-year probability of becoming involved in a felony resulting in death. Such a figure is roughly commensurate with the number of people who choke to death on food or other objects each year.

The same figure—5,000—is less than one-third the number of people who die each year from some kind of fall (an accident which often takes place in the home). But few people I know, myself included, give a moment's reflection to the possibility of getting hurt slipping in the shower or falling down a flight of stairs. We are, it appears, much more fascinated by the idea of injuries that come to us at the hands of other people.

I am not trying to imply that fears about crime and violence are without any basis. The crime rate has certainly increased during the last decade. According to a recent issue of the Uniform Crime Reports published by the F.B.I., the average person's chances of becoming victimized in a crime have risen 55 percent during the last ten years. Still, according to a recent estimate by the National Center for Health Statistics, close to 24 million injuries—four million of which resulted in either temporary or permanent disabilities (loss of a finger, blindness, paralysis of one or more limbs)—were caused in a single year by accidents in the home. This figure must be contrasted with the number of muggings and robberies where some kind of injury to the victim resulted. The estimate (extremely crude, to be sure, for such crimes are notoriously underreported) is on the order of 100,000 during the same year. Nevertheless, given this kind of disparity, why is it that we tend to magnify the one kind of threat and underrate the other, if not to dismiss it completely? Why is there, for so many of us, such an odd discontinuity between dangers as they exist and dangers as we perceive them? Perhaps there is something special about a certain kind of fear—the fear of violence. Perhaps, as recent experimental work has indicated, this fear embodies particular qualities, primarily psychological in nature, which tend to enhance it and make us experience it far more vividly than a cold look at the statistics suggests that we should.

Research into the nature and anatomy of fear—as an emotion, a motivating force, an acquired drive—was inaugurated in the early nineteen-twenties when the great behaviorist-psychologist John B. Watson demonstrated that fear could be produced experimentally. In a study which, a half-century later, strikes the reader as cruel as well as ingenious, Watson and a student collaborator, Rosalie Rayner, "conditioned" an eleven-month-old child to experience intense fear at the sight of a white rat.

Albert B., known as "little Albert" to generations of later psychologists, was the son of a wet nurse at a children's home in Baltimore. The boy was a cheerful, stolid child who, as Watson and Rayner noted, in their paper, had never been seen in either a state of fear or rage. As the two psychologists presented him, in succession, with stimuli which *could* have frightened him—a white rat, a rabbit, a dog, a monkey, masks with and without hair, etc.—the baby was no more than delighted and pleased. He appeared to enjoy contact with the animals, especially the white rat.

But Albert did show fear when Watson suddenly clanged two steel bars together, creating a startling, unexpected noise. This kind of "startle stimulus" was, as the psychologist had noted in an earlier paper, innately fear-evoking. The sound caused the child to rear back violently, hesitate in his breathing, fling his arms upward in a self-protective gesture and then burst into a fit of crying.

Watson and Rayner commenced, soon afterward, a series of "classical" or "Pavlovian" conditioning trials. They simultaneously presented the white rat and the sudden frightening noise. In the first two sessions, whenever Albert stretched out his hand to touch the white rat, Watson clanged the steel bars together. It actually took but those two brief experiences to cause the child to fall forward on his face and begin to whimper. A week later, when the rat was introduced again, Albert refused to touch it. He had, clearly, established a mildly negative emotional response to the animal.

It took but seven such trials for Albert to establish a hardy association between "fearful noise" and "white rat." At the end of that period, the sight of the white rat *alone* produced intense fear. Even in the absence of any further startling, shock-producing noises, the previously "neutral" stimulus—the rat—was in itself enough to make Albert turn, cry and crawl away as fast as he could. It had taken on the fear-eliciting properties of the sudden sound. And when the baby was tested five days later, it was evident that his conditioned emotional reaction to rats had generalized to other "furry" stimuli. He had now become afraid of the rabbit, the dog, of a Santa Claus mask with white wool on it and even a sealskin coat.

It was, suggested Watson, through a process similar to this that most human fears were acquired: That is, a child, in his or her natural environment, learned to associate a variety of previously "neutral" stimuli with painful or alarm-evoking events. (As to those psychological theories which proposed that many or most human fears arise from intrapsychic conflicts, linked to incestuous strivings directed toward the parent of the opposite sex, Watson commented: "The Freudians twenty years from now, unless their hypotheses change, when they come to analyze Albert's fear of a sealskin coat—assuming that he comes to analysis at that age—will probably tease from him the recital of a dream which upon their analysis will show that Albert at three years of age attempted to play with the pubic hair of the mother and was scolded violently for it. . . .")* Our fears, maintained Watson, spring from experiences in the environment: If one knew the learning history of the individual, in all its minutiae, one could readily ascertain the true source of those fears which appear to have been spontaneously produced from within.

The Watson-Rayner study was a dramatic demonstration that fear could be produced in the laboratory—could be, as it were, isolated, measured, analyzed, teased apart into its primitive emotional and motivational components. The many experiments which followed were, however, conducted for the main part with rat and dog (happily), rather than human subjects.

One study, carried out in the early nineteen-forties by Professor Neal Miller of Yale University (now at Rockefeller) attempted to measure the relative strengths of fear and of the primary drive of hunger. Miller found that albino rats that had been trained to run down an alley to their food, would—when restrained by a harness, and very hungry—pull toward the food with a strength of 50 grams. Other rats, trained to avoid receiving an electric shock at the end of the same alley, would pull against the restraining harness—away from the goal—with a force of 200 grams. Furthermore, animals first trained to get their victuals, and then given an electric shock at the end of the alley, would *not* return to the goal to get food again—even though they were nearly starved. As a variety of other experiments have demonstrated, fear interferes not only with eating, but with drinking even in the presence of extreme thirst, and with sexual behavior.

In a 1948 paper that was to become a landmark in the experimental study of fear, Miller demonstrated that this emotion was more than merely a reaction to painful or innately alarming stimuli: It was in itself an acquired drive, at least as powerful as the primary drives—hunger, thirst, sex, etc.—in promoting the learning of new behaviors. In other words, just as a hungry rat could be motivated to learn to run a maze in order to obtain "rewarding" food, so a terrified rat could be trained to perform rather complicated, unratlike tasks to obtain a "rewarding" reduction of fear.

Miller's study was elegant and simple. He designed an apparatus

---

*Albert's mother left her job at the orphanage soon after the experiment, and many subsequent attempts to locate "little Albert" were unsuccessful.

which consisted of two compartments, one white with a grid floor, the other black with a solid floor. Electric shocks could be delivered through the grid in the white section, and the animal could escape the painful stimulus by running through an open door into the black room.

When a series of brief electric shocks were begun, the animals reacted with all the behavioral signs of intense fear—urination, defecation, squealing, agitated running about. They soon learned the escape route through the open door into the "safe" black compartment. Before long the animals had become conditioned to fear the white side of the box: "White walls" and "grid floors" were in and of themselves cues for terror. Whenever the rats were placed in the white side of the box they scurried frantically into the black half of the apparatus. This behavior persisted for literally hundreds of trials *after the electric shock had been turned off*.

A habit motivated by fear was, clearly, extraordinarily persistent. Certainly an animal running down an alley to get a food reward would have stopped after a number of trials in which no food was found at the goal. What seemed to be happening in the fear experiment was that the rat, having learned a response that could enable it to avoid danger and pain, was unlikely ever to return to find out whether that danger still actually existed. The fear of the white compartment was so intense that merely getting out of it appeared to be rewarding. Miller demonstrated this by closing the door separating the compartments and arranging a small gate which would open (enabling the rat to escape the white side) if the animal rotated a wheel just above it. The rats soon learned the effect of the wheel. On being placed in the white compartment, they would scurry to the wheel, give it a turn, and open the way into the black compartment. After learning the new response, reported Miller, their general behavior took on a somewhat casual appearance. Yet the relentlessness with which they would run to rotate the wheel was extraordinary to observe. Like many neurotic behaviors in humans, the rats' stereotyped conduct appeared incomprehensible, but, Miller wrote, "if you know the history, the bizarre behavior is understandable."

Miller's pioneer work on so-called "avoidance conditioning" was followed by a host of related experimental studies. One series, carried out at the University of Pennsylvania under the direction of Dr. Richard Solomon, used thirteen dogs as subjects. All were given avoidance training, as follows: The dog would be placed in one side of a box which was divided in half by a high barrier. The compartment into which the dog was placed was well-lit, but whenever the lights were dimmed, the dog would receive a painful electric shock. The animal could escape the shock by leaping the barrier into the other side of the box.

The "lights out" signal soon became a cue for intense fear. As in the Miller study, the shock was then turned off, and the researchers commenced a series of "extinction trials" to see how long it would take the dogs' acquired fear-reaction (jumping the hurdle when the lights dimmed) to dissipate. Because the barrier was fairly high, making the jump quite an effort, the psychologists believed this would take place readily. To their astonishment, however, the animals continued jumping through hundreds of trials. Indeed, they improved their style, becoming speedier and more accomplished. At the same time their behavior, like that of the rats, became markedly less agitated and emotional. Yelping, trembling, defecation, urination all diminished, for they had a response which enabled them to avoid remaining in the terrifying "lights out" situation. Still, the dogs would not unlearn the fear-motivated jumping reaction.

Puzzled by this perseveration in the absence of any further shock or punishment, the Solomon team tried a variety of methods for "counterconditioning" the animals—that is, teaching responses that would oppose or be incongruous with jumping. For example, the experimenters arranged the apparatus in such a way that, when they jumped on the dimmed-lights cue, the dogs would receive a shock on the other side of the barrier. Nevertheless, ten out of the thirteen dogs continued to leap the hurdle throughout 100 extinction trials. In general, as the animals jumped *into* shock, their jumping styles showed improvement—they jumped faster and better. Punishing the fear response only seemed to strengthen it.

In this situation, the need to escape fear appeared to be more powerful than the desire to escape predictable pain. The sheer craziness of the dogs' reactions indicated, at least to this reader, the degree to which strong fears may underlie and motivate very maladaptive kinds of behaviors. On the other hand, the merits of this kind of emotional conditioning ought not to be overlooked: An animal (or human) that is "wired up" in such a way that it learns very quickly which cues are associated with danger, and then attaches anxiety to those cues and persistently avoids them, is not—as one psychologist remarked to me— "going to get eaten up by tigers very often."

In a sense what this emotional conditioning urges upon the organism is the adoption of a very conservative strategy, a strategy which, in the language of game theory, has a minimax character—minimizing the maximum harm an opponent can do to you. Such a strategy is, obviously, adaptive in the broad meaning of the term: It promotes survival. But as the Solomon study demonstrated, it contains a crucial disadvantage: one may spend a good deal of time avoiding things that actually are not there. Avoidance stratagems are expensive to the individual inasmuch as they place stringent limits on flexibility and freedom, and interrupt behaviors which might be directed toward positive, enjoyable goals.

The fact that humans and lower animals readily learn to attach fear to previously neutral stimuli—so that those stimuli become in themselves autonomous cues for anxiety and alarm—does not, of course, explain why one kind of fear may be experienced more intensely than another. What, to return to my original question, can serve to explain the ease with which we become conditioned to fear those stimuli (streets at night, lonely places, parks, etc.) associated with violence and criminal strangers, while our fears about things like automobiles, highways, home and work accidents appear to remain somewhat unrealistically low? Some clues may be found, perhaps, if we return to the handful of studies using humans as subjects which followed Watson's "little Albert" experiment.

In 1929 C.W. Valentine, an English psychologist, did a study in which he used his own child as the subject. ("One hesitates," he wrote, "to perform experiments causing even momentary discomfort to one's little ones, but 'Y' was an exceptionally healthy, strong and jovial youngster, and I hardened my heart sufficiently to try one or two simple tests with her . . . ") What Valentine did was to place his small daughter, then just over a year old, on her mother's lap, near a small table upon which an ornate pair of opera glasses had been set. Each time the child reached out to touch the glasses, the psychologist blew a harsh blast on a whistle. His daughter, observed Valentine, "quietly turned round as if to see where the noise came from"; the process was repeated several times, but the whistle failed to alarm her.

Later that afternoon, the child, seated upon her father's knee, was presented with a woolly caterpillar which a favorite brother had brought in upon his hand. She had seen such insects before, but had never touched one. She shifted away slightly, then turned back to look at it. At this moment her father blew a loud blast on the whistle: She screamed in terror, and turned away from the insect. This process was repeated four more times. "It is remarkable," reported Valentine, "that the blowing of the whistle, which that same morning had caused only a slight interest, should now so accentuate the reaction to the caterpillar. It can only be explained, I think, on the assumption that the attitude towards the caterpillar was a very *unstable* one, ready to be changed to great excitement and fear . . . The loud whistle, in itself undisturbing, provided just the slight added shock to make the fear of the caterpillar burst forth."

If all human fears were, as Watson had said, simply conditioned reflexes resulting from early painful experiences in the environment, little "Y" ought to have formed a negative association to the opera glasses as easily as she did to the caterpillar. But there was, it appeared, something "special" about stimuli like white rats and caterpillars—perhaps there was, for human beings, something "special" about animals and insects in general. They might have a very particular kind of significance.

To examine this possibility, psychologist Elsie Bregman tried to condition a group of young children to fear stimuli which were indisputably "neutral" (a wooden block, a triangle, a swatch of cloth). Bregman, working in the early nineteen-thirties at the Home for Hebrew Infants in New York—I assume that orphanages no longer permit these experiments—used an electric bell hidden behind a high chair to startle her child subjects each time they reached toward one of these objects, which were among other playthings on the high-chair tray. Of the fifteen children, all in "little Albert's" age range, none showed any measurable change in emotional responses toward the block, triangle or cloth. Bregman concluded that the white rat in the Watson study had not been a "neutral" stimulus after all: It appeared to have had some intrinsic biological significance. Perhaps Albert had displayed an innately human tendency to learn a specific, easily arousable kind of fear—the fear of animals.

Are we as a species—as the Bregman study suggests—genetically "prepared" to learn to fear certain classes of stimuli? Are we neurally "prewired" for acquiring fears about certain objects, or situations, which have perhaps affected human survival over the long course of our evolutionary history? In *The Biological Boundaries of Learning*, edited by Martin Seligman and Joanne Hager, experimental studies—some new, some dating back to the twenties—have been gathered together which tend to support the hypothesis that humans, as well as lower animals, are remarkably choosy about what stimuli they are actually willing to learn to fear. One of the studies, an intriguing experiment carried out with rats, demonstrates this "finickiness" about fears. In essence, it was a replication of the 1948 Miller "avoidance" experiment, except for one crucial difference. The black and white compartments were reversed. The rats were shocked in the black area and from there ran into the white area.

Under these conditions, the animals were extremely slow to learn the avoidance response (running through the door). *Some even failed to perform it at all.* Why? The natural history of a cavity-dwelling, night-adapted animal suggests the answer: Black walls, signifying darkness, might be experienced as a signal of safety, while whiteness (daylight) might be an instinctual cue for danger. Running, therefore, from the black part to the white part of the apparatus may be something for which the rat is biologically counterprepared.

In other words, there may be bred into the rat as a species a selective advantage for those individuals that learn readily to fear daylight (for which the animal is ill-adapted) as there may have been, during our long prehistory in the wild, a selective edge favoring those human beings who acquired fears about animals with great rapidity and maintained those fears with great persistence. As psychologist Martin Seligman notes in a critical essay at the close of *The Biological Boundaries of Learning*: ". . . animals and humans do a great deal of learning about contingencies which their species has faced for aeons. Not only do birds learn to turn wheels for grain [in learning experiments] . . . which their ancestors never did, but they also *learn* to migrate away from the North Star in the fall . . . a contingency their ancestors faced before them. Not only do humans learn to fear crossing busy streets, but also to fear the dark. All of this learning may not be the same." There are, Seligman suggests, stimuli associated with regularly recurring kinds of dangers, which human beings are biologically *ready* to learn to fear.

In our species, in which the original adaptation was for food-getting during daylight hours, for sleep during night hours when predatory animals roamed, and in which social communities early became a major source of protection for individuals, it does not seem unreasonable to suppose that certain kinds of fears (of darkness, of animals, of violent strangers, of lonely or exposed places) might spring up more readily and persist more stubbornly than, say, fears about auto accidents, exploding aerosol cans or the possibility of getting one's hand mangled in the garbage disposal. These later, "modern" kinds of fear have clearly no evolutionary significance; no selective environmental pressures have prepared us for learning about such dangers with the same degree of emotional reactivity and alarm. We fail, therefore, to experience them with the same kind of intensity—and often to evaluate them as being as dangerous as they actually are.

In a conversation I had with Dr. Seligman, who is an associate professor of psychology at the University of Pennsylvania, this issue was explored further. "If you look at the phobias in humans," he remarked, "by which I mean those persistent and irrational fears which some people attach to certain stimuli (such as snakes), then you'll notice pretty quickly that the phobias fall into a quite limited set. That is, fear of open spaces, of specific animals, of insects, of heights, of closed-in spaces— there may be a dozen of them, all told. They include xenophobia, the fear or mistrust of strangers, people who seem foreign. . . . The current alarms about crime in the streets surely partake of phobic elements of this latter sort—that is, fear of people with skins of different color, who may not look like oneself."

Phobias in humans correspond, Seligman believes, to those objects or events in the environment which we are biologically "prewired" to learn to fear. "We know," he explained, "that for children things like pajamas are often paired with psychological trauma; yet you don't see pajama phobias. Also, objects like hammers and electric outlets are commonly linked with very painful experiences: I know of no instance of an electric-outlet phobia. A child may, after an unfortunate experience with an outlet, learn to fear it (wisely); but you won't see him tremble or become rigid with fear at the mere suggestion that he's anywhere near an outlet, as would, for instance, a cat phobic if he spied a cat in the distance." The more neurally "set" the organism is, at some primitive, noncognitive level, for learning to fear a certain kind of stimulus, the "more robust a fear you are going to see, and the harder that fear will be to get rid of. . . ." We respond, with disproportionate emotional force, to those objects and events which have, during the long course of our evolutionary past, been reliable predictors of danger.

Biological "preparedness" is not the sole factor which might tend to make our fears about violence more intense than are our fears about other dangers we face. According to Dr. Seligman, violent situations encompass other dimensions which are known to amplify and increase subjective feelings of fear. One such dimension is that of unpredictability. In an experiment which he carried out in 1966, which used rats and electric shock, Seligman demonstrated that unpredictable punishment arouses much more fear than does precisely *the same amount* of pain when the organism has some means for predicting it.

"Consider two situations," explained Seligman, "in which hungry rats are pressing bars to obtain 'rewarding' food pellets. In the first condition, we present a tone that is paired with electric shock. When the tone is on, as he rapidly learns (rats become exquisitely sensitive to this contingency after a brief period of training), he is going to get that jolt. And so he'll feel fear at the signal, and he'll stop bar pressing.

"On the other hand, he'll have learned, also, that when the tone is off, he is perfectly safe. This will put him in a quite different position from, say, another rat who is receiving exactly the same number of tones and shocks but who is getting them randomly. There is, for the latter animal, no relationship at all between tone and shock. For him, the experience is one of complete unpredictability. There's no stimulus which tells him he is all right (as the absence of the tone does for the first rat) and not going to get shocked. There is, in other words, no sanctuary."

Seligman compared two groups of rats, one receiving shocks reliably paired with the warning tone, the other receiving shocks and tones at random intervals. Those animals in the latter category, he reported, spent most of their time huddled in a corner and lived in a state of unrelieved fear. Of the eight rats in this group, six developed stress ulcers; among the group receiving paired shock and tone, no stomach ulcers were found. "Unpredictability," Seligman points out, "makes the fear continual; it stretches out in time. There is a much greater degree of strain and worry, because the organism has no signal, such as absence of tone, which lets him know that the bad thing won't be happening—that it's possible to relax."

Street violence has, he notes, a certain built-in "unpredictability": it can descend upon anyone, anywhere, at any time. "You can't slip in the shower unless you're *in* the shower," remarks Seligman. "You can't get into an automobile smash-up unless you're riding in an automobile. But where random crime and violence are concerned, one reads, all the time, about someone who's just walking along a street—or is even at home in bed—who suddenly becomes embroiled, as if out of nowhere, in some terrifying event. The lack of any clearly defined places where it can't, and won't, happen—where we know we are perfectly safe—is one aspect of this kind of fear which tends to make it more hardy, more chronic. . . . For some people it becomes an unremitting anxiety, like that of the rats huddled in the corner."

"Unpredictability," of course is intimately related to the overarching problem of control and mastery of the environment. Humans and lower animals have a psychological need to feel that their actions—what they do as individuals—will affect what happens to them. The opposite of mastery is helplessness, and feelings of helplessness demonstrably intensify the experience of fear. In a series of studies carried out at Yale University in 1968, psychologist Jay Weiss showed that albino rats which were given the opportunity to learn a "coping response"—rotating a small wheel or jumping up on a platform—that enabled them to escape or avoid shock, developed far fewer stress ulcers than did passive partners who were receiving precisely the *same amount of shock* but could do nothing about it.

The feeling that one can make a difference, can act effectively in the environment, has, it appears, a generalized influence upon the total magnitude of the fear one experiences.

Worries about potential loss of control invade our thinking about "violence in the streets," Dr. Seligman observes, and tend to amplify our feelings of fear: "Random crime is a rather good example of something which renders an individual personally helpless. It's not something which he brings upon himself, nor something which he can readily escape from once it's happened, nor something which, generally speaking, he's been trained to cope with. Of course, a person might be able to do things to avoid its occurring in the first place—within limits—but there's very little he's going to be able to do about it when he becomes caught up in some ongoing violent event. . . . That's what gives so many people the feeling that there is this thing that, should it happen to them, will render them powerless to affect their own fates."

Crucial to the experience of fear is the issue of whether one will be able to respond meaningfully to a situation—to cope. As one ingenious study showed, merely *believing* that one's coping response is working—even if it is making no realistic difference whatsoever—serves to diminish fear and stress markedly. In this experiment, carried out in 1970 by three psychologists at the Stony Brook campus of the State University of New York, forty male student volunteers were the subjects. In what purported to be a study of "reaction times," each man first received a series of electric shocks, each lasting precisely six seconds.

The group was then divided into two sections. Half of the subjects were told that if their reactions to the onset of shock were swift enough and they pulled a nearby switch rapidly enough, the shocks they received could be reduced to half—three seconds—their timed length. These men were, thus, led to believe that something they *did* could vitally affect what happened to them.

The subjects in the other half of the group were simply told that the shocks they received in the second part of the study would last three seconds no matter what they did. In reality, both groups received precisely the same amount of shock—three seconds—throughout the latter part of the experiment.

Curiously enough, the men who *believed* that they were doing something, who thought they were acting upon and exercising some control over their environment, were far less emotionally reactive (as measured by galvanic skin response) than were those who thought that there was nothing they could do about it. The first group—the "copers"—also appeared to find the shocks, subjectively speaking, far less painful; and indeed were able to withstand higher levels of shock. In summing up this study, the authors, James Geer, Gerald Davison and Robert Gatchel, quoting the anthropologist Malinowski, wrote: "Man creates his own gods to fill in gaps in his knowledge about a sometimes terrifying environment . . . creating an illusion of control which is presumably comforting." The psychologists added: "Perhaps the next best thing to being master of one's fate is being deluded into thinking that one is. . . ."

Still, there are circumstances which are so threatening—or which an individual perceives as so threatening—that a sense of mastery over them is deemed impossible. Then fear may become a chronic rather than a transient state or mood (which is the way most of us experience it). The individual will exist in a state of constant mobilization, of readiness to meet the expected threat—and therefore in a state of continual tension. The common effects of living with this kind of fear are fatigue, feelings of depression, a slowdown in mental processes and bodily movements, restlessness, bursts of aggression and irritability, loss of appetite, a tendency to startle, insomnia and nightmares.

Many internal bodily changes accompany feelings of fear, for one of its "uses" is that it facilitates high-speed responses in the face of danger. When one is frightened, more sugar pours into the blood (producing a burst of energy), breathing becomes more rapid as the blood circulates faster; blood pressure rises and the heart beats faster; more adrenalin is secreted; the pupils of the eyes dilate, so that one can actually see more clearly—one becomes physiologically prepared for taking the necessary action. (Such changes are not clearly distinguishable from those occurring when a person is angry.) If, however, an individual remains in a fearful state for long periods without relief, it is as if he were running his motor too fast and without letup—he puts pressure upon the system itself. Eventually this "racing engine" condition can harm a human being—as well as a rat—physically. It can cause symptoms which range from severe headache to ulcers, high blood pressure, cardiac arrhythmias and hypertension, genitourinary problems, and diseases such as asthma, which are known to be linked to and exacerbated by emotional stress.

                                                                    1974

Terror in the City
Memoir of a Girl Alone

To millions of Americans," commences a staff report to the National Commission on the Causes and Prevention of Violence, "few things are more pervasive, more frightening, more real today than violent crime and the fear of being assaulted, mugged, robbed or raped." This report, quite staid and solemn in its overall tone, was submitted in 1969—and in the intervening few years, the apprehension about street violence seems not, as we can all attest, to have abated. Most of us continue to live with a heightened sense of fear, a feeling of personal vulnerability, an uncomfortable awareness that a role in a horror drama may suddenly be thrust upon us.

The crime statistics, of course, contain the objective assessments of the situation; fear, which rides above them, is a subjective state of being, a natural reaction which serves to alert us to dangers in the outside world. To feel fearful involves not only bodily arousal, including a complicated train of hormonal and neural changes, but the experiencing of disturbing and averse psychological sensations. Fear is a noxious internal condition; human beings, as well as lower animals, will do their utmost to avoid those situations which are associated with its arousal. Where humans are concerned, however, the capacity for merely mentally picturing the threatening circumstances often leads to attempts to circumvent the *imagined* dangers.

Considering this power of imagination, and confronted, as we currently are, not with an explicit menace but the possibility of being victimized in a random criminal event, we all find ourselves in an odd kind of dilemma. We do not know how frightened we ought rightfully to be. How reliable are our emotional responses as a guide to action? In an environment that actually does contain some degree of realistic danger, how much ought we to permit our fears to modify our behavior and our daily activities? Since worry about potential violence is a source of disagreeable stimulation, is it wiser to discount the threat, relegate it to the background of one's life and thoughts because one can do nothing

222

about it in any case? Or, on the other hand, ought one to remain in a perpetual state of mobilization for possible action?

Like it or not, we are being forced, I believe, into making a set of strategic choices. We all must, according to the hazards we perceive within the context of our personal circumstances, try to assess what things could happen and then respond to those conjectures appropriately. What we become involved in is a kind of chess game in which we work out a series of moves intended to counteract or escape the risks as we see them. The difficulty remains, however, the subtle one of ascertaining the point where fears that might be viewed as prudent and in a broad sense "adaptive," may begin to fade into, to merge with, psychologically unhealthy, neurotic and energy-sapping modes of defense.

"Fear has its own smell." So says Mary Lu in a tone of contempt. "More people use deodorant here in New York than they do anyplace else in the country." A young divorcée, Mary Lu lives in the Greenwich Village area of Manhattan—a neighborhood with the diversity and charm of Paris in the twenties, upon which has been superimposed the somewhat sinister disquiet of New York in the late sixties and early seventies. A sense of threat, a possibility of something catastrophic just around the next corner, pervades Mary Lu's existence, indeed motivates and underlies much of her behavior. Her fear is different in degree, but not in kind, from those twinges of anxiety which prevent most of us from going to certain sections of the city, or from using this park or that library or such-and-such a subway line at certain times of the day or evening. Mary Lu, however, has a sense of herself as particularly vulnerable—not only because she is a woman but because she is physically small. Much of her energy is spent in mobilizing herself to meet the assault, mugging, robbery or rape which she fears and fantasizes. Survival is the dominant priority in her personal hierarchy of goals and values. She has become a karate expert, and moves through the streets as if through enemy territory, always watchful and ready.

"Fear isn't, of course, completely a bad thing." Mary Lu shrugs. "It keeps a lot of people on their toes. A friend of mine, for instance, whenever he parks his car, always just sits there a while before getting out, surveying the landscape, making sure there isn't anyone lurking in the hallways, that no one suspicious-looking is coming down the street." Mary Lu, having no car, uses a bicycle much of the time. When returning home, however, she never pedals directly up to her front door. "Usually, I bike past my place, looking up and down the street to see whether anyone is coming. And then, if there isn't anyone, I turn around and go back to my building." Once inside, Mary Lu locks her bicycle in the hallway. Then there is a long staircase to be climbed, and a second door, the one to her own apartment, to be unlocked. She often strings thread across this entryway, or uses a "shim," a little matchstick which, should its position be different from the way Mary Lu had left it, would reveal to her at once that someone had opened the door.

Not only is Mary Lu painstaking about her return home, she is equally so about going out. "I never simply walk out onto the street— not without observing the situation carefully through my mailbox slot. If it happens to be after dark, I'm careful to turn out the vestibule light so I won't be silhouetted. I listen to hear if people are talking out there or for footsteps on the sidewalk. Then I open the door so I can peer out. If I see anyone on the street, I close it at once and wait ten minutes, then repeat the ritual."

To live this way, like a spy in an occupied land, is, concedes Mary Lu, "grotesque"; nevertheless, she considers her watchfulness a necessity from the point of view of survival. "I want to avoid an encounter at any cost," she asserts, looking, with her slight frame, short-clipped straight dark hair and eyes wide with a kind of endemic panic, like a Joan of Arc in slacks and pea coat. "But *should* I have an encounter, I want to be prepared for it. I take karate . . . actually, a whole part of my hand is black and blue, and I'm a mass of sprained fingers from punching. I work very hard to be as formidable an opponent as I can for my size— I'm only five-two, which makes it easier, I feel, for people to pick on me as a good mark, to say, 'Ah, look, there's a midget; she'll be easy.'"

Mary Lu is aware that she has harmed herself more, physically, in the course of preparing to *meet* violence than she has in any real encounter, for she has never been the direct victim of a crime. There was, however, a "near thing" that did occur just recently: she was bicycling home from an evening karate class when suddenly she found herself surrounded by three large, menacing youths in their late teens. Two of the boys were riding together on one bicycle; the third was on a bike of his own. They had, she says, made no movement toward her aside from blocking her way in a very dark street. The karate feeling, she believes, had lingered with her. "I became totally outraged. I immediately started yelling, 'Hey, what do you think you're doing?' And it surprised them, since they'd expected me to cringe—kind of got them off their guard. Then I hauled off and punched the guy nearest me as hard as I could—which is pretty hard. I knocked him and the boy sitting behind him on the bicycle into the street. Then I picked up my bike chain from around my handlebars and started waving it over my head so that the guy behind me wouldn't be able to attack from his direction. Then I snatched my own bicycle upright—it had fallen with the impact of that punch—and rode away. I got about four blocks from the spot where it had all happened, and then I went to pieces."

Despite the terror it had held, that experience, Mary Lu feels, was not completely a bad thing, for it gave her the first opportunity to make use—real use—of her karate prowess. "It was good to know I could act, that I wasn't going to freeze. And in punching those boys, I felt I was teaching them a valuable lesson—that not every woman can be victimized. I believe women are naturally chosen as victims because men don't expect them to be able to take care of themselves. It's even true on my own part: when I encounter another woman in a dark or lonely situation, I never fear death from her. To me, death is associated with men only."

Mary Lu is aware, however, that had one of those youths pointed a gun at her she might have been rendered powerless, paralyzed. Not long ago, she muses thoughtfully, one of the neighboring shops was rented out for a while to a vagrant furniture-moving company. Many of the men who worked in the place were drifters, ex-convicts; one of them, in particular, used to stare out the back window and watch Mary Lu at her karate practice in the grass courtyard. One hot summer afternoon, meeting her by chance on the sidewalk out front, he had stopped her and said in a voice drawling contempt, "You're a karate expert, aren't you?" She answered that she knew some karate. "Well"—he smiled—"what do you think you could do against a gun?" What did she reply? "I just walked away. He was so ignorant, it frightened me." A wincing expression crosses her face.

Mugger, junkie, street criminal. In many people's minds, this frightening specter has come to occupy the place which the escaped lunatic as fantasy-figure once held. The mugger, like the madman, carries with him the unspeakable potential for senseless violence, the aura of having burst through civilization's confines. He is beyond reason, past control; he would, in that phrase which has become as common as a slogan, "just as soon kill you as rob you." In an environment in which the threat of becoming a mugger's victim is not totally unrealistic—in which most of us have a friend or acquaintance with a frightening account to report—the hairbreadth which divides what may be thought of as "normal" responses from "neurotic" ones becomes increasingly difficult to ascertain. Is Mary Lu's behavior, for example, to be seen as "adaptive" and suited to the terrain in which she lives and works? Or is it to be considered maladaptively constricting of her personal growth, as well as wasteful of her time and energy?

In a situation which contains a real but indefinable degree of actual danger, these become peculiar questions to tackle. Certainly, anyone who, like myself, happens to carefully observe the way Mary Lu lives, to listen to her conversation, to comprehend the nature of her preoccupations, to watch her attention to and elaboration on a variety of survival strategies—she has a scenario which involves handing over her wallet to the mugger with one motion while at the same time executing a quick backward jump which will get her out of reach of a knife-thrust—might call her either crazy or prudent, paranoid or sensibly conscious of a menacing reality. The eye, as Shelley long ago remarked, sees what it brings to the seeing.

And other New Yorkers *do* view the situation quite differently. Many people consider the current "crime-wave" concern to be nothing more than a form of social hysteria, masking (but only slightly) a fear of rapid social change—especially insofar as granting equality to nonwhites is concerned. One acquaintance of mine, a lawyer, dismisses the entire "crime thing" as nothing more than a hard-hat device designed to sell more newspapers and titillate an audience of late-night televison-news viewers. Not that street violence hasn't increased to some degree, due to the mushrooming of the city's ghetto areas—but, says my friend, where crime has increased arithmetically, the fear of it has increased geometrically. "And this," he observes, "is due in part to the sensational play that the problem is receiving in the media."

Another friend, a woman editor who, like Mary Lu, lives in what sociologists call an "interstitial area"—that is, a neighborhood in transition, diverse in terms of class and race, and one in which poverty-ridden ghetto and "good" sections are not territorially well-defined—

insists that New York is neither more nor less dangerous than it ever was. "I grew up in Manhattan," she says. "And there always *were* places—neighborhoods—that were off-limits, parks that you'd never venture into; that hasn't changed. The city isn't completely safe, sure; but then, it never really was. The only difference you sense now is that everyone's being whipped into a panic about a certain margin of danger which may have moved up a fraction—or may not have; I really don't know—but which always existed here anyhow."

Because she appears less ruffled than other people I've spoken to, I was curious as to whether or not this same editor feels secure in using certain transportation facilities—the subway system, for example. "I never take subways or buses, only taxis," she replied at once. "But that isn't because I'm worried about crime or about being mugged; I just happen to be slightly claustrophobic. I never could even bring myself to go down into a subway tunnel, because I've always had these anxious feelings about places that are enclosed. And buses at the rush hour are so jammed they make me feel the same way."

One needs, of course, a certain standard of living before being able to afford such phobias. Mary Lu, despite her frank and blatant fear of some "encounter," some violent collision, uses subways often; she hasn't the money for taxis and feels that buses take forever to get around town. But riding the subway does evoke in her anxious, trapped feelings similar to my claustrophobic friend's. "It's always midnight down there. I hate those dark holes," Mary Lu says. She has, she admits, been more worried than ever since a mugger—"he worked with a knife"—was arrested at the subway stop which she herself uses most often. The man, she has since heard, had been making a regular living out of robbing people at that particular station. "He put up a terrific struggle when he was captured. And now he'll go through the courts, but so what? He'll be back at Twenty-third Street and Eighth Avenue soon enough, mugging people again; that's how it goes."

Although she continues to use the subway, Mary Lu has friends whose activities have become seriously curtailed because they are too terrified to do so. "The girl I work with has been simply unable to bring herself to ride the subway ever since she got roughed up on a train several months ago." The incident, reports Mary Lu, involved a gang of tough high-school kids who were beating up on one of their own group, a boy wearing glasses. And when the glasses fell to the floor during the fracas, Mary Lu's friend, a pretty woman in her early thirties, picked them up and tried to hand them back to the boy. For this "interference," for this "crime," the whole mob now turned on her—they began punching her, threw her down and started grinding her face into the floor of the train. "As things turned out, she was lucky," says Mary Lu. "This very large, very strong-looking black man saw what was going on and came to her rescue. He was so tough, he scared the kids off. But that was luck, and that kind of luck can't be counted on. Don't ever think that if the subways are crowded and there are lots of people around you're safe. Busyness isn't the same thing as safety—just like motion isn't the same as progress."

Mary Lu's apartment, two large rooms and bath with bead-curtained doorway, is in the old Gansevoort Market area on the western fringe of the Village. Now mainly occupied by rows of wholesale meat-and-provision suppliers, the market dates back, she believes, to the early seventeenth century, to the time of the Dutch settlers; the building in which Mary Lu has her "loft" is, of course, much newer—probably only about 140 years old. Her place is on the second floor, just over a beef-and-poultry concern. It is well-arranged and tidy, yet filled with the signs of diverse industry. Mary Lu is primarily a designer—"mostly pop stuff and graphics"—but photography equipment, carpenter's tools and jewelry-making gear are also in evidence, along with some ingeniously fashioned copper rings and bracelets decorated with tiny enameled metal plaques "rescued" from the face of an old piece of machinery. "I've done everything." She smiles. "I've renovated houses, made musical instruments, even been a home economist on television." At present, her main income derives from a part-time job designing and decorating (with acrylic paints) fancy T-shirts. She is also beginning work, along with a friend, on an encyclopedia of handicrafts.

Like the old houses of Montmartre in which the starving artists of Fauvist Paris had their ateliers, the building in which Mary Lu lives contains some surprises, unexpected luxuries. The rear windows, for example, overlook a pretty inner courtyard and garden; in the summers, Mary Lu shares this oasis with neighbors who also live above the surrounding businesses. The rear room itself contains another architectural gift—a small fireplace with a fragile, delicately molded mantelpiece. It is in this second of her two rooms that Mary Lu, for the most part, works, reads, cooks, eats. The front area is used as a kind of bedroom-parlor, its old pine floors—wide-planked with an uneven surface so that they give one a rocking feeling—sanded down lovingly to their original glow. Her bed, not far from the two oversized windows facing the street, is piled high with an assortment of delicately stitched antique quilts. But the whole domicile's air of benign coziness, of satisfied activity, is belied somewhat by the heavy steel gates' which stretch across every single window. "I put those in," remarks Mary Lu, following my glance, "just after Bruce Pecheur's murder. Because the mugger who sneaked into Bruce and Lucy's apartment could just as easily have come in here instead. And frightened as I might've been before all that happened, I evidently wasn't frightened enough. Because if I had been, this place would've been airtight even then."

The Pecheurs, Mary Lu's close friends and neighbors—they were just a few steps away, if one went through the back courtyard—lived, until exactly a year ago, in the triangular brick building at the corner where Ninth Avenue, Greenwich and Gansevoort Streets intersect. The front door of the building, still bright green, was painted that color by Bruce and Lucy; the name "Pecheur" remains etched in big white letters just over the green mailbox (the new tenant's name, on a card, is scotch-taped directly above). They are both gone now—Bruce, inanely and senselessly dead; his widow, off in California, working as an actress. After her husband's death, Lucy had moved in with Mary Lu and lived with her for several months. "But finally, she reached the point where she had to get out of the city altogether. She was meeting death everywhere—in everyone's eyes, on their faces, their lips. She had to go somewhere far away, someplace where people wouldn't know what had happened, wouldn't keep coming to her with all their mourning, all those stories whose message was, *See, I'm in pain, too.*"

Bruce Pecheur was thirty-one years old when he died, a graduate of Harvard University with a bachelor's degree in political science and a master's in art history. After finishing college, he had taught high school in Massachusetts for a while, then turned seriously toward the notion of becoming an actor. While trying to get acting roles (he did play in Andy Warhol's *Trash* and also had a small part in *The Way We Were*), he had developed an extremely successful career as a model. Sandy-haired, rugged, elegantly handsome, Bruce was naturally suited for posing as the idealized male: the debonair executive strolling toward his Rolls-Royce, the stalwart sportsman puffing on his L&M. Indeed, just before his death, he had completed a series of ads for L&M that were shot on location in Alaska; lest there be any morbid associations, however, the pictures were reshot after the murder, with another model replacing Bruce.

The prowler, it is believed, had come over the roof of The Needle's Eye, an abandoned bar and restaurant next door to the Pecheurs'. This appears to be the only way he could have gotten onto their fire escape. He came in through the bathroom window while the young couple were sleeping. "Lucy wakened to the sound of a man's voice talking to Bruce, very calmly. And she made believe she was continuing to sleep, because Bruce had made some sort of a motion—I'm not sure what—that he wanted her to keep still. And the man talked and talked, Lucy says, for what seemed to be, oh, an interminable length of time."

The intruder was armed with a very large bread knife. "He was telling Bruce that he wanted all their money." He began, relates Mary Lu, to methodically tear up a sheet. Then he bound Bruce's hands behind his back and began to pile pillows and blankets over his head. "Bruce was lying face-down at this point, and Lucy became frightened that he'd suffocate. And so she couldn't keep up the pretense that she was sleeping. 'I'll take you to the money,' she told the man, and got out of bed. She took him out to the kitchen—he holding the knife to her back the whole time—to the desk where she and Bruce kept their money. She wasn't panicked, not at this point. It was all very cold, and everyone was behaving. She didn't feel then that he'd come to kill, because he kept telling her not to turn around, not to see his face. He also said he wasn't intending to rape her. Although Lucy isn't sure that was true, because at one juncture he did try to push her into the little room which belonged to their eight-year-old son—the room was empty, Joaquin being away at camp—but Lucy resisted."

Bruce had, while his wife and the intruder were out of the room, managed somehow to free his hands. According to most newspaper accounts of the story, he had grabbed his revolver from a nearby drawer, then menaced the man with it. "The burglar walked back to find the pistol pointed at him," reported *The New York Times* in their carefully nonlurid description of the events leading up to the tragedy. But that, says Mary Lu, is not the way things actually did take place. "Bruce had gotten himself loose, true, and he'd gotten the gun. But he had the gun *out of sight.* When Lucy and the man returned to the room, the only thing they found different was that Bruce wasn't lying face-down. He'd turned over—to hide the fact that his hands were now free, hidden underneath him."

The intruder commanded Bruce to turn over the the way he had been lying before; Bruce didn't turn. The man, his knife still at Lucy's back, repeated the order. And Lucy, afraid he was going to attack her husband, said very gently, "Bruce, he wants you to turn over. . . ." It was at this moment, recounts Mary Lu, that a lot of things started happening almost simultaneously. "The burglar realized somehow, perhaps through some motion, that Bruce's hands were no longer bound. And so he said—very furiously—'Now I'm going to have to hurt you!' And Lucy doesn't quite know how he did it, but he slugged her on the head, knocking her aside, and in what seemed to be the very same movement, lunged forward. And he stabbed Bruce very quickly, very accurately, three times—in the heart, the liver and the groin. Then Lucy heard a shot and saw the man fall to the floor. Bruce had managed to take aim and shoot at the instant he was being attacked. But the man rose up again, and Bruce hit him with two more shots. Lucy ran to Bruce," Mary Lu continues, her words trailing off, becoming partially inaudible. "He was already unconscious. He never regained consciousness. . . ."

Mary Lu, her hand fibrillating slightly as if from some inward current, fishes a cigarette from a pack lying on her kitchen table, lights it. Many people, she observes, her expression becoming scornful, seem to attribute Bruce's death to the fact that he had a revolver; they believe that, despite his having been an expert marksman and a collector, he was mad to keep guns in his apartment. "But Lucy's quite sure the intruder never saw the gun; *she* never saw it. She thinks the man was simply angered because Bruce wasn't being a good victim, because he'd untied himself and therefore represented a threat. And so this person killed, very swiftly, very professionally, without any notion whatever that Bruce had the means for striking at *him.* The man was a criminal, a drifter; his name was Edward Garcia and he had a long list of indictments against him." Having puffed on her cigarette briefly, Mary Lu jams it into an ashtray and squashes out its light.

Mary Lu still has not been quite able to assimilate what happened last August. It is as if she has amnesia about where she was when Bruce was murdered. "I feel this great blank. It seems as if everything I was doing and planned to do, and everything I believed, suddenly became meaningless." She thinks now that, cautious though she might have been before the crime, she lived in an illusion of safety. It had to do with Bruce and Lucy Pecheur being so close by, and being such understanding friends. "If I got spooked in the night, as I sometimes did being alone, I could go over there," she says, with a short, helpless lift of the shoulders. "Or if I heard some kind of noise, no matter what time it was, I could call Bruce: he'd check it out for me, and it was okay. . . . They were my friends."

The one fact that Mary Lu has not been able to face, and which she believes most of the other people who knew Bruce Pecheur cannot face, is that "this man, who was so well trained, who knew karate and was an expert marksman, who was so strong and so perfect, could be killed in his bed." All the talk about the revolver is, she assumes, the only way frightened acquaintances have of explaining to themselves why what happened to Bruce Pecheur could never happen to them.

What does it do to someone to live, as does Mary Lu, in the constant expectation of danger? What kind of psychological mechanisms might such a threat-filled atmosphere bring into play? Most current psychiatric literature is, as one soon discovers, curiously evasive on the topic. Many books and papers now being written do concern themselves with problems relating to fear, anxiety, unremitting and unrelieved tension; but these works tend to focus on difficulties arising from *internal* sources. Psychiatrists have a great deal to say about the fears and conflicts which are psychological in origin, but far less to offer concerning those which may be linked to realistic outside stresses. Few theorists seem to be interested, at present, in the problems of adjustment which may result from a person's constant exposure to an environment ranging anywhere from partially insecure to extremely dangerous.

By and large, in order to gain some insight into human functioning in a climate of apprehension and fear, one must return to the psychiatric writings of more than twenty years ago, to the body of work that came out of World War II. Best-known of the studies of that period is the classic *Men Under Stress,* a book by psychiatrists, Dr. Roy Grinker and Dr. John Spiegel, about a group of fliers who were engaged in carrying out repeated and hazardous bombing missions. The psychological difficulties and problems faced by these airmen could, as the authors point out in an introductory chapter, be seen "in an enlarged focus as Everyman's struggles with a harsh reality, ending in some cases with strength and mastery of the circumstances, in others with a neurotic compromise and partial defeat." Drawing on extensive case-history material in their exploration of what happens to people in situations of more or less continual fear and stress, the doctors delineate and describe the types of neurotic—sometimes psychotic—reactions which can and do occur. Such reactions are, in their view, failures of adaptation—the individual is simply unable to cope with and adjust to the strains presented by a particular environment. And everyone, they observe, "has a limit to the amount of stress he can withstand."

One of the great problems for people living in fear, as noted in *Men Under Stress,* is that this emotion is inextricably bound up with feelings of rage. The individual who is forced to cope with high degrees of risk and insecurity has the attendant problem of dealing with his own intense and inevitable anger. "In war," according to the doctors, "the internal response to the holocaust raging around the individual is hostility. In civilian life, desertion by supporting figures, losses of all sorts, frustration, etc., also evoke reactions of rage. . . . Some stimuli evoke rage spontaneously as a primitive biological emergency reflex. Especially is this true of real external danger. Other stimuli cause similar responses only because they have dangerous meanings to the ego, and after such interpretations they are treated as threatening noxious agents. Once rage is activated, it is translated into action and its energy must be expended in some form of action. . . ."

After Bruce Pecheur's death, there was no action, recalls Mary Lu, no meaningful task to engage in, not even that of seeking the criminal: the intruder, along with his victim, was dead. And yet the overriding tone of those days, weeks, then months was that of an all-consuming fury. "We were engulfed by anger, Lucy and I. And there was no target for that anger, except perhaps the society that could've permitted this thing to happen." She and Lucy tried to handle their rage, or at least discharge some of it, by going to karate classes every single night. "In karate, you're told to imagine your enemy standing directly in front of you. And suddenly we both began making more progress in our learning than we had in a couple of years of study before that."

Along with the double burden of anger and grief, the two women bore the strain of an ever-present apprehension—an anxious belief, a feeling shared, that what had happened before was liable to happen again, and at any moment. "Before Lucy left for California, she was no longer able to sleep at night. Because, you see, the prowler had slipped into their place while she and Bruce were sleeping. This led to her feeling a compulsion to stay up at night and watch over me, to make sure *I* was safe." When Lucy did manage to doze off, adds Mary Lu, her slumber was disturbed by fitful dreams, nightmares, night sweats—even though they were armed with knives, which they kept under the pillows, and with Bruce's revolver, which had eventually been returned by the police. "The two of us were sleeping, at least for a while there"—Mary Lu smiles wryly—"as if an army were about to attack us at any instant."

Around the first of the year, some six months after Bruce's death, Mary Lu began receiving some help from a therapist, and is now feeling "a bit better." It was impossible, she says, to go on functioning, to merely sustain herself in that same state of high fear in which she'd lived for a period of time. One sign of her psychological improvement is the fact that she is now able, if she wishes, to skip a karate lesson without experiencing a sense of overwhelming anxiety; before going into therapy, she had developed a phobic terror of missing even a single class. "I felt my safety—my very existence—depended on my being at karate every evening. I had the horrible feeling that if I were to miss one night, the technique I missed might be the very one I'd need to know in order to save my life."

Mary Lu still, however, moves through the streets of the city quickly, a billy-club hidden in her purse and tied to her wrist by a string. She still stays out of the shadows, walks briskly—and down the middle of the street, not close to cars or doorways, if she happens to be coming home alone after dusk.

To live in such a way, with the constant belief in imminent disaster, is, I would think, perhaps to be experiencing the disaster itself. Mary Lu smiles again, that same wry smile. "I rarely have a relaxed moment on the street," she concedes. "But I'm alive."

1974

On Anger

Everyone is born with the capacity to feel and express anger. Just as an ordinary piano is built so as to contain certain chords (which can then be played, or not played, as the individual chooses), so we are all structured in such a way that this emotion is part of our basic repertoire. But during the process of early development, many people learn to fear and avoid any manifestation of anger. They disapprove of it, not only in others, but in themselves. Little Timmy, for example, may declare that he hates the new baby. "Of course you don't really," his mother will object. "He is your own baby brother." Timmy will then become confused about the anger and jealousy he does feel; and the emotions that the beloved adult tells him he ought to be feeling. This is a part of the common experience of becoming socialized: we teach our young how to control their angry feelings. But in a distressing number of cases, the lesson is learned far too well.

Anger is a normal human reaction to certain stress-provoking stimuli—that is, situations, real or fantasied, in which an individual believes himself or his self-esteem to be endangered or threatened. It is also the natural response to circumstances of intense conflict and frustration; even very young babies can be provoked to great anger simply by having their arms and legs held down in such a way that they cannot move them. The anger response is one we have in common with many other animal species: we all recognize angry emotion in a cat whose back is up, and whose hair is standing on end; and in the dog when he stands rigid, lays his ears flat back against his head, and emits a low growl. But the dog or cat, unlike the human being, cannot be experiencing angry feeling on the one hand, and at the same time be telling himself that "it isn't important" or, worse yet, that he isn't even angry at all.

Very recently an acquaintance of mine, a woman in her mid-thirties, told me that she wanted more than anything else to find some meaningful kind of job. Her husband was all in favor of her doing so;

and as far as her children were concerned, nothing could now be more easily arranged. But she felt paralyzed—too terrified to expose herself to possible risks of rejection. Since she appears, to those who know her, to be a perfectly composed, competent and attractive person, I asked her why in the world she should feel this way.

She replied that she was "unfocused"; she didn't think of herself as an "effective person," and she felt that she did things badly. Then she added that she spent a good deal of her time tearing herself down and brooding on her own failings. In short, she felt worthless as a human being. And this inner reality was having a great impact on the outer realities: her feelings were so crippling that they prevented her from even trying to find any satisfactions or validations in the outside world.

As we talked on, my friend related an experience which had been the central trauma of her adolescence: her mother's suicide. She said that her mother's last words to her were : "I hope you've enjoyed your short happy life, because this is all the happiness you are ever going to have." This remark had been made on the night of the high-school senior prom, which was also the eve of her mother's death. The next morning her mother's body had been found; she had left only a cryptic note containing instructions for her burial.

It was an ugly tale. My own response to it was to say to my acquaintance carefully: "I suppose that must have left *you* with enormous feelings of anger and helplessness and fury which you couldn't do anything about."

"Oh, no," she answered emotionlessly. "I wasn't angry. I understood what my mother had been going through."

Her voice sounded so flat and strange that I asked her whether she knew that most psychiatrists viewed suicide as the angriest of angry gestures. Did she know that it was considered to be an act of self-directed hatred which always contained, at least in part, a desire to hurt and gain vengeance upon others—upon those who have "failed" the individual, let him or her down somehow?

But my friend insisted that she felt no shred of blame or anger toward her mother. "My father was slowly dying at the time. And my sister and I were, I suppose, being horrible adolescents. She just felt nothing in her life had worked out well. I never condemned her: I understood."

I asked her then whether, if someone stepped down on her toe very hard, and she "understood" the person's reasons for doing so, she would fail to *feel* the pain and rage which naturally would follow. She looked at me for a moment without replying.

Then she said thoughtfully that it was indeed after her mother's death that she had begun to feel great onslaughts of inadequacy and inferiority, and feelings that "nothing much mattered." She had never, however, despite the bitterness of her mother's last remark, considered the suicide as an act connected to anger in any way. Nor had she responded to it with any conscious anger on her own part.

And yet she was angry, angry to the point of paralysis. This emotion, which appeared inappropriate to her—what she "ought to" be feeling were sorrow, guilt, pity for her mother—had never been consciously confronted. As she spoke I began to feel that the very lack of focus of which she complained was tied to a need *not to know something*: the depth and intensity of her own rage. My friend had spent a good many years denying her very real anger; and yet it lived on within her, a shadowy but powerfully influential existence. She could only let it surface in a disguised form—as intensely negative feelings about herself.

According to the well-known New York psychoanalyst Dr. Alexander Lowen, there is a common tendency for individuals to refuse to face up to and admit their feelings of anger and rage. Many people repress these feelings, sit on them, force them out of awareness—and thus, instead of experiencing and working through their anger, they carry it around within them like a live emotional charge. "Suicide and depression are good illustrations of what the suppression of very powerful angry feelings can do to a person," say Lowen. "If you can get an individual who is depressed to admit to and feel his fury, you can always get him over his depression."

Dr. Lowen, author of several books including one on depression and the body, believes that the individual who is depressed is invariably someone who is angry about something—or at somebody—and yet finds his own feelings too dangerous or threatening to tolerate. "Instead of having experienced his hurt and rage at the appropriate time," observes Lowen, "the depressed person has coped with his particular situation by "armoring" himself, going into a state where his feelings are deadened. He's no longer aware of hostile attitudes, his own or anyone else's. In this way, he defends himself against his hurt and pain. And not feeling his pain, he can't feel his anger. He can't feel life, either."

The depressed individual's rage however, albeit unacknowledged by himself, simmers just beneath the surface of conscious life. The anger which he has failed to discharge outward turns in, sometimes with such vehemence and fury that the person may in fact takes his own life. "And yet all of this can and does often happen," notes Lowen, with a bemused nod, "without any inkling on his own part that he is simply *furious*; and that it is his own angry feelings that are at the source of all his suffering. No one actually appears less angry, or more sad and pathetic, than the poor fellow who is in a depression."

Lowen considers the ability to get angry one of the qualities of being normal, and the inability to feel or express anger a sign of emotional illness. "Anger isn't a negative emotion. It's a hot feeling, something positive, expressive, communicative. Its purpose is to mobilize the energy needed to help a person break free of a restriction, or get past an obstacle, or beyond whatever is binding him, holding him down, endangering his sense of his own wholeness and integrity. To tell a person: 'You shouldn't be angry,' is like telling him he should be dead, that he oughtn't to feel things. There's no reason in the world why an individual shouldn't experience his anger (and plenty of reasons why he should)! The point is, these feelings must be handled with discretion."

The dilemma is, however, that sometimes our angry feelings seem so irrational—or hypocritical—that discretion seems to involve not facing them at all. Take as an example the situation of a man who is truly grateful to his immediate superior for all sorts of kindnesses, patronage and assistance; and who feels nevertheless that this same person is holding him back, or overworking him, or just plain irritating him in some way. The man's positive feelings toward his boss might make his negative feelings unthinkable, so much so that he would repress them completely from his conscious thought.

In that event, the man's irritation and rage could be mounting daily without any real awareness on his part that this was happening. A very possible consequence of this state of affairs would be that one day, on coming home and finding his dinner not yet cooked, or the house unusually dirty, or his wife in a complaining mood, he might explode with a fury out of all proportion to the incident itself. Unaware himself of his rage at his boss, he could discharge his feelings on someone less ambiguous and threatening to him, his wife.

The man's displacement of his anger, from his boss to his wife, will not be without domestic after-effect: very likely before long she will be quarreling with one of the children in an "unrelated" incident. Indeed the burden of anger may be passed from one family member to another, and end with the youngest child giving the cat a good swift kick! But the man's persistent angry problem will by no means be solved or even clarified.

"I would never suggest," says Dr. Lowen, "that a man in this predicament would be *ipso facto* better off expressing his angry feelings directly to his boss. But he would undoubtedly be better off knowing where the anger is coming from; and whom he is truly angry at. Then maybe he could be talking with his wife about the problem, rather than fighting with her. I want to say, by the way, that she should be a real friend to him—as he should to her—and let him talk out these feelings, and empathize with them, and help him to work them through.

"But the problem may sometimes be more complicated than an ordinary interpersonal friction. Maybe the man's anger at the senior person stems, in fact, from an underlying rage at his father, or at some other authority figure, which he failed to work out during his childhood." One of the main purposes of therapy, points out Lowen, is the releasing of long-suppressed feelings and emotions. "There are people who are chronically furious— I mean, just plain mad all the time—who are totally unaware of their anger. A man can be loaded down with these feelings, literally ruin his physical health; and still, at the very same time, believe he hasn't a negative feeling toward anyone. I've seen such people, patients of mine who discover, in the course of psychotherapy, that in fact there's enough anger locked inside them to kill."

Anger is not only a psychological response; it is also a bodily reaction (physiologically identical to what occurs in a fear situation.) Our rate of metabolism changes when we are experiencing anger: Hormones, notably adrenalin, are released into the bloodstream: the blood vessels expand, the breathing rate quickens, and blood sugar concentration rises, bringing a spurt in energy. The senses become more finely tuned and alerted; the pupils of the eyes dilate, for example, so that we literally can see better when we are angry. The body is thus keyed up to maximum readiness for "fight or flight"—meeting the emergency or fleeing it rapidly.

But what if a twentieth-century civilized individual, despite the metabolic changes taking place within his or her body, failed to register consciously the fact that he or she was angry? Imagine as an example that I am someone who was raised in an atmosphere in which expressions of anger were completely inhibited, where people might feel one way but act another way. Suppose that when someone in my family was angry, he or she acted sweetly, or froze, but virtually never did anything to communicate that anger. Now one evening, as it happens, I go out to see a motion picture which I am anxious to see, and find myself waiting for almost two hours in a long queue. Just as the line starts moving, a women pushes in right in front of me. Her aggressive act is a stimulus to my anger; and my body quickly (and involuntarily) prepares itself to meet the stress. But, since I have never learned to recognize or respond to my anger, I am separated from these feelings: I do nothing, say nothing, essentially feel nothing. What happens to that upsurge of angry tension within my body?

In his recent book, *Anger: How to Recognize and Cope with It,* Dr. Leo Madow, a psychiatrist, writes, " . . . if there is no discharge of this buildup, as is usually the case, we remain in a chronic state of preparedness, with heart beating rapidly, blood pressure up, and chemical changes in the blood; and eventually this condition can harm us physically."

The suppression of angry feelings may indeed have concrete physical consequences. There are numerous somatic complaints, such as migraine headache and attacks of asthma, in which buildups of hidden rage are a known or suspected precipitating factor. Anger can also affect the skin's appearance: it may lie at the root of such disorders as itchy rash, pimples, hives. The fact that the skin is a particularly good indicator of a person's emotional health ought not to be too surprising when one considers that skin develops from the same highly sensitive embryonic tissues as do the nervous system and the brain. In his book *Anger,* Dr. Madow quotes a fascinating experiment during which one patient, encouraged to talk about a particularly painful family situation, immediately showed a distinct change in skin tone and burst forth with hives on his forearms.

Depressive moods—very commonly linked to repressed anger—may actually lower the body's resistance, leaving us more vulnerable to certain diseases, such as flu. Certainly, physicians are aware that when an individual is suffering from a psychological depression, his body temperature is chronically subnormal. (It works in the other direction also. When recovering from flu, our body temperature is subnormal, and many people become depressed during that period of time.) Dr. Madow goes so far as to suggest that a person's emotional state may even be a determinant in whether or not he catches a common cold. "In dealing with colds," he observes, "the fact that viruses cause them is less important than the question of what lowers the resistance. If we get chilled or expose ourselves to marked alterations of temperature or accumulate excessive fatigue, resistance may be lowered and a cold develop. However, people who have been out skiing, enjoying themselves and obviously under no emotional stress, may be chilled and exhausted and yet not take cold. . . . (M)any people are aware that they develop colds after emotional frustration. . . . I have seen people develop nasal congestion and mucoid discharge when talking about an unhappy marriage, or anger at parents, or at someone who has hurt them."

Chronic pains in the neck and in the back are problems which are also often bodily expressions of unacknowledged rage. Interestingly, many common expressions such as, "Get off my back!" or "He gives me a pain in the neck!" mirror a folk assumption that it is taut angry muscles that are at the root of the distress, rather than plain physical strain. One friend of mine, who always believed she had a "tennis back," recently told me that she had always assumed it was the distortion of her body as she jumped up and raced and twisted into the air to reach the ball, which caused the awful muscle pain that sometimes followed the game. But she had come to notice that when her husband kept sending her balls which she couldn't possibly reach, and which he knew she couldn't reach, she was very liable to "throw her back out." On the other hand, if she was managing to return every ball, her body could well tolerate all manner of stretching and distortion!

Instead of neck or back muscles, the genitourinary tract may become the body's "organ of choice" for expressing angry arousal. The need to urinate very frequently seems to be linked in some mysterious way to suppressed wrath: such frequent urination may result in mild or serious bladder dysfunctions and sometimes in permanent disabilities.

As is commonly known, repressed emotions can also affect the activities of the stomach and the bowel quite critically. We are all acquainted with that person who is eternally good-natured, always at the service of others, and who one day blossoms forth with a dangerous peptic ulcer or colitis or ileitis. Such an individual has controlled his own anger to such a degree that he may literally have mortgaged his physical survival in the service of maintaining his "never angry" self-image.

His situation is not dissimilar to that of the other "good guy," also a non-angry person, whose blood pressure shows a steady and predictable rise. As mentioned previously, when the body mobilizes to meet an outside stress, there is an immediate quickening in the rate of circulation. If the crisis or emotional problem is never recognized as such, never confronted or worked through, no discharge of inner tension will take place: a chronic state of hypertensiveness may result. Or the never-angry individual, sitting on his stockpile of accumulated, unacknowledged fury, may simply blow up one day—he may have a stroke. Such a person may have convinced himself and others that he is uniquely without anger, but he has by no means fooled his own capillaries, arteries and heart. Writes Dr. Madow: "In an individual with coronary artery disease, anginal attacks may be precipitated by emotions, particularly anger; and the role of anger in coronary thrombosis is fairly well accepted."

Anger, it seems, will out—in one form or another. If a rising reservoir of unexpressed rage does not manifest itself in physical symptoms, it may appear in the guise of a persistent behavioral pattern or problem. The "accident prone" individual, for example, communicates his inward-directed anger in his doggedly repetitious "chance" misfortunes. I have seen one such person, in the course of the past several years, manage to scar his face and most of his body in an endless series of household, bicycling and automobile accidents.

Rage, turned back upon the self, may be discerned in other malfunctional behavioral patterns, such as that of the "unlucky" lady who gets involved in one emotionally disastrous and self-punishing romance after another, or that of the girl who continually gets "caught" by unwanted pregnancies. There is anger being expressed in the behavior of the chronic undereater or overeater too: one psychiatrist, reporting on an obese woman patient, described her as a person who considered herself always "happy, good-natured and jovial." She was, nevertheless, capable of enormous anger, which expressed itself only in the form of uncontrollable eating binges. During the course of therapy this woman lost 150 pounds, let go of her "happy" self-image, and became overtly angrier, thinner and healthier.

Insomnia is yet another problem associated with hidden rage. The angry person's body is aroused, hyperalert, in a state of preparedness to meet a crisis—little wonder that he finds it impossible to sleep!

The woman who finds herself impelled to flirt with every man she meets is very probably, at some level, angry at men. Her behavior, which she may describe to herself as "high-spirited but harmless," follows a predictable course: she invites, teases, excites and eventually frustrates her admirers. Perhaps this is why she often arouses such anger in men.

She is in a sense the counterpart of the Don Juan, who lovelessly "loves women," viewing them as obstacles to be stalked and outwitted rather than as fellow human beings, capable of participating in a real and affectionate relationship. These sexual athletes are not loving, but are angry men.

Ideally, the best way for any of us to handle our angry feelings would be, first, to become aware of them consciously as soon as we are stimulated to feel anger; and then, to communicate the emotion at once. In this way, motor tensions arising within our bodies would be discharged immediately; and hopefully, we might also achieve the removal of whatever obstacle or frustration had aroused us in the first place. But in the course of our lives most of us have learned to have complicated feelings about anger—and a good deal of anxiety about both feeling it and showing it.

Human behavior being what it is, so elastic and intricate, we all devise our various methods for attempting to control and handle anger. Some people, for instance, try to deny it entirely, both in themselves and in others. Some are always conscious of the anger in themselves, but fail entirely to recognize it in those about them. Some see anger in the behavior of other people, but never in themselves. This last-mentioned individual would be someone who constantly seeks, in the behavior of others, confirmation of his own self-rejection; who provokes those close to him to show how little they truly care. This sort of person sees himself as someone without anger, who simply has had the misfortune of being surrounded by angry people. Unfortunately his own anger can only be admitted as a human response when he perceives it as a reaction to *someone else's* anger.

At best, no matter how honest and open we may try to be about anger—our own and other people's—life is full of circumstances which force us to suppress our expressions of this emotion. Take, for example, an instance in which a young wife is expecting a visit from her mother-in-law. As it happens, the two women have a tense relationship; and the younger woman is particularly disturbed by the fact that Grandma overindulges the children. She specifically asks that this time gifts be limited to one toy per child. When her mother-in-law arrives, however, it develops that there were a number of things that she "just couldn't resist" when she went shopping. In fact, she has twice as many presents in her suitcase as usual.

Needless to say, the young mother would be angry. Indeed there would probably be a mutual recognition, on the part of both women, that she *was* angry. But the rules of the situation would generally not permit any free communication of her anger to take place.

Such social situations do hamper a display of anger of which we are quite consciously aware: there are also situations, however, in which we are positively rewarded for manipulating our very consciousness of, and perception of, angry feelings. Suppose a certain man, an intensely patriotic person, happened to see a group of protestors desecrating an American flag. He would probably become agitated and aroused by the sight. His initial impulse might be to communicate his rage directly; but at the same time he could have competing urges: fears that he might get hurt during such a confrontation, or might hurt someone else, or simply make a fool of himself. So instead of acting on his initial emotion, he might dilute and "miniaturize" it by saying to himself: "Why should I involve myself with those crazy young bearded slobs? You can't get any sense out of such people. They're not responsible, not even worth thinking about. . . . " If the protestors are not worth getting angry at, he needn't take the trouble to get angry—he is, in fact, freed of the necessity to take any action. And by diluting his anger, even as he evaluates it, he avoids any possible retaliation on the part of those toward whom it might be directed.

It is the fear of possible retaliation, points out Yale psychiatrist Dr. Leonard Zegans, which perhaps most often prevents us from communicating angry feelings with straightforwardness or openness. "Although retaliation may," he notes, "consist of nothing more than a feared loss of affection on the part of the person with whom we are angry." Therefore, explains Zegans, many of us tend to resort to "appeasement covers" in our everyday lives. "These are little tricks, or candy coatings, which make it possible to deliver a hostile communication while at the same time reducing the other person's reactive options."

A standard "appeaser" is, he remarks, always to be discerned in the sentence which begins with such a phrase as: "I know you'll think this is none of my business, but"— or —"Well, dear, I think for your own sake you ought to know"— or —"Stop me if I'm out of line for butting into this. . . . "

Says Zegans, "What comes after a solicitous opener like this is invariably going to be a hostile belt in the stomach. But the person's come-on will have disarmed his victim. Because after all, what can you say when he's only trying to be helpful?"

Another appeasement cover-up for angry communication may be seen in the innocent prattle of the person whom Zegans calls "the infantilizer." This individual presents himself, or herself, as a harmless well-wisher who is certainly unaware that the things he or she is saying might be having a dreadful emotional effect upon you. This person may be the neighbor who asks over and over again about that child you were forced to have institutionalized; and just what was it that led you and your husband to make that decision? Or the infantilizer may be the fellow who keeps asking you why he hasn't seen you with Ruth lately, even though the question clearly makes you uncomfortable. (Why is it that everyone *else* knows that Ruth threw you over without explanation, and the rumor is that she's seeing your closest friend?) This person has no idea of how painful his or her questions or remarks might be. "This is what I call the It's Only Me, Baby Snooks, approach," says Zegans, with a smile.

The individual who presents himself as "helpless" may also be availing himself of the opportunity to express his anger, while at the same time stripping his victim of any open way in which to defend himself or herself, or even to answer the charges. Remarks such as: "I'm glad you're so happy with your new job and house and car, but I guess now you don't have time to visit your old mother and father," or: "Have a good time on your ski trip and don't worry at all about the kids and me being here by ourselves over Thanksgiving," are, Zegans observes, statements which in translation mean: "You are a rat. And you are abrogating one of your fundamental responsibilities—what happens to me and my concerns." However, the "helpless" person cannot express things in so many words; the justice or injustice of his accusations can never be examined. His angry communication merely peppers his victim with a spray of guilt—and the victim himself will probably be in a rage shortly afterwards, too. But even if he does happen to realize why he is angry, there will be little the victim can do in the way of offering a straightforward response.

Another interesting appeasement ploy is that of the: "I'm in this with you" individual. Such a person cannot be criticized for telling you the truth about yourself, because he is confessing to the same truth about *himself*. While telling you of your deficit he is identifying and empathizing with you: "Don't you wish you and I could get the same kind of brilliant insights as Joe Blow always seems to be getting?" one researcher might ask another. Or an "I'm in this with you," woman might say to a friend, "Don't you wish you and I knew how to dress like Joanne does? She can put on some little scarf, or some pin, and look so well put together. But you and I, no matter how much we've spent, or how carefully we've tried to co-ordinate, always look like we're—you know—sort of coming apart at the seams." What can one answer to such a statement? There probably is no defense against this one. Dr. Zegans confides that he calls this method: "Isn't It a Shame That We Lepers Can't Go into Church?"

The friendly bearer of ill tidings is also, says Zegans, an individual whose motives should always be assessed quite carefully; he is often an angry appeaser. "I look at him as someone who, more often than not, is falsifying his intention—which is to bring you aversive and painful information—under a guise of objectivity and helpfulness. In my view, he is the man from the Colgate ad; only he is good enough to tell you that everyone is talking about your bad breath. What he is actually doing is telling you off; and at the same time, abrogating his personal responsibility for doing so. Because after all, it's not *he* who is saying he detests you, or he who is spreading those awful stories about you. It is that other guy, or maybe a whole group of other people. And how can you hit back, or defend yourself, when he's the one who's being your best—or maybe your only—real friend?"

Nearly everyone has some "angry problems"—problems in translating the angry messages coming from others; and in knowing where, when and how to express one's own anger. But angry emotion need not always be looked upon as "a problem." Yale psychiatrist Dr. Albert Rothenberg recently observed at a meeting of the American Psychiatric Association: "Anger is an alerting phenomenon, for the individual and for others, which provides a basis for communication. . . . " It thus offers potentially constructive possibilities. "Regardless of the explanation," said Rothenberg, "it is a consistent observation that the most truly *violent* people are those who have difficulty dealing with angry feelings."

Anger need not always be seen as something synonymous with aggression, the gateway to violence and self-destruction: angry feelings, straightforwardly discharged, may indeed remove the threat or obstruction before intense verbal or physical abuse appears necessary to an individual. There are certainly circumstances in which, of all options open, anger may very well be the best.

1973

Elation and Despair

Manic-depressive Psychosis and the Related Disorders

The course that Julie N.'s case had taken had not been atypical. In the three-month period preceding her current depression, Julie—mother of a three-year-old girl, wife of a young lawyer, heiress to a modest family inheritance—had experienced an amphetaminelike "high," felt full of energy and enthusiasm, and as she later described it, "practically omnipotent, on top of the world, able to do or accomplish just about anything. . ." During this time she had become involved in trying to establish a small business, and had thrown herself into this project with an almost eerie focus and intensity. The tiny firm preoccupied her thoughts totally, to the exclusion of everything and everyone about her.

Julie's business was primarily a weaving enterprise. She designed, and then had woven—according to her own specifications—unusual and striking "designer" fabrics. She had located a group of women in a village near Mexico City, who did the actual weaving; she herself purchased the raw materials (mostly wools), and tried to make the sales contacts, keep the books, and attend to the thousand other details which the running of the business required. She was working some eighteen hours a day—occasionally more. And the fact that the firm had begun showing fairly serious financial deficits had not in any way affected her high spirits, hyperactivity, and elated frame of mind.

But those around her, particularly close family members, had become increasingly alarmed. The money situation was in and of itself disturbing: The initial outlay of funds to set up Julie's business had not been inconsiderable. Then there was the rental on the little store, the costs of the raw materials, the salaries for the Mexican weavers. And above that there were the strange, almost irrational purchases which she would make from time to time. For example, following upon a dire accounting which demonstrated her firm's rather shaky financial condition, Julie had gone out and bought a glamorous five-thousand-dollar white leather sofa for the anteroom of her shop. (She seemed to have lost, in her rush of optimism, her self-protective wits.)

Her insistently "happy" mood, too, was accompanied by a certain

248

growing irritability—especially toward her little daughter's needs and demands—as well as an inability to relax, a need to be moving about which was so strong that it affected even her sleep patterns and made it impossible for her to remain in bed throughout the night.

At a time when her business was moving inexorably toward financial collapse, Julie's confidence and energetically bright outlook had only continued to grow (though always coupled with that excitability and tendency toward querulousness). Her husband, and then her parents, had carefully suggested that she might profit from some talks with a psychiatrist. But this idea had been dismissed with incredulity because, as Julie later told her therapist: "I felt so wonderful; I couldn't see any reason in the world why I'd *want* to go for help. I mean I was fine—and not simply fine, but superb. I was in that marvelous mood, and so excited about the business and by all of the interesting things I was doing."

This state of euphoria, which was affecting Julie's judgment and understanding, had enabled her to remain impervious to the impending disaster. And when her business enterprise, after a last brief "wobbling" period, finally did fail—and fail decisively—she plunged with an almost dizzying rapidity from the exalted heights of an Olympian joy to the very pit of an acute depressive attack.

A few weeks afterward, sitting limply across from her newly found psychiatrist, Julie sagged in her chair like a creature without inner structure, without bones. Her hair was unkempt, her complexion sallow, her skirt and sweater ill-fitting and selected haphazardly. The brisk businesswoman of a few weeks earlier seemed to have disappeared almost magically; it was as if Julie had been transformed totally by the touch of some malicious wand. Her mood, her experience of her life was, as she described it, "black. . .one of blackness, awful, awful blackness. . . ." She saw herself in terms of utter worthlessness, of a creature destroyed; she could, she confessed, see little reason or sense in continuing to live. Eyes puffy, her cheeks splotched with "crying rashes," she said that she had begun to think that it might be best not only for herself but for her husband and child if she were dead. She had nothing to give to them, nothing to give to anyone. . .life was unendurable. She felt totally isolated and alone.

What Julie N.'s story reflected was the more or less classical outline of a *manic-depressive* (or "bipolar") mood disorder. She had, for a period of months, been feeling "too good to be true," too immune to any of the problems or difficulties which she ought, rationally speaking, to have been confronting. Now, following upon the failure of her shop, the picture had entirely reversed itself; things were "too bad to be true." The collapse of her weaving business was being equated with the destruction of her worth as a human being. She now called herself a "useless," even "loathsome" individual and was seriously questioning her right—and willingness—to go on living. The disappointment she had sustained was being magnified beyond all proportion. Her despair was as exaggerated, and apparently on its way to becoming as prolonged, as had been her mood of joy. And indeed the high mood and the low mood, though on the surface so strikingly different, did share one important feature: They both rendered Julie incapable of sustaining realistic contact with her environment. This inability to correctly read and assess the signals from outside the self is one of the hallmarks (and dangers) of manic-depressive illness—and Julie was suffering from a relatively less severe, which is to say not psychotic, form of this disorder.

Manic-depressive psychosis is, as most textbooks on psychiatry like to point out, one of the oldest psychiatric disorders to have been described in the literature of Western civilization. Medical literature, as well as prose and poetry, dating well back into the fourth century B.C., contain references to individuals who suffer extreme mood swings, alternating between glee and what the ancients called *melancholia*. A doctor living in the second century B.C., one Arateus, wrote a clinical description of the manic-depressive cycle which remains valid to this day: Such patients, after an initial euphoric period were, he noted, "sad, dismayed, sleepless. . . . They become thin by their agitation and loss of refreshing sleep. . . . At a more advanced stage, they complain of a thousand futilities and desire death."

So striking in its roller-coasterlike progression of highs and lows is the illness that in the last century a French psychiatrist, Falret, called it *folie circulaire*—that is, "circular or cycling madness." But the term *manic-depressive psychosis* was not invented until the early nineteen-twenties when Dr. Emil Kraepelin first used it to delineate a form of mental disturbance most characterized by disorders of mood-state.

In Kraepelin's schema, the individual who evidenced mania with no sign of depression—as well as the person who became depressed without any prior euphoria—was to be classified as manic-depressive. (Actually, mania in the absence of depression is extremely rare, while depression without mania is common.) Kraepelin was making the supposition that even if the depressed individual had never evidenced any signs of mania, the manic phase had still somehow been "there." More recently, however, this view has come to seem increasingly questionable. For one thing, the development of different types of psychoactive drug treatments—such as Lithium and the antidepressants (Elavil, Tofranil, and the like)—has demonstrated that certain drugs which are helpful for "plain" depressives may be utterly useless in the treatment of manic-depressive disorder. If the two kinds of patients were really suffering from the same illness, then they ought (or so a number of psychiatrists have reasoned) to be responding to the same kinds of "cure."

Generally speaking, there is a tendency among most experts in the field of depression to view manic-depressive disturbance and "simple" depression as fairly separate and distinct disorders. Manic-depressive disturbance is now often referred to as *bipolar disease*—i.e., a mood disorder encompassing both "poles" of emotion, high and low—while depression in the absence of mania is called *unipolar disease*. According to Myrna Weissman, a faculty member in psychiatry at Yale University and author of *The Depressed Woman*, the depressive phase in both unipolar and bipolar disease manifests itself in symptoms which are virtually indistinguishable: "In both cases, there is sadness; there is hopelessness, loss of interest, loss of energy and usually what we call 'vegetative signs and symptoms' as well. These," explained Professor Weissman, an empathetic woman in her mid-thirties, "would include such things as weight loss, sleep disturbance, general apathy. And frequently, there are a variety of nonspecific complaints as well—aches and pains, headaches, things like that."

Often these clinical indicators of depression are accompanied by suicidal impulses and feelings. "One of the things you do right away in working with a depressed person," said Ms. Weissman, "is to ask: 'Do you feel a little like life isn't worth living?' And if the person says that he or she does, then you go on and say: 'Have you ever thought that you would be better off dead?' And then you ask if he's made any actual plans and what those plans might be. And you continue probing very carefully, going through a whole scale of levels of questions to make very certain that you've covered the waterfront. The person, I might add, is usually relieved, and finds it comforting to be able to talk about these things at last. Because they are, of course, terrible secrets."

There are, she observed, a number of fairly reliable "depression-rating scales," which enable clinicians working with a new patient to estimate the severity of the problem. "Now in bipolar or manic-depressive disease one encounters—and it's very dramatic and memorable, which must be one of the reasons why it's been described down through the ages—the very opposite signs and symptoms. There is overactivity; there is expansiveness, a lot of pressive speech—that is, talking fast—grandiose ideas. . ." The patient may be going on spending sprees, or promiscuity sprees, or gambling, drinking too much, or engaging in cockeyed business deals. The manic person is, in other words, like someone who is mildly drunk. "It's a similar kind of loss of inhibition," said Weissman, with a smile and a slight shrug.

While in this elated phase, as both Weissman and a number of other experts with whom I spoke remarked, the sufferer will often display quite bizarre kinds of behavior. One New York psychiatrist told me of a patient who had first evidenced mania by leaping into her open convertible and driving toward her summer home in East Hampton, totally in the nude. Another doctor told me of a case which had erupted when a young scientist, visiting at the home of a colleague, had suddenly torn off his clothing, run through the house naked, and begun a series of frantic phone calls to the heads of government of Cuba, Mexico and Ceylon. Mania frequently has a terrible kind of funniness. But the manic individual, when in this high, overexcited, overactive phase, can get into wild and self-destructive business deals, gamble away everything he or she owns, drink for days and nights continuously, engage in crazily promiscuous sexual behavior, and even get into physically dangerous kinds of situations. One psychiatric casebook describes the onset of a manic attack in which a wealthy Philadelphia businessman ran his car out onto a metropolitan expressway and began handing out twenty-dollar bills to motorists whose oncoming cars managed to screech to a halt in time! (Fortunately he was stopped before meeting with a driver who failed this "test.")

This state of elation is, however, usually accompanied by a growing irritability. "The manic person is feeling good; but it's not a warm glow, nothing that includes other people. It's all focused on the self, and it has to be protected at all costs from intrusions from the outside." This, pointed out Weissman, was the reason why Julie N. (a pseudonym for one of her patients), though full of energy and hyperactive in her business activities, had screamed at her child whenever she made even the mildest demand. "She just couldn't be bothered with anyone else's needs. There's very little empathy in this so-called mood of happiness: In fact it has an almost desperate quality."

The buying sprees, wild business deals, the gambling, drinking and indiscriminate sexual behavior which are among the common symptoms of mania represent, in the view of many clinicians, the individual's frenzied flight from what is actually an underlying depression. The person's self-references are positive—indeed, super-positive—but they appear to be of a very fragile sort; they must be protected, at all costs, from incursions from the real world (hence the irritability). It is as if the manic-depressive, in order to stave off the oncoming depression and all of its attendant negative feelings, has gone to the extreme opposite end of the spectrum in order to maintain her or his positive sense of self.

Some psychiatrists view the manic episode as not only a denial of an underlying, depressing reality; but as something similar to the acting-out of a metaphor, a wished-for dream. As one therapist remarked to me: "The woman who, for instance, goes on a clothes-buying spree, or redecorates her whole house or becomes sexually promiscuous, is really saying to the world: I am what my dreams desire me to be . . . In my dreams I am all beautiful, and can wear all the clothes, or decorate the most beautiful house, or absorb all the men in the world. And there are no bounds to my reality—no boundaries to social convention, the size of my pocketbook, the capacity of my vagina, or to my body's ability to do without sleep or nourishment." The manic patient does exert a certain kind of dramatic appeal, for we all have in us part of that same dream—that wish to make our overly expansive fantasies real.

This is probably one of the reasons why, according to Dr. Fritz Redlich, professor of psychiatry at Yale and former dean of the Yale Medical School, manic patients tend to become the center of attention on a hospital ward. "During the early stages these individuals can be very sociable, very charming," he observed. "But if it's serious (and if it isn't intervened with, it can become *very* serious), the humor starts to become biting; irritability sets in; and gradually what is merely verbal irritability may turn into assaultive behavior—the person may simply go out of control." He paused, shrugged, smiled slightly: "That's the derivation of the word *maniac*, after all."

Psychiatrists usually reserve the diagnostic label *manic-depressive disease* for the most severe cases of this type—those requiring a period of hospitalization, and in which psychotic delusions or hallucinations have become manifest. Disorders that are similar in kind, though less intense and serious in nature, are known as *hypomania* (less-than-manic) and *cyclothymic personality* (a personality structure characterized by cycling emotions). The mildest of these three conditions is cyclothymic personality: Indeed, the term may be used in the absence of any disorder or abnormality to describe a certain sort of temperament. "The cyclothymic personality," explained Dr. Gerald Klerman, director of the Erich Lindemann Mental Health Center in Boston and a professor of psychiatry at Harvard Medical School, "is simply one which is characterized by swings of mood, from periods of well-being and enthusiasm through periods of the opposite—discouragement, lack of confidence and pessimism.

"I think," he said, "that we all know people who have these protracted mood swings. Some individuals have them on a regular basis; they may say, 'The summer is always great for me,' or: 'I'm always depressed in the autumn'. . .that kind of thing. I have a colleague who just *knows* that come winter her husband is going to be a grouch. He's crabby, feels down, doesn't want to go anywhere, do anything. . .And then each spring he blossoms forth like the flowers. He's full of energy, wants to play tennis, see friends, go to bridge parties, and so forth. In his case the cycle seems to be tied to the seasons; for other people, it's not."

What is striking about cyclothymic individuals is, he noted, that they may seem like such totally different persons during different periods of time. Most of us have a more stable quality to our personalities: We are, even given the fluctuations of our moods, pretty much the same individual during the course of the year. The cyclothymic person may, however, over a period of months, change from a completely extroverted individual to a totally introverted one; he or she seems to be subject to the mild fluctuations of an inner tide that exerts some influence upon his or her thinking and behavior. (One friend of mine, a successful novelist, described her own "mood cycle" in these terms: "There'll be days, weeks, when I just don't feel like doing anything. I'll just lie around watching television, and get on everyone's nerves. And then all of a sudden I'll start waking up early and become a bundle of energy. I'll begin writing at a steady pace, get my wardrobe in shape, clean my apartment from top to bottom, and get involved in a much more active social life. . . That's just my pattern.")

Such people seem to have, in Klerman's view, a wider personality range than most people do. "The difference between this 'happy phase,' as experienced by the cyclothymic individual and the 'high phase' of the hypomanic is," said the psychiatrist, "simply one of degree. Hypomania, unlike cyclothymia, is a clinical state—it requires treatment either with drugs or psychotherapy or with both. The elated period of the hypomanic is characterized by a certain inappropriateness, 'dizzy' kinds of behavior, which are seen by those around the person as completely unlike his or her normal modes of behaving. The person is simply feeling too good: And while she's not psychotic or seriously out of touch with reality, there is that overactivity which is coupled with poor judgment. She is exhausting herself in one way or another, and if you look at it closely, the behavior has, always, a strangely inefficient quality. . ."

The manic-depressive psychotic is, on the other hand, not only overactive but often delusional or hallucinating. In the manic phase, for instance, the person may believe that he or she is in possession of some special powers or magical attributes. "I saw a young woman yesterday," related Klerman, "who believed she had a bewitching and overpowering beauty. (This wasn't, by the way, true.) She thought that her neighbors were plotting against her and persecuting her because she was the most beautiful woman in her area. She was, furthermore, hyperactive—she'd gone on a buying spree and spent hundreds of dollars buying gifts for her friends and neighbors. Then that manic irritability had set in and she'd begun quarreling with everyone around her concerning those 'conspiracies' against her, which she believed to be motivated by jealousy. By the time I talked to her she'd been arrested by the police for having started a brawl in a social club. She was in a frankly manic state; that is, psychotic, deluded, overactive, inappropriate and out of control."

What causes manic-depressive illness? Does it come about as a result of particular kinds of rearing practices or is it "constitutional," that is, built into the sufferer's biological makeup somehow? In reviewing the clinical literature on the subject, and in talks with psychiatrists working in the field of depression, I learned that the pathogenesis of the disorder remains uncertain. One landmark study, carried out in the mid-nineteen-fifties by Mabel Blake Cohen and several co-workers (among whom was Frieda Fromm-Reichmann, the model for the female psychoanalyst in *I Never Promised You a Rose Garden*) consisted of an extensive exploration of the family backgrounds of a group of eleven manic-depressive patients. Cohen and her colleagues found that these people had all come from families which had been set off, for one reason or another, from the surrounding milieu or neighborhood. Either the family belonged to a minority group, or had lost money, or an important family member had become mentally ill. Whatever the onus or burden might have been, it was the individual who later became a manic-depressive who had been the one selected to win, or to restore, the family's honor. Often, this child had been chosen for the task because she or he was brighter, more beautiful, more talented, or superior to the other siblings in some other way. "We also found," reported the Cohen researchers, "that the child is usually caught between one parent who is thought of as a failure and blamed for the family's plight (frequently the father) and the other parent who is aggressively striving, largely through the instrumentality of the child, to remedy the situation. . ."

Was this, then, the particular kind of family and social environment which "bred" manic-depressive disease? The findings of the Cohen study, though intriguing, remain unconfirmed. Later researches on manic-depressive patients have demonstrated that while many do spring from the type of background described by Cohen et al., there are many others who simply do not. Far more fruitful explanations of the etiology of manic-depressive disease will probably emerge from the so-called new biology—genetics, biochemistry, neurobiology, etc.—which is now sweeping through the field of psychiatry.

It is from the province of genetics that fascinating suggestions about the possibly hereditary nature of manic-depressive illness have recently come. It should be noted, however, that even prior to these carefully controlled genetic studies it had been recognized that manic-depressive disorder did tend to run in certain families and groups. Although within the population at large the disease is statistically infrequent (affecting only 1 to 2 percent of the population) there were certain peoples among whom it appeared far more commonly. Jews and Scandinavians, for example, showed particularly high incidences of manic-depressive disturbance.

There is now important genetic evidence, coming from three disparate sources, which supports the notion that there is some kind of inherited vulnerability which renders some individuals incapable of adapting to certain kinds of stress. (Dr. Klerman characterized this as a "subtle interplay between constitutional predispositions and the environment.") Studies of twins have, for example, demonstrated that where one member of a pair develops manic-depressive illness the likelihood that the other twin will have it is extraordinarily high—over 60 percent. "Furthermore," Klerman told me, "identical twins have a higher concordance rate than fraternal twins. What that means—in nonjargon terms—is that if the twins came from the same egg, the probability that if one is manic-depressive, the other will be too, jumps even higher.

"That," he observed, "is one fascinating piece of genetic evidence. The second lies in what are called *pedigree studies*. These are long-range studies of families, running back several generations, of individuals who have been hospitalized with manic-depressive illness. What the pedigree studies have indicated is that, in the families of these patients, there are more manic-depressive relatives and depressive relatives than could possibly be accounted for by chance alone." One large-scale pedigree study, he added, had just been carried out by a student of his who had spent the past two years in Israel. The results imply that the incidence of manic-depressive illness is far higher among the Ashkenazi, or Jews of European origin, than it is among the Sephardic Jews. "Almost all of the manic-depressive illness in Jerusalem appeared to be among the European families, while there was practically none among the North African and Middle Eastern families."

A third kind of evidence which seems to argue strongly for an inherited predisposing factor in the development of bipolar illness has emerged from yet another type of genetic investigation. There are now several studies which have attempted to link the tendency toward manic-depressive disorder with certain other characteristics—such as color blindness and the Xg blood type—which are known to be passed down from parent to descendants and to be carried on the mother's x-chromosome. This research has, generally speaking, supported the notion that the predisposition toward becoming manic-depressive can be correlated with these other genetically transmitted traits. In other words, one may inherit the vulnerability to manic-depressive disease from one's mother, grandmother or great-grandmother in much the same way that one might inherit her color blindness or her Xg blood type.

Although it is, as mentioned, a fairly uncommon disorder, manic-depressive illness is nevertheless a somewhat serious one. While individuals who experience a depression without any mania are liable never to suffer a similar episode again, the evidence indicates that those who manifest the high as well, have an 80 percent chance of experiencing another one. The episode may not occur within the next five or ten years, Dr. Klerman told me. "But," he observed, "if you have had a manic phase, you're at greater risk for the future than the person who has had depression without the mania. That is, you see, an index of some severity; it's probably based on those hereditary factors."

But hadn't the discovery of the drug Lithium, I inquired, changed the clinical picture somewhat? Hadn't it been found to be effective in the treatment of depression alone—and the drug of choice in the treatment of manic-depressive illness?

Klerman shrugged. "I personally think that the Lithium thing has become a little overplayed and is a bit faddist. Lithium is clearly of value in the prevention of the recurrence of mania . . . but even the most enthusiastic Lithium pushers will acknowledge, in their private moments of truth, that about one-third of the patients on Lithium need to take an antidepressant as well. The Lithium, you see, is very good for putting a ceiling on the 'high,' but it only puts a more or less weak floor on the 'low.'"

There is thus, as the psychiatrist pointed out, a fairly sizable group of patients who get intermittent depressions, even with the Lithium. "These people need a combination of Lithium and an antidepressant." The drugs, while "relatively safe," are powerful and must be dispensed with attention and care. Some 10 percent of Lithium patients get thyroid changes after the first year; about 2 percent develop a diabeteslike syndrome. And when antidepressants are included in the medication regimen, there is a danger of cardiac arrhythmia (irregular heartbeat), especially in the patient over forty. There is also the potential for glaucoma and/or an uncomfortable symptom called *dry mouth*. "These drugs are not playthings," said Klerman. "Now I don't think we should panic about that and take them off the market; but I don't think we should be cavalier about them either. Personally, if my own aunt had to be on Lithium, I'd tell her not only to make sure that she had a first-rate psychiatrist, skilled in the use of these drugs, but to make sure that she got herself a first-rate internist as well. And I'd want her to be certain, furthermore, that the two specialists had easy access to one another and were very regularly in touch."

Even in instances where the drug treatment may be working quite well, and there are no untoward side-effects, it may well happen that the patient will simply quit taking his or her drugs. According to Dr. Thomas Detre, chairman of the Department of Psychiatry at the University of Pittsburgh School of Medicine, the manic person often becomes nostalgic for those euphoric highs: "He or she misses the excitement—and stops taking the medications," he said. "In one case, I happened to be treating a very attractive young librarian. She was doing quite well on Lithium. At some point, however, she stopped taking her drugs, and shortly after that she rushed off to New York on a buying spree. She ran up fantastic charge accounts, went to all the shows in town, stayed at the best hotels, frequented the most glamorous bars. . . When she was finally brought back to the hospital, exhausted physically but in a state of frenzy, we gave her her Lithium immediately." The psychiatrist smiled. "She looked down at that capsule in her hand," he recounted, "and then she looked up at me. And then she said, very sadly, 'Hello, Lithium; Goodbye, Broadway.' And then she swallowed her medication."

It is due to this somewhat pleasureful aspect of the high, continued Detre, that it is important for the patient to develop a strong and trusting relationship with the therapist. "It may take several such episodes before the physician can convince the person that it's ultimately not worthwhile to cheat on taking the medications. The problem is, of course, that the individual doesn't feel ill in the elated phase; she or he doesn't feel ill until coming down. And when she's down, she's so *far* down that she becomes totally certain that there is nothing—and no one in the world—that can possibly be of help to her."

In the depressive phase, if the Lithium (either alone, or in conjunction with an antidepressant) provides no relief, there are still other drugs which may be brought into play. These are, however, even more problematical as far as the issue of possible adverse side-effects is concerned. And it is true that only some 60 to 70 percent of severely depressed patients respond to *any* form of drug therapy. "There remain some instances," said Detre soberly, "when electric shock has to be used."

Psychotherapy and family counseling are also important; but, he added, insight alone is usually not enough to prevent recurrence of the attacks. "In these serious cases the most that psychotherapy can do is to enable the person to figure out what kinds of things may be precipitating or aggravating the mood swings. And some therapy is also helpful for the people close to the patient," he added, "because these individuals are disruptive and tend to involve the whole family in their doings."

Perhaps one of the most striking features of the manic-depressive cycle is the way in which the euphoric and depressive phases seem to parody or caricature normally happy and sad moods. A manic episode does, indeed, resemble a good mood gone haywire—or at least one which is for some reason unable to run its course, as good moods usually do. The same may be said of the depressive episode as well. It is an unhappy mood which fails, somehow, to dissipate; whatever grief or loss may have brought it about in the first place, it is the strength and persistence of the emotion which is puzzling. Sad events, many experts feel, do not provide the full explanation. As Drs. Gary Tucker and Jonathan Pincus note (in their recent book, *Behavioral Neurology*), depressive patients frequently either "distort life events or overemphasize their unfavorable side. . .and. . .these allegedly causal events may actually be a product of the depressive feelings themselves."

The suggestion is, in other words, that the depressive feelings— whether or not they have originated with some real setback or sorrow— cannot be normally handled and worked through by the individual; the feelings of sadness and hopelessness have become in and of themselves, self-generating. As Dr. Gary Tucker, professor of psychiatry at Dartmouth Medical School, put it: "The interesting thing is not what turns on a feeling of sadness—we all feel sad at some time or another— but why in some people it goes on for weeks on end. Let's look at it this way: Two women lose their jobs. One feels bad for awhile and then shrugs it off and sets out to look for something else. The other one goes home, starts brooding, falls into a serious depression. Why is one of them able to adapt to the difficulty and work things through, while the other simply cannot? Most of the discussions about depression and about manic-depressive illness get involved in what 'turns on' an episode. But a number of us are now wondering about something else: 'Why can't some people seem to 'turn it off?'"

The answer to this question may, when it is fully resolved, lie within the realm of brain biochemistry. For, as Tucker and Pincus point out in their book, "the clinical and pharmacological evidence strongly implies the existence of biochemical disturbance in mood disorders. . ." Where such disorders of emotional state are concerned, the problem is now thought to involve a group of brain chemicals called the *biogenic amines*. These brain compounds appear to be necessary (and probably in quite precise proportions) for the maintenance and regulation of normal moods. A little too much of one of the biogenic amines, or a bit too little of another, may bring about a marked shift in the individual's state of emotional being and experiencing.

Let us imagine a situation in which there is an overabundance of a particular brain compound called *norepinephrine*. Norepinephrine is known to promote a mood of high spirits, attention, energy, well-being, and so forth. (It is this substance which is released into the bloodstream when a person takes amphetamines.) If we can picture an instance in which an individual is continuously pouring forth norepinephrine, then it is easy enough to see why an initial good mood might fail to end, and why feelings of joy and elation could pass beyond the boundary of normality and into the manic range. The individual who is euphoric, and whose euphoria goes on and on, may be someone whose brain is overproducing norepinephrine.

One somewhat simplistic view of the biochemistry of manic-depressive disease is that the elated phase has to do with too much norepinephrine in the brain and bloodstream; and that the subsequent depression has to do with the depletion of norepinephrine reserves. But this, as several researchers told me, is probably not going to be the precise story, when all of the story is known. The explanation is far more likely to be along the lines of a "carburetor mix" model. That is, it will not simply be a case of too much or too little norepinephrine—or too much or too little of one of the other important brain chemicals—but of the delicate balance between all of them, the particular ways in which they combine, and the manner in which they interact with the body's hormones.

In any case, there are strong reasons for believing that the answers to the problem of manic-depressive disorder will be found, not in the psychoanalyst's or psychiatrist's office, but in the biochemist's laboratory. Such information will, when it becomes available, provide fascinating insight not only into the biological substrata of manic-depressive behavior: It will reveal a great deal about the neurochemistry of normal moods as well.

1975

Time of Transition

The Male in the Mid-life Decade

The age of forty, according to the great Swiss psychologist Carl Gustav Jung, is the "noon of life." Statistics, he noted, show a rise in the frequency of mental depressions in men about this age. At forty, a man is in possession of his full adult powers, but also of the consciousness that his sun is entering a new meridian. His existence is, as it was during the adolescent period, perched on the edge of change. For, as Jung wrote, ". . . we cannot live the afternoon of life according to the program of life's morning: what was great in the morning will be little at evening, and what was true in the morning will at evening have become a lie."

An individual, as he approaches his middle years, often experiences upsurges of turmoil and conflict; ideals, values, goals which in "life's morning" seemed beyond any questioning may now appear doubtful and even inane. Like the adolescent, he begins pondering the real meaning—not to those around him, but *to himself* as a person—of everything he has been, done and become. At the same time he looks toward the future with some uncertainty and a portion of fear. What he may be moving into, suggests a group of Yale University researchers now studying the mid-life (thirty-five to forty-five) decade in males, is a natural and necessary process of personality growth and change. It may occur quietly, no more than a subliminal ripple, or it may explode outward in a volcanic life crisis.

Although psychotherapists have long recognized that there is often a painful phase toward the close of early adulthood, the mid-life period has been, from the researcher's point of view, one of the "dark ages" in the life-cycle. Curiously enough, in a time when studies of infants and growing children, and of the aged, proliferate everywhere, virtually nothing is known of the developmental course of the adult male. Experts are aware, in great detail, of what is happening to an individual during his two-year-old "negative phase," but what is the nature of his experience once he grows up, passes beyond the frontier of age twenty, and moves into the unexplored territory of the thirties, forties and

263

fifties? Is each person's experience absolutely unique? Or do men continue to move through further personality stages for which there are some general, if rough, predictors?

"Historically, our understanding of what might be called adult development (granted that in adult life we do continue developing) has been pretty much nil," says Dr. Daniel J. Levinson, director of the pioneering Yale group now engaged in studying the male mid-life experience. "There hasn't been any comprehensive theory of adult development, no body of hypotheses to be tested. In fact you might think, looking over the sparse body of literature on the subject, that not too much is happening to a guy between the ages of twenty and sixty; he's not changing much. The only trouble is that when you go and take a look at a man in his later years, you find that his personality *has* changed. So the question is, when did it happen? And in what ways? What were the issues involved?"

Levinson, who is fifty-one, is tall and lean and wears a perennial wry smile. His interest in mid-life problems stems, he acknowledges readily, somewhat from his own life experience. "I guess it was a question of asking myself: 'Hey? What hit me when I was forty? What hit most of the men I knew?'" The psychologist, whose coloring is naturally high, reddens almost imperceptibly. He pauses.

There is a long silence which he breaks suddenly. "In Freud's view, you know, once an individual reached adulthood, his personality didn't undergo much more in the way of change. Freud thought of mid-life difficulties as mere replays of earlier conflicts. Only Jung, and more recently Erik Erikson, seem to conceive of this decade as a true developmental period. I mean, a time when a man must cope with an altering image of himself, with new tasks, new dilemmas—and possibilities for change."

Given the complexity of adult existence, however, how does one even attempt to sort out those life issues common among all—or most—men in a given age group, from those which are idiosyncratic, and may concern only one or a few individuals? "At the very outset," observes Levinson, who tends to speak in bursts of words, punctuated by long silences, "we had a choice to make—it was crucial. Do we take a large sample of men in this thirty-five to forty-five-year-old decade and ask them a limited number of questions? Or do we select a smaller group of people in a few, very different kinds of professions, and try to probe into the circumstances of their lives, as they're being lived and experienced, far more deeply?"

The Levinson group opted for the latter strategy. Now in the third year of what is to be a four-year study, they have been conducting intensive in-depth interviews with a troop of forty men: ten are executives, half recruited from a large, settled firm, half from a smaller, more experimental company; ten are novelists, both successful (a few are among this nation's foremost writers) and unsuccessful; ten are biologists at different stages in their academic careers; ten are blue-collar workers, of whom three are black, seven, white. "Obviously," says Levinson, "we aren't assuming that what emerges from these interviews is going to be true for all men in their middle years, in all cultures, at all times. Our work is in the nature of a preliminary foray into a largely unknown area. Although there are certain things we expect to see and find, we're leaving ourselves very much wide open for what we *do* find.

"We did, however," he adds, "start out with a few general questions. Such as: Were all of our men in this age grouping undergoing or heading toward or just recovering from some experience of crisis? And if so, did the intensity of the experience vary quantitatively and qualitatively for men in different occupations? Or were the concerns of most men in the sample—despite all the obvious disparities in type of work, amount of success, sometimes even class and color—similar in some basic and fundamental aspects?"

Currently, with all of the major interviewing completed, and a good number of follow-ups (one interview, two years later) finished also, the mid-life research team is sorting through complicated stacks of data, trying to cull major thematic issues from case after case. The study group itself, having changed shape slightly over the course of its three-year existence, presently consists of three psychologists, Levinson, his wife Maria, Dr. Edward Klein; a psychiatrist, Dr. Braxton McKee; a sociologist, Mrs. Charlotte Darrow; and a resident in psychiatry, Dr. Ray Walker. (Walker, a student of Jung's writings, functions in the group as a sort of Jungian guru.) The mid-life workers gather once or twice every week for long, grueling, sometimes exciting, occasionally stormy seminars (while I attended these, three sessions were devoted to an extended, passionate interpreting of one interviewee's dream).

Has the group come to any tentative conclusions? Do they, for example, find that males do experience a critical period in the transition between early adulthood and middle age? "Would you," I ask, "compare the male crisis or climacteric, if there is such a thing, to the female menopause? Do you think *all* men pass through such a crisis? And if so, what sorts of things does it involve?"

Levinson shifts in his leather chair, leans forward. "Since we aren't looking at a life event which is directly tied in to male physiology, I think the phrase 'male climacteric' is misleading. I don't see how these two processes, the menopause and the mid-life transition, could be looked at as usefully comparable. And besides, the period we're studying is some ten years earlier than the female change of life ordinarily begins . . ."

His voice trails off. However, just as I am about to speak again, he suddenly resumes. "As to whether or not a male *crisis* exists I would say that if you mean it in the sense of 'turning point,' then indeed such a thing does take place. I think it generally begins somewhere in the late thirties, and that the most fundamental thing about it is that it's a part of normal development: a man at this stage can't go on unchanged. He's at the end of something and moving into another period—middle age. There's a discontinuity at this place, a qualitative difference to his life. He's coping with a variety of new circumstances, like the first indisputable signs of aging; and at the same time, assessing old things, fantasies and illusions about himself which he's sustained up until this point." The psychologist hitches up his shoulders, shrugs, smiles slightly. "I'm not saying, of course, that the men in our sample all undergo crisis in the sense of experiencing profound depression, misery, even feelings of intense uncertainty. We do have people who appear to pass through this transitional period with very little stress—just as certain adolescents move into adulthood with relative ease. On the other hand, we also seem to encounter a number of men who describe themselves in interviews as happy, content, on top of the world. Then, after we've done some psychological testing, we're surprised to stumble across unconscious themes of despair, humiliation, disintegration.

"These are men," he adds soberly, "who haven't yet been able to confront the nature of their fantasies and their unconscious experience. There is a crisis in their lives; but they can't face it, take responsibility for it, and meet it at a conscious level."

The range of individual responses to upheavals of turbulence at mid-life varies, according to Levinson, as widely as does the degree of the turbulence itself. At one end of a behavioral spectrum would be someone like the artist Gauguin, who, in his mid-forties, shed wife, family and job like a dead skin, and struck off for the South Seas to become a painter. On the other extreme would be the man who feels depressed and upset as he moves toward age forty, but makes no change at all in his career, marriage or life style. "And then, of course," says Levinson, "there is the guy who goes through a crisis period, has a lot of affairs, does badly perhaps in his work. Then the flurry dies down; he simply stays put in his life structure and doesn't change anything at all."

But regardless of whether a man alters everything, a few things, or nothing in his life during this decade, he emerges from it "different," the findings seem to indicate—restabilized (in the mid or late forties) at another personality plane. "Even if nothing whatsoever in his external life is different," remarks Levinson, "*he* is, and it's all going to have a different meaning for him."

If men between the ages of thirty-five and forty-five undergo some process of personality change—in the sense of profound psychological reorientation—what are the sorts of life issues which might be involved in this change? In order to extricate themes which were of universal concern among men in this age group, the Levinson workers began by trying to set the mid-life period into a new, developmental type of context, to assess it as one part of an unfolding sequence of maturation. If the experiencing of this phase of life was in some meaningful sense age-linked, then were there other, earlier life periods or stages in the mens' adult lives which could also be identified? The investigators, painstakingly comparing case history after case history, found that there were. The first such period occurred, roughly speaking, around the time of the early twenties. At this point, the men interviewed had all been getting into the adult world, exploring sexual and marital opportunities, different occupational possibilities, varying kinds of adult group memberships—but without making firm internal commitments.

A man at this stage of life, the researchers suggest, is trying out (and casting off) new identities, sets of values, modes of relating to other people, professional options. His inner commitment to any choice, however, tends to be shifting and tenuous. Quite often, during this exploratory phase, a person may be pursuing contradictory goals—for example, working toward success as a businessman and as a writer at the same time. Later, as he integrates his life into a meaningful pattern to which he commits himself, those pursuits which have no place in the pattern will be relinquished.

Says fifty-year-old Charlotte Darrow, the lone sociologist working with the groups; "One man's exploratory period may last throughout the twenties, while another's is, we find, quite brief. One person may be all over the map, trying everything, while another looks around very little before moving into the next phase, that of building a life structure—a period we've called *settling down.*"

During the settling-down phase, which begins some time in the twenties ("And normally not later," remarks Mrs. Darrow, "than age thirty to thirty-two,") a man becomes involved in the major tasks of his early adult life: proving himself in an occupation, establishing a family, working out a coherent set of beliefs and values that will cement together and give meaning to the life structure he is creating. During this "building" phase, a man is less free to explore alternate options; his main energies are absorbed into the career-marriage-family life he is shaping; and those aspects of his personality which do not fit into this dominant schema are pushed aside, left dormant or repressed. During this period, a person is deeply influenced by the values and judgments of those around him; he wants to succeed in terms of beliefs he shares with his group at large. Spurred on by some vaguely perceived promise or goal (for many of the biologists interviewed, it was related to early dreams of winning the Nobel Prize), he struggles forward toward some distant horizon. It lies ahead of him, always, this incoherent but deeply experienced vision, giving him energy, spurring and luring him forward.

But by forty a man has reached his horizon. The promise of the future is no longer that; it is a presence. Whatever fantasies and illusions have moved him hitherto, this is a time of assessment. "He knows fairly clearly," says Mrs. Darrow, "just where he has placed in life's battles— and just about how much further he can go." If a man has failed, either in his own eyes, or in others', or both ways, there is the pain of making peace with that knowledge. But even where a man has not failed— indeed, where he has won the very professorship or high executive position he set out to achieve—he often must come to terms with feelings of futility and meaninglessness. The dream realized turns out to be far more limited in reality than was the original vision.

'At this point," explains Mrs. Darrow, "many beliefs and values—all of those obvious 'truths' which supported a man while he was creating his life space or structure—may suddenly come into question. For, after all, it's a huge effort he's been engaged in, and he's thrown himself into it completely. And then all of a sudden, things don't seem so clear. And he starts asking himself, 'Is this what I really wanted? Was it worth all that struggle? Was it worth all I had to give up?'" The sociologist pauses, blinks several times behind her large round-framed glasses. "And maybe he's also asking whether or not he wants to go on doing all those same things for the years he has left—and if not, what doors are still left open?"

One of the great difficulties of the mid-life period has to do with an individual's realization that many of those things which were supposed to make him happy in some distant, glorious future simply are not doing so. "And that realization kicks off a questioning of the whole structure-of-living, this whole life they've worked so hard to achieve. The men start wondering about many assumptions they've simply taken for granted: are these ideas their own, or simply a reflection of everyone else's? And this questioning of their relations with the external world sets off an internal questioning, a questioning of the self."

At the same time, those voices in the personality which were silenced or pushed aside earlier, now speak out, with renewed urgency. "After all," notes Mrs. Darrow, "a person, in order to do his masculine, ego-involved thing—I mean, to move out and to achieve in the external world—simply has had to sacrifice, to do away with certain parts of his Self. For example, if he's a biologist, he's had to emphasize those parts of his personality which are rational, consciously intelligent, tough-minded. And this means defending against another whole area having to do with more emotional, softer, less masculine wishes and feelings."

A man's occupation, in effect, connects with and helps to realize and gratify certain aspects of his personality; at the same time it helps him or forces him to suppress those parts of his Self to which it is opposed or unrelated. The same kind of thing, points out Mrs. Darrow, occurs also in marriage: "Every man has more than one fantasy of a woman, and himself in relation to her. These different, to some degree contadictory, 'women in his imagination' correspond to different parts of himself. If he should marry a nice, loving, caring woman, he's connecting to those aspects of his personality that are more socially acceptable, and with his fantasy of the good, nurturing mother. But then he's leaving out another whole area, which for many men goes along with the idea of the 'illicit woman'—and with those parts of himself which are sensual and aggressive, or even exploitative and phallic.

"And obviously the built-in problem is," she adds, "that no job and no woman are going to connect to all parts of a given man."

The crisis of the middle years revolves, in large part, around upheavals of those areas of the personality which have been left out of a man's life structure, and which now demand expression. As he approaches the midpoint of life the individual's dominant thrust—which had been outward into the world, toward achievement, toward "making it"—is veering and returning; a man's psychic orientation is moving inward toward the Self. The long work of the early adult period, that of creating and expanding upon an identity and place in the world is completed or almost so: to confront that identity, and those things which he has given up to achieve it, are among the staggering tasks of this problematic decade.

The restlessness, despair, discontent which a man may begin to experience more and more intensively toward the close of the thirties are, in the view of the Levinson group, presages and stirrings of new personality growth and change. During this period, a new kind of freedom from external compulsions comes to be felt; but at the same time an often-painful process of re-evaluation and reappraisal gets under way. And this process is accompanied by inner changes, affecting a man's view both of himself and of those about him.

Such internal change may happen almost unnoticed. The biologist mentioned above, for example, experiencing a new need to be related to people rather than ideas or things, might quietly shift into more administrative kinds of activities. Or the changes might involve a silent but profound modification of a man's ideas about himself. As a thirty-nine-year-old novelist taking part in the study explained it: " . . . phrasing it melodramatically, I feel a weakening of the need to be a great man. And an increasing feeling of: 'Let's just get through this the best way we can. Never mind hitting any home runs, let's just get through the ball game without being beaned.'" As the same man noted in a later interview, his whole early adult career had been guided by a dream of success, notoriety and fame which had never been realized; but now: ". . . when I think of giving these things up, it doesn't pain me anymore."

The change may be overt and dramatic, as it appeared to be for one forty-four-year-old executive, whose marriage was suddenly flowering after twenty years of what he called "dormancy." "From an emotional standpoint," related this subject, "ours has probably been a very one-way relationship, with my wife doing most of the giving. I suspect . . . it hasn't gone very far in terms of enrichment. I know I'm the one who's contributed most of the control, kept us on this lousy monotonous plateau. But I'm going through some kind of change, becoming less intellectual about feelings and so on. Like, the other night my wife had her menstrual period, and we got into bed; and well, she was just very nervous. You know, rolling and tossing. I don't know why, but I just started rubbing her back, and soothing her. And then I just held her, face to face. I put my arms around her, and we just stayed that way. And this seemed to comfort her quite a bit, and she quieted down and had a good night . . . . You see, I felt this might do her good, and I tried it. Which I'm not sure I would have thought of six months or a year ago. In fact I suspect a year ago I might have lain there for awhile and then said, 'Well, I'm going to have a cigarette.' And then I'd have gotten a blanket and gone to sleep on the couch."

The keynote of this decade is: something changes. The mid-life decade is, according to the Levinson researchers, a crossroads in the maturational process—a time when new personality growth is possible. An individual may now move toward a new kind of intimacy in marriage, toward greater self-fulfillment in his occupational role, and toward deeper, less fantasy-ridden relations with his children. This is the period in life during which, Jung believed, the individual had a chance to achieve true identity. But, he wrote, " . . . there is no birth of consciousness without pain."

If adolescence may be said to involve the advent of social identity, then the mid-life crisis, as one Levinson worker phrased it, "has to do with the advent of the Self." The mid-life period, like that adolescent phase which it parallels and resembles, holds the promise of new enrichment, positive change, sometimes even a kind of "rebirth" of the personality. It holds its threats too: in these years the incidence of alcoholism, hypochondria, overeating and obesity, all connected to depression, show a marked rise. Sexual difficulties, if they existed before, are exacerbated. The divorce rate leaps upward. As far back as

1965 statistics indicated that nearly one-fourth of all persons filing for divorce in this country had been married for more than fifteen years. And the incidence of marital break-up among those couples in the "twenty-year slump" was, experts agreed, growing every year.

What, then, are the difficulties and concerns a man must grapple with during this critical mid-life period? And if he does emerge from the decade different in some fundamental way, what are the areas and dimensions of that change?

Although their voluminous material is not yet fully analyzed, the mid-life researchers have found that certain key issues do appear to cluster together in core problems common among most men in the study sample. The clearest (and yet most complex), the most obvious (and yet in many ways complicated and obscure) set of difficulties has to do with the plain fact that an individual has reached the midpoint of his life span. He has lost the sense that he is still growing up; now he has begun growing old. He is no longer in the stage of apprenticeship, of dependence on older, more authoritative adults. The wheel of generations has revolved a notch; he stands in a new position. And beyond, as he perceives with a new and painful clarity, lies his own old age—and death.

The knowledge that one will someday die, easily understood from a chronological point of view, is not so easy to deal with psychologically. As Freud observed: "No one believes in his own death . . . in the unconscious everyone is convinced of his own immortality." But in the mid-life decade, death's reality presses in upon a man in a host of new ways: through the aging or dying of parents, through the deaths of friends and peers, through growing signs of his own aging process— balding, graying, wrinkling, even mere physical fatigue. It is at this time of life that a person must confront the growing evidence that his control over his own body is limited and truly circumscribed. As one forty-four-year-old writer taking part in the Levinson study recalled the event: ". . . I understood (suddenly, waking up after a party one morning) that I could not, that I did not have an absolute capacity for sleeplessness and alcohol . . . It was a very dramatic and distinct change because up until then I could stay up until dawn or seven or eight . . . The bacchanal, you know, that one might meet the dawn having drunk a bottomless amount of alcohol, go to sleep for three or four hours, wake up exhilarated but able to go through the next day without any problems . . . But in the summer of my thirty-seventh year I realized that I could no longer do that. I felt terrible. It was as if I'd gotten a message. I got the message very radically. I suddenly realized that I was no longer twenty-four years old. I was getting on toward forty."

Said the same man, in a subsequent interview; "I tend to notice it in the newspapers nowadays, when people my own age die . . . Which is something you don't seem much to see when you're in your thirties. But then, people at that age die in accidents; in their forties, they start to keel over from heart attacks . . . Hardly a day goes by when I don't say—I don't mean it preoccupies me, by any means—but I play the awful game. I'm sure many people do. Where you say: 'God, in six years I'll be fifty.' Of course, it is a game because there is that six years and six years is, of course, a considerable length of time. But the idea, you know, of time encroaching and the possibilities of this elysian amplitude of foreverness shrinking . . . "

The shrinking of time, the awareness of bodily decline: here is the way in which one subject, a black industrial worker in his early forties, expressed it: "I'm working in the business, hard . . . And I'm getting older, and the energy I started with is running out . . . it's going away. And I'm coming to the point where sooner or later I'm not going to be able to work as hard as I have, and I really haven't gotten any place . . . As you get older, you begin to think of a man in a hurry. The years are going by and you want to know your life meant something."

And another subject, a novelist who had several years earlier thrown over an extravagantly successful business career to go into full-time writing, described his mid-life experience in this way: "I don't make love as much, I play doubles instead of singles, I don't swim under water as far. I try to substitute technique for that earlier, more animal energy." He currently does, he noted, suffer from bouts of insomnia, and ". . . when I'm awake like that I think about my own death."

The paradox of this time of life, the years of a man's "prime" and his "fulfillment," is that they bring to a person an ineluctable realization of how dated are those years, and that prime. It is this—the new and vivid encounter with death, which takes place at mid-life—that lends this period its somewhat painful tone, precipitates its often critical nature.

Another central and somewhat related set of issues has to do with a man's changing experience of his paternity. During this decade there are generally new demands, cries and criticisms coming from his own, near-adult children; at the same time, aging or dying parents are often also in need of a man's care and protection. He stands in a generational crossfire: as well as being parent to his children he must be, in essence, father to his parents too. And if his own father is dead, he must assume the psychological burden of replacing him, identifying with him, being more fully "the father" himself. Whatever the circumstances, an individual at mid-life is having to give up sonhood and dependency. And as these old supports are withdrawn, a number of fresh and sometimes overwhelming demands are being made.

Here, for example, were the situations of four men, chosen at random for the mid-life sample, in regard to their older or oldest children:

1) *executive*: His oldest daughter had just had what he termed a "tantrum" and dropped out of college . . . His "Number One Son" was not working up to the level of his ability; it was not clear what sort of future this boy could possibly aspire to.

2) *industrial worker:* The oldest child, a stepson, "cannot seem to learn . . . he's not as smart as he might be." His own son was brighter, could get all A's, but "doesn't cooperate . . . seems emotionally unstable, never hears what you say, can't keep his mouth shut."

3) *novelist:* His oldest son, age thirteen, was in a "terror of a rebellion." He was a "dropout," had "run away," was "into drugs," and was doing no work at school.

4) *second novelist:* His oldest child, a boy aged eighteen, was "tall, handsome, swinging away . . . " But he was a political revolutionary, had been picked up by the police three times, had used and transported dynamite. He was in another state, attending a private boarding school: "That is, *when* he is there . . ."

Says Dr. Edward Klein, forty, a mid-life staff psychologist: "Being a father to an infant is dramatically different from being father to adolescent or older children. As father to babies, you can entertain all kinds of illusions about your own power and omnipotence: there is that child whose very fate depends on you, whom you're going to mold and shape into some ideal being . . . " During his children's adolescence, however, a man must compare that fantasy with what has become reality, and accept the limited nature of his own influence. And, as mentioned, he is almost simultaneously being forced to rework his relationship with his own father. If one examines the case histories of the same four individuals—all normal, stable men in the mid-life decade—one finds them in the following situations vis-à-vis their own fathers or parental guides:

1) *executive:* His father and mother were both dead; his older sister and his brother-in-law, to whom he had been deeply attached, were dead; his closest "parental figure," an older man with whom he had formed a warm bond, had, he said, "been gone from this area for several years now."

2) *industrial worker:* His father was dead, his mother "lives far away, and is going strong, but I don't get to see her." There was no figure in his life upon whom he depended: his own recent attempts to "father" and care for a younger brother had just failed.

3) *novelist:* This man's father was ill and dying during the course of the interviews: "There is no possibility of communication with him . . . My father can't talk clearly, his mouth is partially paralyzed . . . he is quite helpless. He seems appreciative that I am there . . . 'Painful' is the way I would describe my own feelings—this isn't the man of my childhood. . . ."

4) *second novelist:* Both father and mother, in this instance, were alive, but "quite aged. When I think of them I see only two very old people . . . they are frail. My father works around the house, builds fences and re-roofs the place, but neither he nor my mother is strong now. And I can't in any way come to terms with the idea of their dying. . . ."

"The essence of what is happening," observes Dr. Klein, "is that during the mid-life decade a man not only has to give up the vestiges of his sonhood, but he gets a lot of flak from his own sons—and from his 'symbolic sons' as well. Because his paternity, at this point, isn't something which extends only to his own children and perhaps to his parents: it comes to be expected of him by other, younger adults."

That this is so can in itself come as a shock. Many men in their late thirties retain the illusion that they themselves are still young or, as Klein says with a smile, "simply ageless." A chance word, however, a remark made by a junior colleague, or the friend of an adolescent child, may bring to them the sudden realization that people in their late teens and early twenties see them as vaguely parental—as middle-aged or even old. As the writer Proust once observed, to the very young man the older "established" generation, seen on the horizon, seems to mark the fixed boundary of a world. But then, with the passage of time, " . . . we ourselves move forward, and soon it is *we* who are at the horizon from the point of view of the generations advancing behind us . . . ."

A man in this decade of life is moving (perhaps feeling shoved) forward, and into a variety of new relationships which involve caring for, "bringing up"—in the widest sense of the word—the succeeding generation. This is what the psychoanalyst Erik Erikson calls the *stage of generativity*. It involves, in his words, "overcoming the ambivalence of obligation." Erikson views the development, during this phase of living, of a newer, more altruistic, more "fathering" stance toward younger adults, as an inborn phase of normal maturation. "The principal thing," he writes, "is to realize that this is a stage of growth of the healthy personality and that where such enrichment fails altogether, regression from generativity to an obsessive need for pseudo-intimacy takes place, often with a pervading sense of stagnation and interpersonal impoverishment. Individuals who do not develop generativity often begin to indulge themselves as if they were their one and only child."

The problem is, however, that assuming paternity in its fullest sense does involve letting go of certain fantasies about the self—such as the illusion that one still is, and will remain, young. Explains Klein, "In a way this final taking-on of responsibility is like the last bite of the biblical Apple. You're no longer the son, the one who can or can't do certain forbidden things without full, conscious awareness of the consequences—you're the guy who's in charge of the whole show, the one who's entrusted to *take care* of others . . . The trouble with all of this," he adds, with a rueful laugh, "is . . . Who wants to let go of the Apple?"

Letting go of the Apple—concerns about sexuality—were, not surprisingly, another of the major thematic issues which emerged from the mid-life study interviews. Among the forty men in the sample, all fairly well adjusted, and all, generally speaking, doing well in life, it was found that, as one Levinson researcher put it: " . . . they're commonly making love less, liking it less, and not infrequently, blaming it, for one reason or another, on their wives." There were widespread allusions to worries about declining sexual attractiveness and to fears about the possibility of waning virility. And often, among men who consciously felt themselves to be in a period of change, and who wanted to change, there was guilt about what it might mean to the marriage. In these cases, the individuals interviewed expressed great uprushes of anxiety, both about being trapped in an old sexual commitment; and about what might happen if they ventured beyond it.

Less than one third of the group taking part in the mid-life study were actually involved in extramarital entanglements. But there was a marked degree of fantasying about possible affairs, and a good deal of psychological conflict around the issue. A number of men were, for the first time, consciously and seriously considering beginning a new relationship with some other woman. Said one individual, an executive who had recently become, as he phrased it, "emotionally involved" with a neighbor (after almost twenty years of a happy marital life), " . . . I haven't had the nerve to begin a physical sexual affair with her. I set these things up and then I don't go through with it . . . (but) I cannot pass her house, I cannot be with her, I cannot think of her without the greatest excitement and energy change coming over me . . . "

Another executive taking part in the study described the way in which, as he sat working, his thought processes were diverted by fantasies of women. Even while he was at home, telling stories to his children, he found that a woman often appeared on the horizon of the tale, interjecting herself between the King and the Queen, and laying claim to the male. "I'm rarely at peace inside," remarked this man during the course of an interview. "What I'm torn about is whether my commitment to my wife is the thing I really want. It's too easy to imagine being fulfilled by other women."

The relative ubiquity of sexual fantasy among men in this decade has to do, according to Dr. Ray Walker, with a "heightened sense of loneliness." Walker, thirty-eight, began working with the mid-life group while still a medical student; he is now a psychiatric resident, in training to become a Jungian analyst. "For most men this doesn't have to do with, simply, a search for sexual variety or adventure," he says. "The whole question of one's marriage and family are part and parcel of the general question of one's life. And in this decade, where a certain reordering process gets under way, where there is a search for new kinds of goals and values which are truly connected to the Self, a man may suddenly come face to face with something fairly disquieting. And that is an awareness of what is limited, of what is missing in the character of his relationship with his wife." (One subject taking part in the mid-life study, a biologist, practically paraphrased these remarks during the course of one interview: " . . . I do feel much more lonely now than I did in the earlier years of marriage. There is this feeling I have, yes, that maybe out there is someone who might share a more intellectual kind of life with me. . . . ")

Perhaps the most fascinating and suggestive phenomenon to emerge from the mid-life material has been the appearance, in the life histories of most of the participants, of a kind of relationship which the Levinson group has come to call the *mentor* relationship. Almost every subject who had achieved a degree of success in the external world had had, along the way, one or more mentor figures. During the period of early adulthood, when the men had been engaged in "making it" in their occupations, such relationships were the common experience; after about age forty, mentors were rare in a man's life. As for the subjects who never did have mentors, they were usually the same people who had failed in achieving their goals.

What is a mentor? Explains Dr. Braxton McKee, the only practicing psychiatrist presently working on the mid-life project, "He is a person who's at least a bit older, generally some eight to ten years, and who has some expert knowledge or wisdom, or personal qualities or skills, which he offers to share with the younger man. A mentor could be someone like a professor, a teacher, a more established executive, an older relative, but he is usually (not always) someone connected with a guy's occupation. He has, in turn, the function of the instructor, the exemplar—and someone who, on his side, cares about you."

The mentor, for the younger man, represents a point of development which is higher, and to which he aspires. The mentor is in this sense a parental figure, and yet he is also a friend. He offers, as the true parent never can do, the possibility of a true equality with him. He is thus someone who, according to McKee, more or less says, "Here is the world, of which I am a part; and into which I invite you—to become my peer and colleague." The mentor has the function of a "recruiter," drawing the younger adult into the larger society.

"What surprises me," observes McKee, who is thirty-eight, blond and handsome, "is the way in which this mentor thing really does leap out at you. Generally speaking, most theoreticians have had the idea that once a person separates from his own father and leaves his home he's independent. But that's simply not *true*! What seems to be consistently overlooked is the parental function of the institution or organization he becomes involved with; and also the fact that, despite a man's new-found independence he starts almost immediately to seek out these semi-parental mentor figures. And develops much further, by the way, if he succeeds in finding them." Mentor relationships, the Levinson investigators are currently hypothesizing, may be a crucial part of early adult development: they may possibly be *the* crucial part.

The developmental framework that the mid-life study group has been working with is, thus, somewhat in the nature of a ladder: a young man moves first into an exploration of adult life; then into a period of intense engagement with the external world (during which he "settles down" and creates his life structure) and finally into a phase which the researchers call *Becoming His Own Man*. This stage, occurring in the middle or late thirties, marks the peak of early adulthood, and the launching-place into the complex currents of the mid-life transition. "Very often," says McKee, in his quiet, southern-accented voice, "it is the break with the mentor which signals the fact that an individual has reached this point."

In becoming his own man, an individual does just that—he assumes more responsibility for himself in the world, insists on speaking with his own voice, becomes more autonomous, less dependent, more authoritative in his work and family life. This new state is often facilitated by external events: he may have just reached the top of an occupational goal ladder, received his professorship and tenure, gotten a writer's prize, or achieved a top executive position.

"Or," explains McKee, "this new feeling about himself may be something totally self-generated. . . . Somewhere around the late thirties, for a sizable number of men, there just seems to be this sense that one ought to be making a step toward something a little better, more responsible, or creative. Something that comes out of a man's own inner goals—something independent of whatever tasks he's been working on before, and of the mentor. Maybe it's a new kind of position, a new book . . . One writer in our study was just into this phase when he brought a half-finished work to his publisher, who said to drop it, it was no good. But our guy insisted on hanging in and finishing the book even though it meant going deeply into debt.

"In becoming one's own man," adds McKee, "a person seems to be saying to himself: 'I've got one last chance to realize this dream, in my own terms, in my own way. Up until now I've made too many compromises, let myself be diverted in too many directions.' Whatever it may be, the movement a man makes now—call it a gamble, a risk of some sort (we refer to it as the *inflated act*)—represents an attempt to engage with the world and people around him in a totally new, much more autonomous way. Whether it succeeds or doesn't, it is in itself a quantum leap toward something else: call it inner independence, a new kind of fidelity to the Self.

"What intrigues me," he concludes, "is how in a sense the men in their early or mid-thirties show signs of what you might call anticipatory ripples, premonitions of turmoil to come. And the men at the end of the decade, feeling somewhat restabilized, are able to indicate what that turmoil was about, and how they've worked it out, how they came out of it. But for the men who are just *at* forty, there's a feeling that they're holding their breath, almost waiting for something to happen: they can't even talk about it. Very often this tension, this waiting, is connected to that bet a man has placed on himself—he's standing by to see how that will work out." Becoming one's own man marks the conclusion of the individual's main struggle with the external environment and signals the beginning of a newer, more internal battle which commences in its wake.

"The mail we receive from wives is all very much alike," remarks Dr. Levinson's wife Maria, the third psychologist working on the mid-life project. "They tend to write in (from 'the two of us') on behalf of a husband who appears to have caught some kind of a 'virus,' something which attacks men at mid-life. The wife's initial response is in the nature of this frenzy of mothering: her husband is sick with this thing, and her question is, how can she cure him?"

"But," I inquire, "if a woman has lived with a man for some fifteen or twenty years in a state of some happiness and equilibrium and suddenly he begins changing, then how is she to view it?"

"As a stage in the developmental process," answers Maria Levinson without hesitating, "not as a kind of flu. As a period when a man is very naturally going through some painful changing of gears—when he's moving away from that earlier, determined building of his life to an assessment of what he's done, how it's been. When he's starting to experience himself as older; and having to come to terms with that, and with the task of ceding to those of the next generation *their* place . . .

One might think of this as a time when a shift in the drives is taking place. And like all transitional phases, it's unsettling and can involve a lot of turmoil and distress."

"But what words of advice," I persist, "might one have to offer a woman whose husband happened to be going through this period of upset and distress?"

Mrs. Levinson, who is in her early fifties, smiles a short but kind smile, runs her hand swiftly through her slightly curly, graying bangs: "You know," she remarks thoughtfully, "in some of our cases it was the wife, not the husband, who upset the equilibrium, who made demands suddenly for the man to get off his behind and start changing. It was she who initiated the new directives for ceasing-to-be in the old relationship, and it was she who got a new kind of development going." She pauses momentarily.

"My speculation on the wife is," she resumes, "that what happens to her depends very much on the stage *she* is at; and on her capacity to tolerate his depression and everything that goes along with it. And of course it depends on the amount of understanding and intimacy that existed previously. You know, in the love of young adults there is a great deal of projection and fantasy: a young wife projects onto her husband many of her feelings and fantasies about her father, and a young husband projects onto his wife his own feelings and fantasies about the mother. But now, in mid-life, when one is being freed of many of these earlier burdens (these fantasies and illusions which prevent one from truly seeing the other person), the question is: What was the relationship in the first place? Can that younger love become something more adult? If there is good communication between the two people, if they are developing in parallel ways, then there will be change on both parts; they'll reintegrate at a higher, more genuine and honest level."

"But on the other hand," I ask, "suppose that a man moves into a time of great distress, and won't talk about it to his wife? Suppose he can't show his weakness that way? Or suppose his dissatisfaction with himself has something to do with a dissatisfaction with her—and he finds some *other* woman to talk about his problems to . . . ?"

Mr. Levinson hesitates, looks at me, her gray eyes widening. "Well, if that were the case, I'd say"—she blinks rapidly several times—"I'd say . . . That's too bad."

                                                                    1972

The Wish to Die

On Women and Suicide

Ellen Winston" was a patient on a psychiatric ward in which I happened to be doing some research several years ago. She was twenty-six at the time, a college graduate (Phi Beta Kappa), the wife of a flight surgeon in the Air Force, and the curator of a rare-books collection housed in a major eastern university library. One hot June afternoon, about two months before I came to know her, Ellen had swallowed an overdose of sleeping pills and then gone out to her car, which was parked in the enclosed garage attached to the house. She climbed into the front seat, rolled up the windows tightly, switched on the ignition, and then stretched out full length, as if for sleep. Inside, on a kitchen counter, a note scrawled on the back of a groceries list had been left for her husband Tom. It said: "I just can't face things anymore. I'm sorry—I'll love you forever."

Tom was away on a tour of duty (he was absent from home, as a matter of course, some 60 percent of the time). But, almost a full day later, when his wife was discovered unconscious in her car, he was summoned back directly. It was at some moment during this highly confused, distressing period that Ellen's diary, kept faithfully for the past year and a half, was found sitting on top of a pile of books and magazines. Tom had actually seen this ordinary lined copybook many times before, for it had always been left out in plain sight; but he had never asked his wife about it. Opening and reading it now, he found a careful account of her descent into what had become an intolerable hopelessness and despair.

In her journal, Ellen sounded not at all like the well-trained, competent, attractive librarian that she was, but more like a creature abandoned, stranded, astray in an empty and darkening wasteland. Here, for example, is a series of random night thoughts, written at a time when Tom had been away for a period of some weeks:*

---

*Excerpts from Ellen's diary have been altered extensively in order to ensure her privacy. What has been retained is the general flavor of the document. The diary has been used, with the permission of the patient and her family, as a teaching aid in furthering the understanding of the psychodynamics of suicidal behavior.

... Hello, Room; Hi, Pictures; Hi, Lamps. It's barely Tuesday and after monumental attempts at getting at least some sleep, I've blown it. Everything seemed to conspire against me . . . the noisy refrigerator motor, that g.d. fire engine, the whining of the MacKenzies' dog. So, after two half-assed drinks and an encore on the sleeping pills, I'll have to admit that I'm licked. For nights I've been wondering when the sleeplessness was finally going to get me. I've been wrestling with it, just barely fending it off for weeks, but tonight, Jesus, it's unspeakable . . . .

In this long entry, written when she began to keep her diary, Ellen goes on to muse about the impoverished drabness of her daily routine, the loneliness of her existence. These thoughts and preoccupations soon start to merge—and this happens throughout the journal—with more gratifying and "self-loving" ones . . . with sexual fantasies, memories, desires.

I started thinking about that guy from the library, David, awhile ago . . . naturally. I remembered the hurt, wounded look he gave me. He never said a word aloud, but he *was* asking with those gray eyes of his: "Ellen, Ellen, why has it got to be like this?" I can still feel my own revulsion, the sense of guilt so nauseating that it almost made me dizzy . . . I wanted to hurt him, to be cold, to denigrate everything that was happening by my lack of any real feeling for him. And I suspected that he, in some strange way, was secretly turned on by that indifference . . . It's been weird, this whole goddamned parade of men, having me willingly or otherwise—guys I hardly even or don't know. Boy, things are getting pretty foul. . . .

At this juncture, as in other places in her diary, the distinction between what is true and what may be Ellen's guilty fantasy is not completely obvious. What is clear, however, is that all such flights into sexual thought and reverie bring an inevitable backlash of disgust and self-hatred. It is only during Tom's sojourns at home that Ellen is free of her bleak unhappiness, her thoughts of other men and of the self-directed contempt and anger that these thoughts bring in their wake. When the couple is together, during Tom's regular rotations back to the base, all sense of misery vanishes magically from the journal.

Her physician husband's presence brings Ellen a joy which she experiences as something "like exquisite, intense pain." She is able, during these relatively carefree intermezzos, to feel protected, safe, even "normal." The sight of Tom, dozing off to sleep while reading on the sofa, fills her with a loving amusement. "He looks so peaceful, so vulnerable, with his eyes closed and no expression at all on his rugged, bearded face. The way his hair falls forward, slants down over his forehead. How much I love, so far beyond my capacity for saying . . ."

Each of Tom's successive departures was, nevertheless, making her more and more panicky; she had a deep and increasing conviction that she somehow no longer "existed" aside from those times when he was with her. Alone once more in April, over a full year since she had begun keeping the diary, she was sounding more and more desperate. She recorded a sadness "so terrible that I can't even cry to ease it," a pain deeper and more intense than anything she had ever known. Exhausted by "nervousness, overwork and crying," she was beginning to suspect that she might be going insane.

Distraught, in June she wrote to Tom, "I NEED YOU BADLY." But a day after mailing the letter—and too soon for him to have received it— she made her devastating suicide attempt. Ellen was discovered, through a chance accident, some eighteen hours later; she had survived only because her car had run out of gas. She remained unconscious for a total of thirty-six hours; and at the end of a week's hospitalization she was still incontinent, played with her feces and was able to make only garbled sounds.

By the time I met her, she had achieved a far greater degree of recovery. But she had been unconscious for a dangerously long time, had had several brain seizures, and had probably suffered some carbon-monoxide poisoning as well. There had been organic and irreversible brain damage. The former Phi Beta Kappa student now had a measurable I.Q. of 94.

Ellen's intelligence and acumen had not, however, been so drastically reduced that she herself did not understand the seriousness of the change that had taken place. This was, I believe, part of her reason for insisting that I—along with some other nonmedical staff who happened to be there—be given a copy of the journal. She seemed to want us all to know who she "truly" was; or, at least, who she had been. And her diary did surprise me. For the Ellen on the ward, with all of her multiple social and intellectual deficiencies, could not have seemed more remote from the expressive, subtle, self-scrutinizing person who sprang from the pages before me. I realized then that her suicide attempt had to some very considerable degree succeeded. The "Ellen" of the diary had, in more than a mere metaphoric sense, annihilated herself completely.*

The literal meaning of the word *suicide* is "self-murder," and the question of what brings an individual to the point of wanting to commit the act of murder upon her or his own self is one that has never been adequately answered. Years of study and the growth of a whole new area in the social sciences—suicidology—have contributed much to understanding which people tend to commit (or attempt) suicide, and at what point in the life cycle a woman or man is more likely to make a suicidal effort, and which methods she or he is liable to use. But the ultimate understanding of the problem—the profoundly difficult *Why?*—is one that remains mysterious, resistant to analysis, and tinged with a shamed incomprehension.

What causes an individual to want to blot out her own consciousness, to "erase" her existence—to die? (Or, in the case of a suicide attempt, to gamble with death?) One explanation of suicidal behavior, appearing over and over again in psychoanalytic writings on the topic, has it that the person who attempts or commits suicide is expressing an overwhelming hostility that she feels *toward someone else.* The act, when one thinks about it, is an angry one. The person may not have articulated her anger consciously—she may even be unaware of her own aggressive feelings—but the aggression and anger are there. Because she is unable to acknowledge such feelings (for any one of a number of complicated psychological reasons, but most probably because of a deep-seated belief that one cannot be angry with someone one loves) they are never expressed or discharged. Instead, they are turned back against the self in the form of self-criticism and self-hatred.

The suicidal act is, when seen in this light, like a lethal boomerang; it is retroflexed anger, hate that has been turned back upon the self—and in the most radical expression of hatred, which is murder. As Dr. Wilhelm Stekel, a colleague and contemporary of Freud's, observed at a 1910 symposium on the subject of suicide (this meeting, called by Freud, was

---

*Ellen was able, after a long recuperation, to return to her job at the library (her lowered I.Q. was still within the normal range) and to function there in a far more limited capacity. Tom, given the circumstances, decided to resign from the Air Force in order to be able to remain close to his wife and to give her the care that she needed; he went into private practice as a surgeon. Ironically enough, the upshot of the situation was that Ellen got what she wanted all along; but she got it at an amazing cost.

the first academic discussion of the topic ever undertaken): "No one kills himself who did not want to kill *another* [my italics], or at least, wish death to another . . . ."

Ellen's case is interesting to view within this particular theoretical framework. Throughout her entire journal, Ellen had no word of criticism for the absent Tom. Indeed, she wrote of her husband in terms of a not-quite-human paragon, a supremely moral, courageous, "manly" man. There was no hint of the rage and anger at him which she must have been feeling after each of those painful departures. All that Ellen seemed to be aware of and to express was that she loved Tom and needed him and missed him. There was never a whisper of the intense hostility and perhaps murderous impulses which she might have been harboring toward this person who continually refused to recognize her powerful dependent needs and who "abandoned" her time after time. And yet it was such rage-filled feelings as these, turned against the self, that very probably provided the psychic "fuel" for her stunning and sudden attempt. Suicide has been called an inverted form of homicide— "murder in the 180th degree"—and the supreme interpersonal insult that one individual (the victim) can deliver to another (the survivor).

The highly communicative function of the suicidal act is an element which ought not to be overlooked. An attempt to die is an open declaration of sorts, and one made in a compellingly dramatic way. When the suicidal person survives, the reactions to what she has done are extraordinarily complex and involuted. The people around her, as psychiatrist Edwin Stengel has noted, tend to behave "as they feel they ought to behave had the outcome been fatal . . . ." They are shocked, guilty, anxious to make amends. The suicidal attempt, therefore, exerts an undeniable "appeal effect" upon those close to the individual. It is for this reason that the failed attempt is often considered a cry for help.

The suicidal act that results in a fatality has an equally potent communicative potential. One suicidologist has described the suicidal death as "the last word in an argument." The effects upon those people closest to the victim have much in common with ordinary grief and bereavement; but they are more intense. According to Dr. Stengel, there is "an upsurge of posthumous love associated with guilt feelings and self-reproach for not having cared and loved enough. . . ." It is the knowledge of the effects that the suicidal act will have upon one's loved ones that—at either a conscious or an unconscious level—prompts and motivates many an individual toward actual commission of the deed.

It is an odd but arresting fact that males, in all known contemporary societies, and at all ages, commit suicide much more frequently than do females. The rates may vary—in some countries they are as high as four men to every one woman—but nowhere is the ratio less than two males to every one female. Women, on the other hand, *attempt* suicide far more often; and, according to a recent study carried out by Dr. Myrna Weissman at Yale University, the number of such attempted suicides has been rising dramatically during the past decade. (The reasons for this rise remain unclear.)

There are, observed Dr. Weissman, who is director of Yale's Depression Unit, rather striking differences between the kinds of people who "complete" and those who "attempt" suicide. "The individual who succeeds in killing himself tends to be a man, someone who is older, who is single, widowed or divorced; and is living alone. He is usually somewhat isolated socially—he may have lost his job recently, or been retired. Or he may be unemployed."

The "attempter" is, on the other hand, more often a woman. "She is frequently someone between the ages of eighteen and thirty . . . most commonly, she's under twenty-five. She tends *not* to be someone who is living alone; but she is embroiled in a set of interpersonal relationships that are filled with conflict, unsatisfying and difficult." The attempt itself, added Weissman, often occurs within the context of some serious interpersonal friction: "Usually, it follows upon a quarrel with someone who's terribly significant to her." The use of alcohol prior to the act seems to be, both in the case of the suicide completer and of the attempter, a standard factor in the situation. "Also, there's commonly been a lot of 'suicidal ideation,' " the researcher observed. "That is, thoughts of suicide, talk of suicide, suicidal feelings. . . . The attempt itself is, however," she added, "usually totally impulsive in nature."

The sudden decision to "go ahead and do it" is probably, she speculated, linked to mighty upsurges of angry and hostile impulses that the individual is unable either to handle or to discharge. A suicidal gesture of this impulsive type was made recently, related Weissman, by a young female patient who was in treatment for a depressive disorder. "This person was in her early twenties, and had two young children. She had been married in her late teens to a medical student . . . and he wasn't paying a great deal of attention to her. This was a problem for her; the children were giving her problems; and she was someone who had great difficulty in asserting herself and making known her needs and demands."

The patient, said Dr. Weissman, had already begun responding to the treatment she was receiving for her depressive disturbance. But it happened that, late one evening after classes and hospital duties were over, her husband came home in the company of a fellow student. The two young doctors-in-training sat around the kitchen, drinking beer. The wife had had a difficult day; she wanted to talk to her husband about some predicament regarding the children. "He simply kept ignoring her and passing off everything she was trying to say. Finally, he turned to his friend and asked, 'How about going out somewhere and having some coffee, or maybe a drink of something stronger?' At this point, she became so furious and frustrated that she went straight into the bathroom and swallowed everything in every bottle in the medicine cabinet."

The woman then came out and told her husband what she had done. And so, added Weissman dryly, he had to give up his other plans and rush his wife to the hospital. "She got what she wanted: His attention. I don't think her behavior was very constructive," she continued, with the trace of a smile. "But it *was* adaptive for that moment."

An unfortunate aspect of this sort of strategy is, however, the fact that a certain percentage of suicide attempters eventually become completers—and not because they intend to. There are, according to Dr. Weissman, many instances in which the person makes a fatal misjudgment. "Our research indicates, for example, that women— especially younger women—who use pills as a suicide method, often don't mean to kill themselves and are not very disturbed psychiatrically. Their attempts tend to be more along the lines of a 'cry for help' than of a real wish to die. But many of them do come quite close to dying, closer than do people who might have appeared to be using far more drastic methods, and who are, in fact, much more mentally disturbed." The reason for this unintentionally high success rate among young pill-takers is, said the psychologist, due to the fact that there is often a total misunderstanding about the actual toxicity of the pills or other medications that they may be swallowing.

People seem to assume that drugs prescribed by a doctor—such as sleeping pills or antidepressants—are somehow less lethal than are illicit drugs. Any antidepressant is a poison in large doses. "And often," pointed out Weissman, "when a person is attempting suicide, she'll take a combination of things—say, for example, Amitriptyline, which is a commonly used antidepressant, some digitalis that just happens to be in the medicine cabinet, and probably some alcohol as well. If she should take all of those drugs together . . . well, she's mixed herself a pretty potent cocktail. And one that's far more lethal than she might ever have imagined."

It is because of the general lack of knowledge about the real potency of many prescribed drugs that the clinician cannot really judge the seriousness of the person's intention to die merely by assessing the amount of self-harm that she or he manages to inflict. The medications may be, as a recent article in the *American Journal of Psychiatry* pointed out, far more poisonous than the person possibly could realize. A sleeping pill that used to be prescribed fairly commonly, Doriden, is fatal if ten capsules or tablets are swallowed at one time. And there are, furthermore, synergistic or "additive" effects when different types of medications are taken together. As is widely known, for instance, a lower dose of barbiturates than would otherwise be effective can be lethal if the person taking them has been drinking and has a high alcohol level in her bloodstream. What is less well known is that there are many other drugs and medications that, when taken together, combine in an equally powerful, additive fashion.

The method of suicide (and suicidal attempt) most favored among females appears to be self-poisoning—either by pills or other drugs, or by gas, or by means of some toxic household liquid. Women sometimes cut their wrists as well, but very rarely do they shoot themselves. Men, on the other hand, use guns as a weapon of self-murder more than they use anything else; jumping from high places and hanging are also far more frequent among males than among females. These deadlier methods account, perhaps, for the higher number of "successfully completed" suicides among men.

Why do the preponderant number of potential female suicides turn to pills and drugs, while men for the most part tend to shoot, hang themselves, or jump? Some experts have suggested that it may be related to female passivity as contrasted with the male's more active approaches—even in this extreme situation. My own guess is that women, even women who may be seriously intent upon dying, probably have some deep-seated aversion to mutilating their bodies. Even though one will be dead, and therefore not around to view the carnage, the idea of disfigurement and/or ugly dismemberment of some sort is far more unthinkable to a sex so well schooled in the care, maintenance and importance of physical appearance. There may be, as well, some deep and unspoken fantasy that death will be a kind of peaceful and calm "waking sleep"—that, like Snow White, one will someday reawaken, alive and physically intact, the problems of the present having magically vanished.

The typical "sketch" then—drawn from statistical data—of the suicide attempter is someone who is: female, under the age of thirty, frequently single or divorced although not usually (as tends to be true of the older, male, suicide completer) living alone. Her personality is often characterized by strong dependency needs, immaturity, problems in recognizing and dealing with her own hostile feelings, and low frustration tolerance. The attempter is likely to be a person who clings to others for emotional support, whose feelings of worth and self-esteem come not from inside but from "outside supplies." "Most of the good and positive things that this kind of individual has in her life," observed Dr. Malcolm Bowers, chief of psychiatry at Yale-New Haven Hospital, "are things which come to her from other people—and most frequently, from the affection and approval of some crucial other person."

If, therefore, a situation arises in which the relationship with the crucial other person is threatened, the emotionally dependent individual may experience this as a threat to her existence—to her very *being*—itself. This may lead, explained Bowers, to an extremely desperate state of affairs.

"The person who feels herself utterly needful, utterly dependent upon a particular relationship—whose whole sense of self is in jeopardy when that relationship is in jeopardy—may feel compelled to do something to turn the circumstances around. . . . There is often, then," said the psychiatrist, "an attempt to demonstrate to the other person how important he is, either by threatening to end one's life or by actually attempting to do it.

"This is," he added, "simply a way of upping the ante, of saying very dramatically: 'If you don't want me' or 'If you won't do whatever I want you to do . . . I'll kill myself.'"

According to Dr. Bowers, the individual who thus uses her own welfare and her own well-being as a means of exacting certain kinds of behavior from others is often doing so because it conforms to an old pattern of behavior that has worked for her in the past. Very frequently she is someone who has emerged from a family situation in which her own mother was preoccupied, distracted—depressed, perhaps—and had, in essence, very little time for the daughter during her childhood. "The child—that is, the person who later becomes suicidal—had no means, therefore, of communicating her needs and wants to her mother in the context of an easily flowing reciprocal relationship. And so what has happened is that she's had to learn to communicate grandly, strongly, in a way that will demand attention—by throwing tantrums. In children tantrums commonly have to do with no attention from, and no reciprocity with, the mother."

There are many situations and circumstances in which the suicidal attempt can be viewed in the same light—as the biggest behavioral tantrum of them all. "An act of this sort delivers a message: 'I want what I want and I *must* have it now.' And the person is prepared to put her very life at risk in order to get it. She is, of course, only behaving in the ways that she's learned to behave. And what she's learned during her childhood is that the kinds of behavior that get results are those that are dramatic and flamboyant."

Other features that tend to be present in this general type of suicidal situation are feelings of helplessness and hopelessness, as well as the strong dread of an insupportable loneliness, completely beyond the person's capacity to endure. "Loneliness," observed Bowers, "is a basic bad situation for human beings. It probably is the basic human demon, second only to—if not ahead of—guilt."

We are, he noted, all engaged in a more or less lifelong struggle against feelings of loneliness. "If you're a child, and first going to school, then the thing you are fighting is loneliness—because when you're at home with Mommy, you aren't lonely. So, risking school is risking loneliness. And if you go away to camp as a teenager, you're risking loneliness, too. Because homesickness is loneliness too; that is, it's being lonely for the person or people who could make you feel not lonely anymore."

In a way, continued the psychiatrist, all the time spent growing up into adulthood is a time of learning to master loneliness. If, therefore, a twenty-year-old woman makes a suicide attempt, her dilemma can often be understood in terms of deep and unmastered fears about being stranded, isolated, abandoned, helpless. "What she has done, in order to stave off these fears, is to latch on to a single and overwhelmingly important 'love object'. . . . Someone who is to her—in the configuration of the mother, a be-all, an end-all—the source of all the solace and support she can expect. Absolutely everything, for her, rides on this one relationship, upon which she feels herself completely dependent. And so you see, if the relationship has come into question, the person experiences herself as 'abandoned,' without options, without love, without any emotional supplies whatsoever. And *that*"—Bowers lifted his shoulders in a slight shrug—"is loneliness."

Everyone, of course, finds being alone and lonely a circumstance that involves pain. "But," he pointed out, "for the immature person, being alone is Death. She's had to clutch on to someone else in this terrified way because she hasn't yet mastered the fundamentals of coping with human existence on her own. And so, for her, being alone isn't merely a challenge or a kind of a test. It's a catastrophe."

The more mature individual can certainly get into close relationships with others, and can certainly be hurt and anguished should an important relationship fail. But, given similar sets of circumstances, she will have a broader repertoire of behaviors with which to respond. She can show more flexibility in reaction to a devastating emotional loss than that of rushing headlong toward the bottle of sleeping pills in the medicine chest. Said Bowers, "One patient of mine put the matter very well when she remarked: 'I'd never do that kind of thing to myself, never harm myself because of someone else. . . . I think too much of *me* to ever want to hurt *me* in that way. . . . And so killing myself is simply not among my options.'"

Transient feelings about and thoughts of suicide are, he noted, quite common to most people in situations occurring around the loss or ending of important emotional relationships. But a wide gulf separates those people who harbor temporary suicidal feelings from those who actually begin to make plans and then perhaps try to carry them out. Among this latter group are many persons who, should they survive a fairly delimited suicidal crisis period, may never desire to harm themselves again. "It's often just a matter of giving them some time to get their heads together, so to speak," remarked Dr. Bowers. "Many people's lives can literally be saved if you can just protect them from themselves for little more than a two-to-three week interval."

The question of "treatment" for the potentially suicidal person is one upon which there seems to be no clear medical agreement. No one has been able to point with certainty to the most effective types of psychotherapy and/or the kinds of drugs and medications that the physician ought to prescribe. In practice, what is done for and with the patient tends to depend upon a series of crucial initial appraisals.

In dealing with a suicidal emergency the clinician must make a careful assessment not only of the individual herself, but of the individual within the context of her own environment. How much help and support can be expected from the people closest to her? And what *changes* in her environment might the suicidal attempt have been directed toward achieving? If, for instance, a woman is brought into a hospital emergency room after having swallowed an overdose of sleeping pills, a critical factor in an evaluation of the situation will be her lover or husband's reaction. As one psychiatrist put it: "If the husband isn't there and isn't awfully upset and scared and saying things like: 'Oh, my God, I didn't realize things had gotten this bad'; but is, instead, staying casually at home, more or less ignoring the whole thing and saying that stunts like that aren't going to get her anywhere—then you worry."

The suicidal gesture made within the context of an interpersonal crisis may, if it fails to evoke the desired responses, "up" the risks for a subsequent suicide attempt soon afterward. The person has, without doubt, attached a great deal of significance to her effort to destroy herself; if her husband or lover fails to become upset and involved, she becomes more convinced than ever that she doesn't matter to him at all. Her next attempt at dying, therefore, is likely to be far more determined. In this kind of circumstance, a period of inpatient hospitalization—in order to protect the patient from herself, and to give the situation that provoked the attempt time to cool down—may be recommended.

All suicidal crises are not, of course, linked to interpersonal problems. A large number of suicide attempts (and completed suicides) occur in connection with some form of mental disturbance or illness. Where serious mental difficulties are present, the person's "motivation" for suicide can often be quite bizarre. The individual may try to kill herself because she believes someone else is trying to kill her. Or she may, as one patient did, try to drown herself because she believed a Sea-God was calling to her from below the water. A psychiatrist working in Middletown, Connecticut, told me of a patient he was treating who went home and slashed her wrists after their weekly session because she felt he had been sending her secret instructions throughout the hour, and that he wanted her to harm herself.

Of all the major forms of mental illness, however, it is depression which appears to be most closely linked with suicide. A seriously depressed person is often burdened by a terrible sense of hopelessness, with feelings that existence is painful and pointless and that the future is only an endless extension of an unbearable present. It is, perhaps, a wish to "stop the future"—to end one's sufferings sooner rather than later— that causes so many depressed people to contemplate, or to attempt, or to commit suicide.

Treatment of the suicidally depressed individual usually involves treatment of that person's depression. Again, this may require psychiatric hospitalization, sometimes on an involuntary basis. This is, many psychiatrists believe, justified inasmuch as it can be a literally lifesaving technique. For it frequently happens that once the depressed mood has lifted, the person loses her determination to end her life. She becomes able—sometimes quite spontaneously and on her own—to recognize that there are strategies for dealing with her problems other than the crude one that she has chosen, i.e., suicide.

It used to be assumed by most clinicians that anyone showing suicidal inclinations *must*, at least to some extent, be depressed. Recent studies have shown that, just as there are many people who are depressed without becoming suicidal, so are there certain individuals who can want to die without showing any of the clinical signs and symptoms of depression (sleeplessness, weight loss or gain, sad mood, bouts of weeping, and so forth).

Most commonly, however, a link between the two phenomena— depression and suicidal behavior—can be found to exist. One study carried out at the University of Pennsylvania demonstrated, in fact, that the seriousness of an attempt at suicide is highly correlated with the number of depressive symptoms that the suicidal individual displays. According to Dr. Aaron T. Beck, director of the study, the key finding of his research group was that the major depressive symptom emerging among suicidal patients was that of "hopelessness."

"Often," Beck told me, "if you interview the person immediately after the attempt, you'll hear things like: 'I did it because there was no other way out. . . .'" The individual who makes such statements has, he suggested, fallen victim to a type of faulty logic, a disordered thinking pattern that causes her to reject any of the less extreme methods of dealing with her difficulties. "The person is leaping from a premise which may be something like: 'I can't live without him,' to a conclusion—'I'll kill myself.' But she's not stopping to question that first premise. It may in fact be totally untrue that she can't live without him," he added. "She may be able to do so quite well. The point is to keep her alive long enough to begin questioning that first assumption."

One patient he treated, related Dr. Beck, who is director of the Mood Clinic at the University of Pennsylvania, was a woman in her early thirties who had nearly killed herself with an aspirin overdose just following the termination of an unhappy love affair. The person's lover was, as it happened, a doctor connected with the same hospital in which she worked as a nurse; and so she was forced to encounter him on an almost daily basis. These meetings had devastating effects upon her self-esteem. "The fact that this man no longer wanted her meant a great many things—sweeping, global things—to her. It meant that she was, as she put it, 'nothing'; that she was unattractive and unlovable; that no one else was ever going to want her; that if no man ever wanted her again, she wouldn't be able to continue functioning; that if she couldn't function, she was 'nothing'; and therefore, being 'nothing,' she might as well be dead. And so she tried to kill herself."

The therapist then asked her, he recounted, whether—since she was 'nothing' after having lost this lover—she had been 'nothing' before meeting him. She replied at once that such had *not* been the case—she'd been fairly happy, efficient, productive at work, and socially quite outgoing in advance of that long affair. "I asked her, therefore, how she had become converted from 'something' to 'nothing' simply by virtue of having been involved with this man. If she'd been functioning well enough before she knew him, what made her unable to function without him now . . .?" Beck smiled slightly. "That prompted her to begin to look again at some of those illogical premises she was operating with— which were in reality shot full of inconsistencies."

Dr. Beck's approach to the treatment of the suicidal patient is frequently by means of one of the newer techniques, devised in his own clinic, and called *cognitive therapy* (*i.e.*, "thinking therapy.") The method is based upon the assumption that human beings respond to their own habitual thoughts—to what they are saying to themselves *about* themselves—and that such thoughts are part of a complicated feedback system. In other words, if an individual is constantly telling herself such things as: "I'm worthless" or "I'm an evil person and a fraud" or "I'm getting old and unattractive and nobody will give a damn for me," then she will soon start *to behave and to feel as if it were true.*

Suicidal and/or depressed individuals are often people who are ruminating upon morbidly self-punishing ideas, thoughts and prophecies. Whether or not this is uniformly due to their having "turned aggression inward" is not the issue here: the main point is that they tend to become involved in obsessive thinking-cycles in which their cruel thoughts about themselves are never checked out in reality. If, for example, a friend or acquaintance says some nasty and unfair things about me, there will be a number of ways in which I can defend myself and discharge my own feelings; I can counterattack directly or talk things over with a third party or respond to the aggressive attack in some other way. If, on the other hand, the nasty and unfair accusations come from within me—I am helpless. The things I am saying to myself will inevitably make me feel certain ways and view my situation and my life in particular ways—and the things I am saying may be both horrible and untrue.

Cognitive therapy is a carefully designed intervention, a "wrench" to be thrown into the workings of this spiraling, self-destructive process. It is a method used first to aid the person in questioning her erroneous and often frankly preposterous set of basic assumptions—viz., Ellen Winston's notions that she had no existence during Tom's absences; that she was "all bad" and he an examplar of every virtue, and so forth. Secondly, cognitive therapy helps the patient to restructure habitual thought patterns rife with accusations against the self, and ideas of negative self-reference.

Among the many suicidal patients whom he has treated using this method, said Beck, was a woman who had been prevented—by her estranged husband—from jumping from a window-ledge. "This person had, it seemed, been quite depressed for an extended period of time.

Because of her depression, she'd fallen behind in many of her obligations and responsibilities . . . which were numerous because she had a full-time job, an apartment to keep up and heavy commitments to volunteer and political activities.

"She'd been feeling 'down' for so long a time," continued the clinician, "that she'd simply let everything slide. And then it all started to seem like too much, and way beyond her ability to cope with, even to catch up with . . . This made her feel hopeless and helpless. She could see, too, that things were going to get even worse, which made her feel more depressed and even more worthless. She got to feeling, she said, that her 'head was going to blow off.' The pain of having shirked her responsibilities was such that the only way she could think of escaping it was to kill herself."

Treatment with this person involved, initially, working out a small list of daily "assignments"—trivial tasks she would be able to complete. Thus, instead of lying in bed feeling miserable because she could do nothing, she was encouraged to move from one little accomplishment to the next. "I had," explained Beck, "to get her over the absolutely illogical assumption that there wasn't anything she could do, no effective way in which she could act; that she would always be depressed, and her situation was hopeless." Part of the treatment-technique included, therefore, getting the patient to systematically record her activities—including each "success" and whatever pleasure she took from it—in a logbook. This is a method which is geared toward forcing the individual to acknowledge to herself that she is, objectively speaking, having some successes; and that she is, furthermore, taking some pleasure from them. "This is something," observed Beck, "that the depressed and/or suicidal individual is often loath to do."

It is because of her disordered mode of thinking and reasoning, he added, that the suicidal person has come to see dying as the only solution during an emotional emergency. "She must, however, be made to realize that she's working within a very narrow time frame—and she's got to be helped to think back to past problems in her life which might have seemed insoluble at one time . . . but which have, in fact, been solved."

One problem facing psychotherapists who attempt to treat suicidal patients is that they are notoriously resistant to accepting help. In a recent survey, carried out at a major university hospital, it was found that only some 30 percent of the patients referred for clinical care after a suicide attempt ever returned to get it, even though it had been arranged for them and they had been encouraged to come back.

A variety of other studies, carried out in different hospitals and clinics, have reported up to 90 percent of suicidal patients refusing any psychiatric aid after an attempt. I asked Dr. Beck, therefore, what he would advise a person to do if she had a friend who seemed to be preoccupied with suicidal thoughts and/or plans. "And what would you advise *me* to do," I inquired, "if I realized that I were obsessing upon suicidal thoughts and ideas myself?"

Generally speaking, he replied, a person who is distressed in this way should "at least" seek a psychiatric evaluation. "If you were thinking about suicide, I'd very strongly suggest that you go and see a therapist on a one-or two-session basis. This would provide you with some outside perspective on your wish to die, and a far greater objectivity about your entire life situation."

Such an arrangement would not, he pointed out, entail my committing myself to a long term of treatment or to any treatment at all. "It would simply give you a chance to talk things over with someone who is an expert in this type of problem. And it would give you an opportunity to gain some distance from the difficulty—whatever it may be—as well."

Many patients who come in for one or two sessions of evaluation find so much relief that they stay on for a full course of treatment, said Beck. "And anything short of getting yourself into professional hands would be, in circumstances where you're seriously entertaining the notion of suicide, really extremely risky."

Should it be a friend of mine who was the person expressing suicidal thoughts and ideas, he continued, the best help I could offer would be: 1) to hear her out fully, and 2) to urge her to seek professional advice. "Should she refuse, the next best thing would probably be to go and speak to some member of the family, to alert her or him to the problem . . . since that person might be in a position to insist upon her seeing one whether she wants to or not. . . .

"Very often we find that, after the suicide or the attempted suicide, the family realizes that there were a great many danger signals in advance. Then they'll start berating themselves and saying: 'Oh, how could we have been so stupid? How could we have ignored the ways in which she was behaving?' But by then it's too late. The important thing a friend can do, before anything does happen, is to help set up channels of communication between the suicidal person and the responsible *caring* people in her environment."

The typical behavior pattern of the suicidally intentioned person usually, he explained, involves some noticeable changes in that individual's ordinary *modus operandi*. If a few weeks ago she was speaking desperately about wanting to end her life, she may now talk cheerfully of going away for two or three weeks' vacation. If she happens to be a working wife, she might start taking off time in the middle of the work day; she may also begin a process of putting her affairs in order. "Often one finds a person like this staying home from her job, doing a complete housecleaning—even down to the last bit of laundry. What she is doing is slowly preparing her death; and the whole theme of this time, if you are alert to it, *is* Death. She may revise her will during this period. She's rather similar to a cancer patient, in that there's the same effort to catch up with things before the expected end . . . But," added Beck, "in the case of the suicidal person, there's a furtiveness, a covertness, an air of secrecy about all of the things she is doing."

According to every expert whom I consulted, and everything that I have read on the subject, there is no truth to the old canard about the person who threatens to kill herself never being the one who actually does it. Quite the contrary: It appears that those who attempt to (or who do) commit suicide have talked about it and threatened it frequently. In most cases there have been multiple advance warnings and signals of the most blatant sort, but these have been shrugged off by those close to the suicidal individual. It would seem, therefore, an unwise policy to ignore suicidal talk and dismiss it as empty threats or mere posturing. Anyone who is even talking in this fashion should be heard out sympathetically and urged most insistently to seek professional help.

As many writers on suicide have stressed, given that there is probably always a deep ambivalence—a tension between the desire to end one's sufferings, and a wish to go on living—present in every suicidal person, a timely and intelligent intervention can serve an absolutely critical function. Objective, professional care can aid the individual, not only in weathering the suicidal-crisis phase, but in working out alternate methods of coping and problem-solving that do not necessitate her dying . . . and, by so doing, tip the precarious balance in favor of life.

1976

Index

Abortion, 4, 6, 7
Accident proneness, 242
Accidents: injury rate, 208-209
Acquired drive, fear as an, 209-211
Adams, Julie, 180, 187, 188
Adaptative behavior, 124, 129-130; attachment behavior, 109-110, 119; compensation, 126, 128; criterion for normalcy, 145; fear as, 216-217; female submission, 102-103; schizophrenia, 173, 176; sleep, 76-77; tool-using, 104
Adler, Alexandra, 132, 133
Adler, Alfred, xviii, 123-136; background, 124-125; influence, 123-124
Adler, Kurt, 135
Adler, Raissa, 130-131
Adolescence, 21, 25, 271
Adrenalectomy, 24
Adrenalin. See Epinephrine
Adrenals, 23; hormones, 30
Adrenogenital syndrome, 33
Affectionless characters, 111
Aggression: chimpanzees, 95, 98, 101, 102, 104; E.S.B., 46, 47, 49; human, 126-127, 154; hyenas, 102-103; testosterone levels and, 19-22
Alcohol: congeners, 59-60; effects of, 56, 57, 60, 67; suicide and, 287; See also Hangovers
Almond, Richard, 193
Alpha rhythm, 65, 85
Amines, biogenic, 261
Amniocentesis, 16
Amphetamines, 67, 261
Androstenedione (AD), 23, 30
Anger, 235-247; appeasement covers, 245-246; displacement, 238-239; functions, 238, 247; handling, 243-246; physical response to, 239-240; relation to fear, 233; repression, 236-239, 240-243; suicide and, 285-286;

suppression, 244
Anxiety, 46, 203-204; E.S.B. treatment, 40, 49; guilt reactions, 57; predisposition to, 176; REM loss, 56, 73; testosterone levels, 22; therapy for, 200-202, 204; unpredictability and, 218-219
Anxiety neurosis, 85
Appeasement, 245-246
Arateus, 250
Assertive training, 204-206
Attachment behavior, 109-119
Aversive therapy, 198-199
Avoidance conditioning, 211-213

Baboons, 104, 105
Bazelon, David L., 141, 142, 143, 155
Beck, Aaron T., 294-297, 298
Behavior, abnormal vs. normal, 137-163, 171-172
Behavior modification, 195-206; unlearning maladaptive responses, 197-198; See also Electrical stimulation of the brain
Behrman, Richard E., 3, 16
Belief systems, 167
Benson, Herbert, 81-86, 87, 89-92
Berger, Hans, 42
Bernstein, Irwin, 19
Biofeedback, 74; control of blood pressure, 82
Bipolar mood disorders. See Manic-depressive disease
Blood lactate, 84-85
Bok, Sissela, 12
Boltax, Sandra, 193
Bootzin, Richard R., 72
"Boston Grave-Robbing Case," 14
Bottome, Phyllis, 132
Bowers, Malcolm, 290-292
Bowlby, John, xviii, 109-119
Bowlby, Ursula, 113, 116
Brain, 42; amygdala, 48; central gray

301

Composed in Times Roman by The New Republic
Book Company, Inc.
Printed on 55-pound Sebago paper and bound by The
Maple Press Co., York, Pennsylvania.
Designed by Gerard Valerio.